Sodomy in early modern Europe

STUDIES IN EARLY MODERN EUROPEAN HISTORY

This exciting new series aims to publish
challenging and innovative research in all areas
of early modern continental history.
The editors are committed to encouraging work that
engages with current historiographical
debates, adopts an interdisciplinary
approach, or makes an original contribution
to our understanding of the period.

SERIES EDITORS
William G. Naphy and Penny Roberts

EDITORIAL ADVISORY BOARD
Professor N. Z. Davis, Professor Brian Pullan,
Professor Joseph Bergin and
Professor Robert Scribner

Already published in the series

SODOMY
in early modern Europe

EDITED BY TOM BETTERIDGE

Manchester University Press

Manchester and New York

distributed exclusively in the USA by Palgrave

Published by Manchester University Press
Oxford Road, Manchester M13 9NR, UK
and Room 400, 175 Fifth Avenue, New York, NY10010, USA
www.manchesteruniversitypress.co.uk

Distributed exclusively in the USA by
Palgrave, 175 Fifth Avenue, New York,
NY10010, USA

Distributed exclusively in Canada by
UBC Press, University of British Columbia, 2029 West Mall,
Vancouver, BC, Canada V6T 1Z2

British Library Cataloguing-in-Publication Data
A catalogue record is available from the British Library

Library of Congress Cataloging-in-Publication Data applied for

ISBN 0 7190 6114 8 *hardback*
      0 7190 6115 6 *paperback*

First published 2002

10 09 08 07 06 05 04 03 02   10 9 8 7 6 5 4 3 2 1

Typeset in Monotype Perpetua with Albertus
by Northern Phototypesetting Co Ltd, Bolton
Printed in Great Britain
by Biddles Ltd, Guildford and King's Lynn

Contents

Contributors

Tom Betteridge Volume Editor. Senior Lecturer in the School of Humanities, Kingston University. Recently published *Tudor Histories of the English Reformations, 1530–1583*.

Maria R. Boes Associate Professor, Department of History, West Chester University. Numerous publications on judicial practices in early modern Germany.

Alan Bray Honorary Research Fellow of Birkbeck College, London. Numerous publications including *Homosexuality in Renaissance England*.

Danielle Clarke College Lecturer In English, University College Dublin. Recently published *The Politics of Early Modern Women's Writing*.

N. S. Davidson Lecturer in Modern History and Tutorial Fellow of St Edmund Hall, Oxford. Numerous publications and is currently completing a study of the Inquisition in sixteenth-century Venice.

P. G. Maxwell-Stuart Honorary Lecturer in the Department of Modern History, University of St Andrews. Numerous publications including *The Occult in Early Modern Europe*.

William Naphy Senior Lecturer in the Department of History, University of Aberdeen. Numerous publications including *Calvin and the Consolidation of the Genevan Reformation*.

Sarah Salih Lecturer in English Literature, School of English and American Studies, University of East Anglia.

Alan Stewart Reader in Renaissance Studies at Birkbeck, University of London. Publications include: *Close Readers: Humanism and Sodomy in Early Modern England* and Biographical Studies of Francis Bacon, Philip Sidney, and James VI and I.

Tom Webster Lecturer in the Department of History, University of Edinburgh. Recently published *Godly Clergy in Early Stuart England: The Caroline Puritan Movement*.

Preface

During the course of putting this collection together I have incurred numerous debts, intellectual, academic and personal. This book would not have been produced without the constant support of Bill Naphy. All the contributors to this volume have been a pleasure to work with. I have gained a great deal from the suggestions and comments made by a number of people who have read parts of this study or listened to my ideas. I would therefore like to thank the following: Kim Coles, Patrick Collinson, Brian Cummings, Allen Frantzen, Tom Freeman, Gabriele Griffin, David Scott Kastan, John King, Erica Longfellow and Alan Sinfield. I would also like to thank my colleagues at Kingston University, and in particular Sarah Sceats for her constant incitements to talk about sex and food. This study would not have been completed without the whole-hearted support of Alison Whittle and Jonathan Bevan at Manchester University Press.

This book is dedicated to the memory of Alan Bray, who sadly died in 2001. Alan was a constant source of help and advice to me while I was putting this volume together. His death has robbed academia and the wider world of a kind, generous man and an inspirational scholar.

Tom Betteridge

Introduction

TOM BETTERIDGE

Sodomy in early modern Europe is a collection of essays that reflect closely the main areas of debate within gay historiography. In particular, for the last twenty years scholars have argued over the nature of early modern sodomy. Was it the same as modern homosexuality? Were there homosexuals in early modern Europe? Did men who had sex with each other in this period regard their behaviour as determining their identity? Who were they? What was the relationship between the grave sin of sodomy and the homoerotic images that fill Renaissance culture? Scholars have responded to these questions in a number of different and often apparently contradictory ways, and the chapters that make up this book reflect this diversity of approach. Indeed sodomy in this book refers to an extremely wide spectrum of acts, desires and discourses. In some chapters sodomy is nothing more than an ill-defined threat lurking in the margins of early modern culture while in others it is used as a self-evident descriptive category.

The large differences between contributors' understanding of sodomy within *Sodomy in early modern Europe* is, however, a reflection of the lively theoretical debates within the field and of the interdisciplinary nature of this book. Literary critics and historians have adopted a wide range of quite different approaches to the study of early modern male sexuality. These differences are perhaps most noticeable in the area of nomenclature; the names or labels that scholars use to define their field or object of study.[1] Literary critics have, on the whole, been concerned with the circulation of homoerotic desire within and through texts. In the process they have tended to question the validity of sodomy as a descriptive category. Jonathan Goldberg, for example, has argued that any inquiry into what sodomy is and how it is recognised 'will never deliver the sodomite per se, but only ... sodometries, relational structures precariously available to prevailing discourses'.[2] Goldberg's approach to the study of sodomy in the early modern period has been very influential among literary critics. In particular the idea that Renaissance sodomy is an inherently deconstructive concept that undermines the textual stability of works in which it appears has become almost an orthodoxy for queer and gay studies of early modern literature. Historians have, however, on the whole adopted a quite different approach to the study of sodomy in the early modern period. For example, Maria Boes in Chapter 2 finds the term *sodomy* quite unproblematic since the magistrates of early modern Frankfurt appear to have had a relatively precise idea of what sodomy was. Bill Naphy's work on Geneva suggests that the leading citizens of the town judged sexual crimes such as sodomy on the basis of different degrees of culpability which related directly to the extent to which those accused of being involved in sodomitical sex were aware of what they were doing. This led the Genevan magistrates to be particularly certain when condemning, men such as Jobert and Lespligny who appear to have been a long-standing gay couple. It seems that in the case of Geneva labelling someone as a sodomite was easier the more they looked like modern gay men. Where literary critics have viewed sodomy as a protean deconstructive category historians like Naphy and Boes have used it as a descriptive category whose meaning is relatively fixed

Sodomy in early modern Europe contains chapters written from literary-critical and historical perspectives. In effect it stages the differences I have discussed in these opening passages, and in the process gives its reader the opportunity to work through her position as regards the status of sodomy in early modern Europe. It was to allow the reader the freedom to do this which led me to resist the temptation to put the chapers that make up this book into any order other than alphabetical by author's name. I did not want to impose a false or misleading ordering that sought to create coherence where in practice what exists is debate and diversity. Indeed as soon as I tried to order these chapters I came up with methodological and intellectual problems. Grouping them by discipline seemed reductive, while putting them into either geographical or chronological sections seemed to create un-necessarily clear distinctions. I have therefore decided to keep the chapters in alphabetic order and to provide the following brief theoretical introduction to this volume and to the specific chapters it contains. Those readers who wish to read this book without my spin should therefore skip the following pages and plunge straight into the world of *Sodomy in early modern Europe*.

The study of homosexuality in the early modern period has been dominated by a debate over whether in this period one is dealing with acts or identities.[3] Did men who engaged in sex with each other view themselves as belonging to a discrete social group? Or were they simply taking part in acts that we would now regard as homosexual but which they saw as simply sexual? These questions relate to a basic historiographical problem since one way of thinking through this problem is to ask whether or not the term *homosexual* has meaning in the early modern period. In the process of stating this question, however, one is confronted with the basic and unresolvable historiographical problem that the use of modern terms to describe past events or phenomena is always potentially distorting. At one level the problems associated with the use of the term *homosexual* to describe early modern men who engaged in sex with each other are no more or less problematic than the use of the any other modern term to describe historical phenomena. Why is it more problematic to use the term *homosexuality* than *feudalism*?[4] The answer to this question is, however, relatively obvious. There must be few places where the term *feudal* can be used as a term of abuse and where people are prepared to argue in public that all the sins of the world can be blamed on feudalism. This is not, unfortunately, true of homosexuality. There are people for whom a world, and therefore a time, without homosexuals is something to be desired and worked towards. It is this that makes the discussion within gay historiography over what term to use, *sodomite* or *homosexual*, *sodomy* or *homosexuality*, so fraught but also important.[5]

What also makes the issue of which term to use to describe early modern men who engaged in sex with each other particularly complex is the relationship between sodomy, homosexuality, homoeroticism and homosociality in the culture of Renaissance Europe. Indeed the multiplicity of terms that have been used to describe the relations, real and imagined, between men during the early modern period is itself indicative of the complexity of the debate that has bedevilled, but also energised, the study of male sexuality during this period.

One of the key theoretical influences upon these debates has been the work of Michel Foucault. In the first volume of *The History of Sexuality* Foucault argues that modern sexual identities are a product of the nineteenth-century scientific and sexual discourses.[6] He suggests that before the emergence of these discourses it is inaccurate to speak of sexual identities. Instead what one finds is acts that do not in themselves define a person's identity. The implication of this is that before the emergence of the modern discourse of sexuality homosexuality, and by implication homosexuals, did not exist. Foucault's theory is complex and subtle. However, it has had a number of rather reductive effects on the history of homosexuality. One of the most problematic has been the way in which historians and literary critics have responded to Foucault's claim that homosexuality first appeared in the late nineteenth century. In recent years there has been a sustained critique of this claim and an attempt to push back the date when one can first use the term *homosexual* without being anachronistic.[7] This search for the holy grail of the first real or authentic gay man is, however, in some ways misplaced. Indeed in terms of Foucault's work the idea of finding the first authentic homosexual needs to be seen as a product of precisely the kind of nineteenth-century discourses that he is critiquing in *The History of Sexuality*.

Another key criticism of Foucault's ideas has centred on his claim that before the nineteenth century one is dealing with sodomy as an act not a discourse. This argument is problematic since it appears to depend on a potentially simplistic separation of acts from discourse. Danielle Clark in Chapter 3, argues that:

> Contrary to the schematic Foucauldian model, the picture of sodomy that has been built up for the Renaissance period suggests a situation where discourses constantly subsume acts, deferring and relocating the physical and sexual experiences that give rise to the disturbingly imprecise areas and actions located within the term *sodomy*.[8]

For Clarke sodomy functions in works attacking the Duke of Buckingham as a metaphor for corruption. In particular, when early Stuart writers refer to the reign of Edward II they draw parallels between the disruptive effects of Edward's relationship with his minions and those created by Buckingham's friendship with James and Charles. Sodomy in these texts works as a metaphor for the way in which the favourite's position subverts social norms because of its emphasis on parity between favourite and king. Sodomy in Stuart political writing symbolises a collapse of distinctions, in particular between public and private, the king's physical and symbolic body. This leads Clarke to suggest that while 'for Foucault sodomy is an act without a discourse; in these texts it is a discourse without an act'.[9]

Another important criticism that has been made of Foucault's argument is that it relies on a rather traditional understanding of historical change and development. In particular medievalists have questioned the bucolic version of their period found in Foucault's work. In Chapter 7 Sarah Salih argues that 'Medieval productions of sexual subjects are not benign: most typically, they call such subjects into being in order to control, expel or obliterate them. If modern histories of sexuality are to evade complicity in such obliterations, they must disavow the innocence of the Middle Ages'.[10] For Salih the medieval period is not an age of innocence when sex escaped the clutches of discourse. In particular Salih argues that specific types of medieval writing, chivalric romance or penitential guides, created equally specific versions of proper and aberrant masculinity. She goes on to comment that 'whether a sexual identity comes into visibility is dependent on the particular needs of the genre: whether acts constitute identities depends on whether you need them to'.[11] Salih's argument is not, however, that Foucault's ideas are inapplicable to the medieval period. Rather it is that they need to be used strategically and with care. Indeed the issues addressed by Salih, and Clarke, are clearly indebted to the theoretical parameters and concepts articulated in *The History of Sexuality*.[12]

If Foucault's work forms the theoretical point of departure for studies of early modern sodomy then one could argue that Alan Bray's *Homosexuality in*

Renaissance England, published in 1982, is the other essential point of reference for anyone interested in this area.[13] The central argument of Bray's study is that sodomy as a discourse in the early modern period was marked by a violent disjuncture. At one level everyone knew that sodomy was a terrible cosmic sin, a crime against Nature's and God's order. Crucially, however, sodomy was not an exclusively masculine sexual crime. As a concept it encompassed a whole range of sinful and wicked behaviour only a part of which related to male single sex desire or behaviour. Bray writes that: 'What sodomy and buggery represented – and homosexuality was only part of these – was rather the disorder in sexual relations that, in principle at least, could break out anywhere'.[14] Sodomy, for Bray, was in the Renaissance a collection of disordering sexual practices and desires. It was not what we now call homosexuality since it included within its scope any form of sexual licence or transgression that in the eyes, and ears, of early modern culture went against the natural order. In Chapter 1 I discuss the way in which John Bale deploys sodomy as a signifier of general papist sexual, political and textual corruption including, but far from exclusively, single-sex male desires and practices.

The other side of Bray's argument in *Homosexuality in Renaissance England*, one that is often missed by his critics, is that the status of sodomy as a cosmic crime meant that people were often reluctant to recognise specific sexual actions as sodomitical. Acts which we would now describe as relatively unambiguously homosexual, for example mutual male masturbation, could be, and indeed appear often to have been, regarded as simply too commonplace or insignificant to warrant being classed under the dreadful label of sodomy. This does not, however, as Bray points out, mean that early modern culture tolerated the sodomite, rather that the emergence of this figure was not simply the product of male sexual behaviour.[15] The work of Naphy and Boes in Chapters 6 and 2 supports Bray's argument. In Frankfurt it appears that it was quite possible for a person to engage in behaviour that by any definition was sodomitical without being reported to the authorities by his neighbours. If anything the situation in Geneva appears to have been even more extreme. Naphy points out that in one of the trials he discusses it was admitted that the accused 'had been publicly called and known as a bugger for the previous eight years'.[16] It is clear that in both Frankfurt and Geneva a *de facto* tolerance existed that required outside factors, competition within the pastry trade or a spy scare, for it to be withdrawn. In the early modern period sodomy emerged at moments of political and religious tension when an explanation was needed for social antagonism and conflict. In Chapter 5 P. G. Maxwell-Stuart demonstrates that this was clearly the case with bestiality in early modern Scotland, where a cluster of cases in the late 1650s can be explained by the precarious and fraught political situation. It is, however, noticeable that the Scottish magistrates investigating these cases were quite clear that they were not dealing with simply another form of sodomy.

Homosexuality in Renaissance England represents the relationship between homosexuality and sodomy in the early modern period as caught constantly in a state of dialectic-tension. At any moment acts and indeed desires that were homosexual could be suddenly and violently inscribed into the discourse of sodomy. This inscription made these acts, and the men who engaged in them, suddenly aberrant and perverse. The tension within sodomitical discourse between act and identity also enabled sodomy to play an important explanatory role in early modern polemical and political writings. By blaming the sodomite for society's ills it was possible to make an explanatory move from the general or social to the individual without actually addressing the real reasons for social conflict, early modern Europe's massive inequalities of wealth and power. As a figure the sodomite represented at the level of the individual the breakdown of social order. The discourse of sodomy, the disjuncture that Bray argues existed between actual male sexual behaviour and the status of sodomy as the signifier of sexual disorder and sinfulness, allowed and indeed incited the move from the social to the individual since it created a situation in which particular acts could suddenly take on new, terrifying and universal meanings.

Before I move on to discuss the individual chapters it is necessary to briefly broaden out this discussion to encompass the status of masculinity and heterosexuality in the early modern period. What it meant to be an ideal or proper man in this period is perhaps less self-evident then one would imagine. Tom Webster's work on Puritan masculinity suggests that, despite its patriarchal trappings, the beards and sermons, it was unstable and fraught. Webster discusses the spiritual writings of seventeenth-century godly ministers (Chapter 9). These suggest a willingness among these men to imagine their relationship with Christ through the use of sensual and feminine tropes. For John Bale, however, as I argue in Chapter 1, real masculinity was based upon an explicit denial of any weaknesses. Bale's men appear as robotic figures locked into an absolute and fixed notion of masculinity. They would certainly have had no truck with the kind of writings that Webster's ministers produced.

Early modern masculinity, and indeed heterosexuality, was quite different from modern versions of what it now means to be masculine or heterosexual. The critical theorist Judith Butler has consistently argued that

> Heterosexuality must be understood as a compulsive and compulsory repetition that can only produce the *effect* of its own originality; in other words, compulsory heterosexual identities, those ontological consolidated phantasms of 'man' and 'woman', are theatricality produced effects that posture as grounds, origins, the normative measure of the real.[17]

Butler is arguing here that heterosexuality is never stable or fixed, although it certainly does constantly claim to be both these things. It is rather based on a repetition of norms that change and are historically specific – but which also tend to deny their historical nature. Once one accepts that the heterosexual, like the homosexual, is constantly being invented and produced anew then the idea of the invention of homosexuality from a bedrock or basis of heterosexuality becomes meaningless. Historically heterosexuality has constantly produced aberrant others that then have to carry the burden of the historical or performative since it invariably claims to be ahistorical and normative. It is impossible to exaggerate the extent to which early modern heterosexuality was simply and profoundly different from that of the present day. In particular, when one looks at early modern masculinity and heterosexuality it is certainly arguable that the space for close, affectionate and intimate relationships between men, which were none the less regarded as heterosexual, was in many ways greater then it is at the moment.[18] Indeed, in the context of the early modern understandings of masculinity, our present understanding of heterosexuality would itself look rather effeminate, with its obsession with the female body as the exclusive proper object of male desire.

These issues can be brought together around the metaphor of visibility. For Butler heterosexuality constantly seeks to deny its status as notable or seeable through its claim to be normative. In other words one is not expected to see heterosexuality since it is the norm. It is the aberrant, the transgressive, that is marked by visibility, that exists to be seen and condemned. It is the status of queerness as visible that guarantees the normative invisibility of the straight. In seeking to make visible a gay past there is therefore a danger that all one is doing is reproducing this straight logic since in the process one simply confirms the status of heterosexuality as the non-seen, non-visible, of history. The gaze of the historian and literary critic has always been drawn to the aberrant, strange and curious however, perhaps what one really needs to make visible is the straight in all its queer weirdness.

The theoretical debate that I have been discussing so far in this Introduction was not, however, alien to the early modern period – although clearly it was conducted in a radically different language. In Calvin's Geneva it is clear from Naphy's work (Chapter 6) that magistrates and clergymen had an understanding of sodomy that embodied a notion of sexual preference as something beyond simply acts. In Frankfurt it appears that people were prepared to tolerate men who engaged in sodomy, even to the extent of ignoring unwanted advances, as long as the magistrates were not involved. Perhaps most surprisingly it seems clear from Nicholas Davidson's work on early modern Venice (Chapter 4) that it was possible for men to defend homosexual practices in print. Davidson writes that 'Throughout the Renaissance, in fact, and well into the seventeenth century, there was a surprisingly self-confident literature available in Venice arguing that sexual preference was a matter of choice, not of law'.[19] Clearly it would be false to regard Venice as a typical early modern state. Indeed as Davidson acknowledges it may be that the defences of sex between men which he discusses in his chapter are no more then theoretical and playful exercises designed to amuse and shock their readers in equal measure. However, as Davidson also points out there clearly were long-term male relationships in Venice and it also seems from the evidence produced by Naphy in Chapter 6 that there were men living together in Geneva as couples.

Sodomy in early modern Europe comprises a diverse collection of essays that introduce the reader to the range of current approaches to the study of sodomy. My Chapter examines the historical writings of two English Protestants, John Bale and John Foxe. The former appears to have been obsessed with sodomy and produced numerous works, not all of which were historical, that sough to display popery's sodomitical nature. His follower Foxe was far less interested in displaying sodomy then in recording the deeds of Protestant martyrs in his major work *Acts and Monuments*. However, while sodomy is rarely mentioned in this massive work, its effects, and those of its suppression, can be found throughout Foxe's work. Maria Boes's Chapter 2 deals with two well-documented persecutions for sodomy in early modern Frankfurt. The details of these cases are shocking, not least because of the apparently gratuitous use of torture even after a confession had been secured. Her conclusions are, however, also surprising since she finds evidence of a tolerance towards such sexual crimes as sodomy that worked to provide a 'protective shield against judicial intrusion'.[20] Danielle Clarke's Chapter 3 examines the use of sodomy in Stuart polemical writings attacking the role of the Duke of Buckingham. In particular she discusses the use of the example of Edward II to produce critiques of James I's and Charles I's relationships with their favourite. Nicholas Davidson's Chapter 4 suggests that Venetians in this period adopted a fingers-crossed approach to Church teaching on sexual morality. They appear to have been quite aware that sodomy was regarded by the authorities as a serious crime and yet, to judge by the works printed in its defence, the pleasure outweighed the risk. P. G. Maxwell-Stuart's Chapter 5 does not strictly concern sodomy. Rather it discusses a cluster of bestiality cases that came before the Scottish courts in the mid seventeenth century. It forms an important part of this book since it has been suggested by some modern scholars that early modern magistrates often simply treated all forms of sexual offence as sodomy. However, Maxwell-Stuart's work suggest that this was at least not the case in Scotland. Bill Naphy's detailed analysis of sodomy cases that came before the city authorities in Calvin's Geneva (Chapter 6) confirms the argument that early modern magistrates were careful to distinguish between sexual crimes and treated those that seemed to be based on sexual preference or predilection with particular harshness. Sarah Salih's Chapter 7 discusses the status of sodomy in the context of medieval culture. Alan Stewart's Chapter 8 examines the way in which humanist pedagogy worked to deny its homoeroticism. He concludes by commenting that 'the humanist model of education [was so] far entrenched in the mind of the humanist pupil-king [that] whether the grown pupil-father like it or no, the schoolmaster [would] "cum uncalld"'.[21] Tom Webster's work (Chapter 9), like Stewart's, is concerned less with sodomy as a sexual act then with early modern masculinity and the homoerotic imagery that it seemed constantly to turn to.

This book is not intended to be comprehensive or even to present an agreed position. What I do hope that it will achieve is to give readers a sense of the vitality of the field and provoke them to further reading and study. It is with this in mind that Alan Bray's Epilogue looks towards the future of gay historiography and the study of sodomy in early modern Europe.

NOTES

1 This is not the place to discuss this issue in detail. However, attentive readers will notice that, while historians prefer the term 'early modern', literary critics tend to prefer 'Renaissance'.

2 Jonathan Goldberg, *Sodometries: Renaissance Texts, Modern Sexualities* (Stanford: 1992), p. 20.

3 For recent work in this field see Ed. Cohen, *Talk on the Wilde Side: Toward a Genealogy of a Discourse on Male Sexualities* (New York: 1993); Jonathan Dollimore, *Sexual Dissidence: Augustine to Wilde Freud to Foucault* (Oxford: 1991); Martin Duberman, Martha Vicinus and George Chauncey, eds., *Hidden from History: Reclaiming the Gay and Lesbian Past* (London: 1989); Kent Gerrard and Gert Hebma, eds, *The Pursuit of Sodomy: Male Homosexuality in Renaissance and Enlightenment Europe* (New York: 1989) Goldberg, 1992); Jonathan Goldberg, ed., *Queering the Renaissance* (Durham, N.C.: 1994); Jeffrey Masten, *Textual Intercourse: Collaboration, Authorship, and Sexualities in Renaissance Drama* (Cambridge: 1997); Bruce Smith, *Homosexual Desire in Shakespeare's England: A Cultural Poetics* (Chicago: 1991); Claude J. Summers, ed., *Homosexuality in Renaissance and Enlightenment England: Literary Representations in Historical Context* (New York: 1992); and J. Summers and Ted-Larry Pedworth, eds, *Renaissance Discourses of Desire* (Columbia, Mo.: 1993).

4 This is a particularly salient comparison since recent historical work has suggested that feudalism, and the idea that there once existed a feudal society in Europe, is itself a modern myth.

5 The political implications of arguing that there were no homosexual men in the early modern period are obvious since one important component of homophobia is the idea that homosexuality is a form of modern degeneracy.

6 Michel Foucault, *The History of Sexuality: An Introduction*, trans. Robert Hurley (Harmondsworth: 1978). For a succinct discussion of Foucault's ideas in this area see Goldberg, 1992, pp. 18–19.

7 For a recent example of this tendency see Michael B. Young, *King James and the History of Homosexuality* (New York: 1999).

8 See below p. 48.

9 See below p. 61.

10 See below p. 127.

11 See below pp. 124–5.

12 It is worthwhile noting that the seventeenth-century texts and the medieval texts that Clarke and Salih discuss were bowdlerised by their Victorian editors in a move that seems to

confirm the accuracy of Foucault's argument that the nineteenth century witnessed a profound change in the way sex and sexuality was understood.

13 Bray's work has been subjected to a number of attacks. While it is clear that his thesis is perhaps a bit too sweeping, many of these critiques have in practice illustrated Judith Butler's claim that gender and sexual norms are based on their compulsive repetition. Bray's sin, in the eyes of some of his detractors, seems to have been that of questioning this norm-producing process in relation to homosexuality. On Butler's ideas concerning gender and sexuality see *Bodies that Matter: On the Discursive Limits of 'Sex'* (London and New York: 1993). For a forceful critique of the idea that there was a time when 'homosexuality did not exist' see Joseph Cady, '"Masculine Love", Renaissance Writing, and the "New Invention" of Homosexuality', in Summers, 1992, pp. 9–40.

14 Alan Bray, *Homosexuality in Renaissance England* (London: 1982), p. 25.

15 *Ibid.*, p. 77.

16 See below p. 105.

17 Judith Butler, 'Imitation and Gender Insubordination', in *The Second Wave: A Reader in Feminist Theory*, ed. Linda Nicholson (New York: 1997), pp. 300–16, 307.

18 James M. Saslow points out that during the Renaissance 'Canon law outlawed as sodomy certain physical acts, ambiguously embracing all forms of non-procreative sexuality, while passionate but chaste male emotional intimacy, modelled on classical notions of *amicitia*, was held up as the highest earthly happiness'. James M. Saslow, 'Homosexuality in the Renaissance: Behaviour, Identity, and Artistic Expression', in Duberman, Vicinus and Chaunecy, eds, 1989, pp. 90–105, 97.

19 See below p. 71.

20 See below p. 37.

21 See below p. 143.

1

The place of sodomy in the historical writings of John Bale and John Foxe

TOM BETTERIDGE

And at this day Meprius [slaughtered] his brother thurgh treson and hym self afterward helde the land ... and after bicame so [evil] a man that he destroied in a while all [the] men of his lande. And at laste he bicame so wikked and so lecherous that he forsoke his own wif and used the synne of sodomie wher for almighty god was wroth ...[1]

What did it mean in 1480, when Caxton published his Chronicle, to 'use the sin of sodomy'? Was Meprius, one of the earliest English Kings mentioned in the chronicle, a sodomite? Or did his sinful sexual behaviour simply reflect his vicious nature? What came first, sodomy or sodomite?[2] These questions go to the heart of the current academic debate concerning the status of sodomy and homosexuality in the early modern period – are we dealing in this period with acts or with a discrete and known sexual identity? Were there homosexuals in early modern Europe?[3] This question is not, however, an easy one to answer. This is partly because it raises a set of difficult theoretical problems relating to the relationship between social norms, sexuality and subjectivity.[4] It is also, however, because the early modern period itself, or at least its men of letters, appears to have shared our contemporary confusion over the correlation between desire, behaviour and identity.

Caxton's Meprius is a wicked man. His sodomy seems largely to be a product of a more general lechery. However, even in this short chronicle entry things are a little more complicated than they first appear since in this text there is an implied causal link between Meprius's rejection of his wife and his use of the sin of sodomy. Why should this be the case if sodomy is simply an act? Indeed in Caxton's text there is a potential separation between sodomy and its enactment or use; between act and meaning. Meprius uses sodomy – which is slightly different from either being a sodomite or indulging in sodomitical acts. It implies that sodomy has an existence beyond or apart from its enactment. But where could this be? Did Meprius keep sodomy safely locked in his closet until he could safely bring it out? Or was it inevitable that his lechery and wickedness would end in a sodomitical embrace? The first part of this chapter will examine John Bale's use of sodomy in his anti-papist histories. It will then go on to discuss the coexistence in John Foxe's *Acts and Monuments* of images of sodomy and homoeroticism. The main argument of this chapter is that one can see in the work of these two Protestants a playing out of the tension that, as Alan Bray has argued, 'exercised a compelling grip on the imagination of sixteenth-century England', the tension between the masculine friend and the sodomite.[5]

John Bale's papist sodomites

The representation of sexual and gender norms in the work of the mid-Tudor writer John Bale is marked by a number of curious slippages and tensions. Bale was a Protestant polemist who produced a large number of works throughout the period 1530–60. He started life as a Carmelite monk but during the 1530s he became an important member of the team of writers that Thomas Cromwell assembled to defend the Henrician Reformation. With the fall of Cromwell Bale went into exile in Germany. He returned during the reign of Edward VI and, after a number of other appointments, ended up as Bishop of Ossory in Ireland. With the advent of Mary Tudor and the restoration of Catholicism Bale again fled to the continent only to return finally with Elizabeth I's succession. Although now largely neglected, Bale was an influential figure in terms of mid-Tudor Protestant writing and, as Andrew Hadfield has recently commented, 'deserves to be better known as a key figure in English literary history'.[6]

Much of Bale's writing consists of historical attacks on papistry's sodomitical nature.[7] For Bale all papists were sodomites and the inevitable result of papistry was sexual disorder. This interest in sodomy has in the past made Bale a notorious but peripheral figure in accounts of the English Reformation. However, if one considers Bale's contacts and the number of his publications it is clear that he was an important figure within English Protestant circles and one of the movement's leading writers.[8]

There are two sides to Bale's understanding of sodomy.[9] At one level it is clear that for Bale sodomy is a general sexual crime. Masturbation, cross-dressing, self-castration and bestiality are for Bale all sodomitical acts.[10] Indeed as far as he was concerned the papists' subversion of monarchical power and their corruption of Scripture could also be seen as sodomitical since in Bale's writing they are invariably represented as being caused by the papist's addiction to sodomy. In *The First Two Partes of the Actes or Unchaste Examples of Englyshe Votaryes, gathered out of theyr owne legendes and Chronicles* (1560) Bale describes how the papists have throughout history attacked the power of monarchs and subverted the teachings of Christ in order to protect and further their sodomitical practices and desires.[11] For Bale Rome is a 'synnefull ... syncke ' and a 'pernicious puddell' that has infected all the world with its 'Sodometrous vow' of chastity.[12] A crucial element in Bale's understanding of sodomy is its relationship to the papist's false or failed chastity. Bale argues that this vow produces a simulated chastity – sodomy. He writes that the Roman Church told its priests that they '... shuld ether live chast, that is to say, become Sodomites (for [that] hath bene their chastity ever se[n]ce) or els be suspended fro[m] al spiritual jurisdiction'.[13] There is therefore for Bale a causal link between the vow of chastity and sodomy, not in a simple or stable way however, since it is unclear in Bale's text if the enforced celibacy produced sodomy or was simply an excuse for it. It appears that Bale could not make up his mind if the papists were sodomites who invented clerical celibacy in order to allow them to indulge their perverse desires or if these desires were themselves a product of the impossibility of male chastity.

At the opening of First Part of *The Actes or Unchaste Examples of Englyshe Votaryes* Bale writes:

> Wheras [God] hathe declared marryage excedingly good, [the papists] have conde[m]ned it / as a thing execrable [and] wicked. And wheras he hath spoken it by his own mouth, that it is not good for man to be alone, they have improved that doctrine and taughte the contrarye, as a thing more perfight and godly.[14]

Bale goes on to spell out the effects of this reversal of God's natural order.

> For this presumption God gave them clerely over, and left them to them selves withal their good intents [and] vowes, wherupo[n] they have wrought sence that time filthines unspekeable. Their chast wome[n], vestals Monials, nunnes, and Begines, cha[n]ging [the] natural use, haue wrought unnaturally. Likewise the men in theyr prelacies, priesthodes [and] innumerable kindes of Monkery, for want of women hath brent in theyr lusts [and] done abhominations without no[m]bre ...[15]

This passage is marked by a number of tensions that run throughout Bale's work. It is unclear if it is the lack of women that makes the papists sodomites although the implication of this passage seems to be that had they had access to the proper outlet for their desires, women, they would not have indulged in sodomy. Obviously one can take this logic a step further and argue that Bale's understanding of sodomy is based on an assumption that all men, if denied women, have the potential, indeed the propensity, to become sodomites.[16] Another important element of this passage is Bale's claim that the crimes of the papist clergy are unspeakable and beyond number. Bale then goes on, however, at considerable length, to describe these crimes in such detail that he is clearly aiming to speak every single one of them. There is therefore a hysterical side to Bale's response to sodomy; he has to name and describe all its manifestations in order to prove himself wrong – that the papist's crimes can be named and numbered.

Bale's desire to display the sexual crimes of his enemies to the public's gaze is central to his historical project of writing the truth of papist corruption back into the chronicle.[17] In the process, however, a tension enters Bale's historical work since the status of his truth, Protestantism, as absolute and non-performative means that it hardly appears at all in *The Actes or Unchaste Examples of Englyshe Votaryes*. This text is full of lengthy descriptions of papist crimes and in particular their sodomitical practices. It is sodomy that fills Bale's text and which is the site of textual play and slippage. In *The Actes or Unchaste Examples of Englyshe Votaryes* Bale acts as a kind of premature deconstructive critic, simultaneously arguing the papistry is based on a subversion of the relationship between signifier and signified and using the possibilities created precisely by just such a subversion to construct the linguistic and sexual corruption of papistry. For example Bale claims that his intention in writing *The Actes or Unchaste Examples of Englyshe Votaryes* is to expose the papist's 'hipocrisy, lies, falshead, unclennesse, Idolatry, prodigious lustes, defilinges of body, chaunginge of the naturall use into an use againste nature, and other unspeakable beastlynesse'.[18] This list represents papistry as being inappropriately textually productive; as Bale piles up more and more words to describe the corruption of the papists, his text itself is infected by a simultaneous excess but also scarcity of meaning. The words spill forth but finally the beastliness of the papists is unspeakable.[19] Bale equates his work explicitly with God's promise to pull the Whore of Babylon's clothes over her head to show her nakedness and exposure her 'uncomelye priuvities', to all the world.[20] In these terms it is clear that *The Actes or Unchaste Examples of Englyshe Votaryes* embodies a frankly voyeuristic agenda in which the reader is repeatedly invited to gaze on the 'uncomelye privities' of papistry with horror but also with desire and fascination. Bale's text invites its reader to consume its accounts of the sodomitical practices; to see them as horrific but also to enjoy this moment of exposure and inspection.

Sodomy in Bale's work is marked by textual, political and above all sexual corruption. Although it is unclear whether for Bale sodomy came before the sodomite or visa versa, it does seem that for him at one level all men, potentially, could be tempted if placed in the impossible position created by the papist's vow of chastity. This means that Bale's representation of sodomy in *The Actes or Unchaste Examples of Englyshe Votaryes*, and in his other works, has important implications in terms of our understandings of early modern heterosexuality. For Bale the heterosexual is a norm that is so reduced and constrained that it is difficult to imagine anyone being able to live up to it. This is, of course, what one would expect in terms of the work of theorists such as Judith Butler. Bale consistently represents heterosexuality, and more precisely heterosexual masculinity, in terms that are not only alarmingly absolute but which reject any possibility of it being anything other then given and natural. Anything that

would or even could make one's masculinity look at all like that of the sodomitical papists is rejected out of hand; passivity, the performative and even
the body itself. This creates a situation in which for Bale true heterosexual
masculinity cannot really be described or put into a text since to do so would
automatically place it alongside or adjacent to sodomy. This in turn would of
course create the dangerous possibility of the one seeping into or crossing over
into the other.

Bale's work embodies a structure in which a moment of making visible,
of exposing papist sodomy and forcing it out of the closet, is constantly
repeated for the reader's fetishistic consumption. Bale invites his readers to
gaze with horror, but also pleasure, on the sodomitical practices of his enemies.
He incites us to regard the acts he describes as beastly and counts on our desire
constantly to repeat this confrontation with sodomy to provide his text with
narrative motivation. In the process Bale makes his readers participants in a discourse of sodomy. He, like his arch-enemies the sodomites, uses textual play
to seduce his willing victims into an endless consumption of sodomy.[21]

This discussion of John Bale's representation of sodomy has, however, left
a number of key questions and issues unanswered. Above all, while it is clear
that for Bale sodomy was a sin that could encompass a number of sexual perversions and practices, it is less certain whether he regarded being a sodomite
as something that was a possibility for all men or if, as far as he was concerned,
one had to have a propensity for this kind of behaviour. Were papists naturally
sodomites or could any man end up indulging in sodomy if his natural desires
were distorted by something as corrupting as clerical celibacy? Bale's confusion
on this point can be seen as reproducing the discussions within modern
accounts of early modern sexualities over the relationship between sexual acts
and identities – did the acts make the man or vice versa?

In his works, historical, polemical and dramatic, Bale spends a lot of time
on and with sodomy. His representations of true or proper masculinity are,
however, limited and restrictive and leave very little room for the possibility of
non-sodomitical homoeroticism or even of any kind of loving relationship
between men. This is not, however, the case of the work of his fellow Protestant historian, John Foxe, whose major work, *Acts and Monuments*, contains a
number of clearly homoerotic moments and images.

Sodomy in *Acts and Monuments*

John Foxe was in many ways a protégé of John Bale. Foxe appears to have kept
a low profile during the last years of Henry VIII's reign when the passing of the
Act of Six Articles in 1539 inaugurated a period when Protestants such as Foxe

were persecuted, During Edward VI's reign he took an active part in the
Edwardian Reformation, publishing a number of works. With Mary's succes-
sion he went into exile only to return, like Bale, with the advent of Elizabeth.
Foxe wrote what was one of the most influential works of history produced in
English during the early modern period, *Acts and Monuments*.[22] This work,
which went through six editions in Foxe's lifetime, two in Latin and four in
English, is a massive work. It details, often in horrific detail, the sufferings of
Christian martyrs throughout history. It is not, however, in any sense a work of
impartial history. For Foxe early Christian martyrs and those burnt by Mary
Tudor's regime were all part of the invisible true Church of God.

Foxe's version of history was almost identical to Bale's. However, he
departed from the example set by his mentor in one important way. While *Acts
and Monuments* does contain plenty of anti-papist polemic it does not reproduce
the stress on papistry's sodomy found in such works as *The Actes or Unchaste
Examples of Englyshe Votaryes*. Indeed in the 1570 edition of *Acts and Monuments*
there are only two index entries to sodomy. One of these, however, perhaps
explains why Foxe was far more circumspect in his area than Bale was.

One of the key moments in English Church history for Bale was the imposition of clerical celibacy by Anselm. Foxe discusses this moment and goes on
to relate it directly to the appearance of sodomy within the clergy: 'after the
restreinte of priests marriage: when filthy Sodomitrie began to come in the
place therof, the[n] were they [the clergy] forced also, to make an acte for
that'.[23] As in *The Actes or Unchaste Examples of Englyshe Votaryes* sodomy is here
seen as a product of clerical celibacy. The punishment for this 'new' sin was
excommunication, with this sentence and its cause being published every week
in parish churches across the country. Foxe explains, however, that

> this grevous generall curse was soone called backe agayne, by the sute of cer-
> tayne: which persuaded Anselme, that the publication or opening of that vice,
> gave kindlings to the same in the hartes of lewde persons: ministering occasion of
> more boldnes to them to do the like. And so to stop the occasion of filthy Sodomi-
> tyre, the publication therof / was taken away, but the forbidding and restreinment
> of priestes unlawfull marriage (which chiefly was the cause therof) remained stil.
> And thus ever since, horrible Sodomitry remanyned in the Clergy, both for lacke
> of marriage more used, and for lacke of publication, less punished.[24]

There are a number of important points to make about this passage. Sodomy in
this passage is a sexual practice produced by clerical celibacy, a desire kindled
in the hearts of 'lewde people' and a personified sin who, like one of the
sodomitical vices in Bale's religious drama, finds a safe place to hide within the
precincts of the clergy. It is also important to note that the term 'lewde people'
has clear class implications. The publication of the clergy's sin of sodomy within

parish churches means that some lower-class people will be, or might be, encouraged to indulge their existing tendency towards sodomy. This argument is not, however, Foxe's. Indeed it is noticeable that it embodies a lack of confidence in the intelligence of the congregation that was common among those churchmen who did not share Foxe's Puritan leanings. This passage in *Act and Monuments* perfectly illustrates the kind of tensions that could coalesce around sodomy within early modern texts. The reason that the curse against sodomy was stopped was, in terms of this passage, because of the dangers of publicity – publishing sodomy was turning medieval parish churches into gay chat rooms where men who desired sex with other men could go to find willing partners. This meant, however, that sodomy remained within the papist clergy, unpublished and unpunished. For Bale it was precisely this lack of publication that provided the motivation for his historical work: however, as has been already suggested, Foxe was far more circumspect then Bale in this area. This lack of explicitness creates a situation in which *Acts and Monuments* itself becomes a site of suppressed or at least non-spoken sodomy; a historical closet containing the truth of the papist's sexual perversities but failing to speak their name.[25] Foxe's work consistently shies away from explicit accusations of sodomy while being prepared to imply that specific papist clergymen did have sodomitical tendencies. The reasons for this more subtle approach can be related to the extent to which in *Acts and Monuments* close and potentially homo erotic relationships between Protestant men are often held up as exemplary and commendable.

These issues can be illustrated by examining a woodcut entitled 'The right Picture and true counterfeite of Bonner, and his crueltie, in scourgyng of Gods Sainctes in is Orchard at Fulham'.[26] This picture is in the first English edition of Foxe's text, 1563, and in all subsequent versions printed during the sixteenth century.[27] This woodcut depicts Bishop Bonner beating a Protestant in the garden of his house in Fulham. Bonner, as bishop of London, was one of the leading figures in the attempt during the reign of Mary Tudor to purge England of Protestants and restore the realm to Catholicism. Protestants writers like Bale and Foxe painted a very damning picture of Bonner as a bloodthirsty fiend. He actually appears, however, to have often gone out of his way to give Protestants a chance to recant in order to spare them the ordeal of being burnt alive as heretics.

Historians and literary critics have used this picture to sustain the argument that some of the illustrations in *Acts and Monuments* are accurate or even mimetic representations of historical events. Bonner is alleged to have commented on this woodcut's accuracy after being shown a copy.[28] Of course it is possible that this is true and that the former Bishop of London welcomed, or at least recognised as minimally truthful, a picture that depicted him as a violent lower-class sodomite – although personally I think this is unlikely.

'The right Picture and true counterfeite of Bonner, and his crueltie,
in scourgying of Gods Sainctes in is Orchard at Fulham'.
From John Foxe, *Acts and Monuments* (London: 1570), p. 2242.
By permission of the Syndics of Cambridge University Library.

Bonner is depicted in this woodcut in a state of passion, his clothes are
disarrayed and his body is bursting out of them. He is sweating and his brows are
creased with anger. The Bonner of this woodcut is a disordered man; one whose
body determines his behaviour; a man of the flesh. The fact that his clothes do
not fit him could be a reference to the common Protestant criticism of Bonner's
relatively lowly background. His clothes do not fit him in this picture because,
like his position within the Church, they were intended for a higher class and a
better-educated man. Bonner is also represented in this picture as a feminine
man. His shaved state indicates an undue and therefore female-like concern for
personal appearance. Indeed the unruly nature of his body is itself a sign of his
femininity since men were meant to keep their bodies under control while, as all
Tudor men knew, women were incapable of exercising any restraint in this area.
This picture also has a historical side. It represents Bonner as sharing the characteristics of morality play vices and, more specifically, of Herod as he is portrayed
in the Corpus Christi drama.[29] It also reproduces in pictorial form the representation of clerical tyrants found in such Lollard works as *Thorpe's Confession*.[30]

Although this woodcut clearly implies that for Bonner beating a man on his buttocks had a sexual meaning, the Bishop's sodomitical desires are not spelt out in the accompanying text. Instead it is left up to the reader to draw the obvious conclusions. Foxe, however, shapes his narrative, and indeed his general account of Bonner in *Acts and Monuments*, so that one is primed to see sodomy in Bonner's actions. Bonner is here shown whipping a man within his garden in Fulham. This is possibly a reference to the similar (alleged) treatment of heretics by Thomas More and, perhaps more importantly, to the supposed tendency of school teachers to indulge their sodomy by beating their charges. The site of this beating is also significant. It takes place within the walls of Bonner's garden in Fulham. This places it within a Biblical discourse – the scourging of Christ – and in a carnivalesque/romance one – gardens as places of courtly love and river banks as potentially liminal sites of carnival, and in particular of sexual transgression. Indeed Foxe constantly emphasises the places within which Bonner beats men. For example in the case of John Milles Bonner is alleged to have taken him to his Orchard and 'there within a little herdaur, with his own handes beat him, first with a willow rod, and that being worne well nigh to the stumpes, he called for a burchen rod, which a lad brought out of his chamber'.[31] Gardens with little arbours, bedrooms with birch rods and ostentatious codpieces – why would a Bishop need these things? The conclusion that Foxe clearly wants us to draw from this evidence is that Bonner used his position in order to indulge his sodomitical desires.

There are, however, a number of other figures in this woodcut, in partic-ular the two Protestants. I want to concentrate on the man who has presum-ably been forced to participate in the beating of his fellow believer by holding the latter's head between his legs. This figure is depicted 'peeping' between closed figures at the scene of Bonner's violence. He knows the scene is horrific and terrifying but he also knows he must look, he has a duty to see and know. The other men in the picture, apart from these two unwilling participants, are all implicated in Bonner's sodomitical desire. This woodcut is clearly inviting its reader to identify with the standing Protestant figure whose role is to wit-ness his fellow believer's humiliation. Sodomy functions in this woodcut to incite its reader to adopt an explicitly Protestant gaze – one stabilised and sus-tained through a simultaneous recognition and rejection of papist sodomy. To read this picture 'properly' one needs to see but also deny the sodomy that its depicts. The woodcut deploys sodomitical desire to position its reader as a pro-ducer of Protestant truth – sodomy here is the unnamed but implicit meaning of Bonner's actions, his 'crueltie', that the viewer of this woodcut is incited to find and reject.

There are, however, two sets of relations between men being represented in this woodcut. Obviously at one level Bonner and the man he is beating are sharing an albeit far from mutual sodomitical moment, but how is one to describe the relationship between the two Protestant men in this woodcut? The standing figure can be seen as being in direct opposition to Bonner. He is helping his fellow believer in an act of comradeship while Bonner's behaviour, as has been suggested, can be seen as a parody of that of humanist tutors who beat their charges for their own good to help them learn. Protestants were not meant to resist oppressions violently but this is not really the issue in the picture since there is no reason why there should be anyone holding the man being beaten down – or rather would it not make sense for this to be a papist oppressor? Foxe and/or his illustrator wanted to make a point about the relationship between Protestants by putting two of them into the picture. Their passiveness could have the effect of raising a question mark over their masculinity. At the same time their beards mark them in iconographic terms as masculine in opposition to the clean-shaven papists.[32] In this woodcut passivity is a sign of masculinity since it is the papists who, like women, have, in the figure of Bonner, lost control of themselves and have become slaves to their bodies. It is they, and not the suffering Protestants who are inverting the natural order and disrupting gender norms.

Amicitia in Acts and Monuments

The relationship between the two Protestant men in the picture can be seen as a pictorial representation of that between other male martyrs in Acts and Monuments. Foxe's work contains numerous letters exchanged between the male leaders of English Protestantism. Many of these texts are formal and are concerned with theological questions. However, a considerable number are pastoral, and these were designed to give succour and guidance to the recipient. The economy of these exchanges, perhaps not surprisingly, reproduces the norms of early modern relationships between men. In 1556 John Careless wrote to John Philpot to thank him for an earlier epistle. Careless opens his letter with a number of verses from Ecclesiasticus celebrating friendship

> A faythful friend is a strong defence; who so findeth such a one, findeth treasure.
>   A faithful friend hath no peer; the weight of gold and silver is not to be compared to the goodness of his fayth.
>   A faythful friend is a medicine of lyfe, and they that fear the Lord shall finde hym Ecclesiast 6.[33]

Careless goes on to thank Philpot for his words of comfort and support.

> Ah, my true louing friend! How soone did you lay aside all other business to make a swete plaster for my wounded conscience, yea, and that out of a painefull paire

of stockes, which place must nedes be uneasie to write in. But God hath brought you into a strait place, that you might set my soule at liberty. Out of your pinchyng and painful seat, you haue plentifully poured upon me you precious narde, the sweet savour wherof hath greatly refreshed my tried soul. The Lord likewise refresh you, both body and soul, by pouryng the oyl of his gracious spirite into your sweete hart. [34]

In this passage Careless is drawing on conventional Biblical tropes, drawn from from the Song of Songs, to represent his friendship with Philpot as part of the larger relationship of Christ to the Church and the believer. At the same time it is important to notice the homoerotic aspects of this passage. In particular Careless's text deploys a metaphor based upon the circulation of healing liquid from one man to another to imagine men taking part in mutual social and loving exchange. Later in this same letter Careless produces an extended metaphor on Philpot's name.

O my good m. Philpot, which art a principal pot in dede, filled with most precious liquor, as it appeareth by the plenteous pouring forth of the same. O pot most happy, of the high Potter ordained to honour, which doest containe such heavenly treasure in thy earthen vessel: O pot thrice happy, in whom Christ hath wrought a great miracle, altering thy nature, and turning water into wine, and that of the best, where out the Master of the feast hath filled my cup so full, that I am become drunken in joy of the Spirit through the same. [35]

Careless seems to have been concerned that he is going a bit over the top in this passage as he goes on to ask Philpot not to be offended 'at my metaphoricall speech'. I find Careless's letter deeply moving. It was written from gaol, in the shadows of the martyr's pyre but manages to be tender and witty. Again, as with the earlier passage, Careless is here using Biblical imagery to equate his friend's wine/words with Christ's.

Careless's letter is his response to an earlier letter from Philpot in which the latter wrote:

Since God hath willed you at your Baptism in Christ to be Careless, why do you make yourself careful? Cast all your care on him. Set the Lord before your eyes alwayes, for he is on your right side, that you shall not be moved. Behold the goodness of God toward me. I am careles, being fast closed in a payre of stocks, which pinch me for very straitness; and will you be carefull. I would not have that unseemely addition to your name. [36]

What we see in these letters is the articulation of a friendship between two men based on the exchange of playful texts, albeit written in terrible conditions, embodying Biblical imagery that is clearly intimate and potentially erotic. In particular, the play that each of these men makes with the other's name is noticeable. At one level this is can be seen as simply a typical piece of humanist display; however, one can also see it as an attempt to subvert the meaning that the Marian authorities had imposed or inscribed upon them. The meaning of the labels 'Careless' and 'Philpot' was a matter of dispute between these two men and their gaolers. While the latter sought to make 'Careless' and 'Philpot' the names of notorious heretics, the letters that Careless and Philpot exchanged can be seen as part of an attempt to wrest back control of who they were from their gaolers. And in this textual struggle the humanist discourse of male friendship proved an important weapon for Philpot and Careless.[37] In this context it is worthwhile noting that Careless's letters to his wife seem extremely formal and impersonal in comparison with those he writes to Philpot.

This is not, however, to argue that Careless and Philpot were lovers. Rather it is to argue that they loved each other but that this meant something quite different to what it would today. The homoeroticism of these letters, and that embodied in the figures of the two Protestant men in the picture depicting Bonner, is not inherently subversive of early modern social or gender norms. It is rather a signifier of order against the social and sexual disorder of the papists. Bonner's sodomy, like his femininity and his low social class, are all represented as a products of his fallen sinful nature while the homoeroticism expressed in the relationships between male martyrs in *Acts and Monuments* protects them from all that is embodied in the figure of Bonner. The proper hierarchical relationship between Careless and Philpot, with the younger man clearly accepting the authority of his older friend, is held up by Foxe as a model for male relationships. It is based on godliness, on humanist ideals concerning friendship – which include care and love – and is constructed explicitly against the sodomitical figure of the papists.[38]

There is, however, an aspect of the behaviour of the Careless and Philpot and that of two Protestant figures in 'The right Picture and true counterfeite of Bonner' which does seem to put their masculinity into doubt, and that is their passivity. As has been suggested in terms of the men in the woodcut, one can argue that their passivity should be seen against the out-of-control corporeality of Bonner. However, Careless and Philpot could also be seen as being dangerously emasculated by their incarnation. Alan Stewart has discussed in detail in his book *Close Readers: Humanism and Sodomy in Early Modern England* the dynamics of humanist friendships. One of Stewart's most important arguments is that humanist writers such as Roger Ascham strategically deploy humanist notions of friendship, *amicitia*, to explain relationships whose politics were potentially dangerous. Indeed Stewart argues that in the case of Ascham the latter 'recognised the possibility of an erotic interpretation of his relationship' and understood it 'as a way of deflecting interest in a *political* interpretation'.[39]

There were a number of attractive reasons for Foxe to encourage his readers to deploy the concept of *amicitia* in relation to male Marian martyrs. Seeing

Philpot and Careless in terms of humanist understandings of male friendship allowed their enforced passivity to be given a positive gloss. Indeed one lesson that the reader could take from the letters that these two men exchanged was that they had found in male friendship a way of resisting their imprisonment and enforced passivity.[40] It may be that for Foxe, and indeed Philpot and Careless, inciting readers to see their letters as homoerotic had advantages since it effectively placed Protestant resistance to Mary Tudor's regime within a personal, even intimate sphere.[41] This would be attractive to Foxe since one of the uncomfortable facts that *Acts and Monuments* seeks to obscure is that Protestant exiles from Marian England constantly plotted the Queen's violent deposition and produced texts that articulated resistance theories quite antithetical to the official teaching of English Protestantism. Foxe's representation of martyrs such as Careless or Philpot as exemplary created the impression that humanist and Protestant stoicism was the normative response of English Protestants to the Marian regime.

The image of Careless and Philpot's relationship produced in *Acts and Monuments* through their letters seems designed to make Elizabethan readers see it as being clearly based upon humanist principles. In *Close Readers* Stewart argues that in the early modern period:

> humanism – in its constant lip service to equality between patron and patronised who are by definition socially unequal – signals an alternative economy of social relations, which produces anxiety; sodomy, too, signals an alternative economy of social relationships which produces another anxiety.[42]

Philpot's and Careless's letters play with ideas of parity while throughout acknowledging the former's seniority. At the same time the play with names creates an image of men reading men, playing with each other's names, that is homoerotic. However, what makes these letters unproblematic is that the readers of *Acts and Monuments* knew that these two men were physically separated. The forced passivity of imprisonment allows the production of images of male friendship that can never slip into sodomy. The masculine friend and the sodomite are kept apart in *Acts and Monuments* by the prison wall. And perhaps it was only such physical barriers that could achieve this in Tudor England.

Conclusion

A distinction is implicitly drawn in *Acts and Monuments* between a homoeroticism that is humanist and ordered and a sodomy that is represented as disordered and bodily. In Bale's work such a separation would be meaningless since for him sodomy seems to be such a dangerous possibility within all men that the only possible protection against it was the maintenance of a fixed, almost robotic, manhood. Perhaps it was Foxe's humanism that encouraged him in *Acts and Monuments* to produce a more positive and subtle image of masculinity, and in particular close male friendships. However, it may be that he had no choice in the matter. Although there is ample evidence that Foxe was prepared to tamper with the texts that make up *Acts and Monuments*, there is also plenty of evidence to suggest that Philpot's and Careless's letters would have been treated by Foxe with care.[43]

The texts that Foxe was least careful with were those of the lower-class radicals whose beliefs clashed with his own magisterial Protestantism. Of course this class hierarchy of textual remains was the absolute norm in Tudor culture. Perhaps more worryingly it can also be discerned in the field of gay and queer literary studies - and obviously in this chapter. Indeed the class tensions reflected in the woodcut of Bonner can be seen also in the work of some late-twentieth-century scholars. Rosemary Hennessy has argued that 'the formation of a gay/queer imaginary in both corporate and academic circles … rests on the suppression of class analysis'. She goes on to argue that if one asks the question 'how the achievement of lesbian and gay visibility by some rests on the invisible labour of others' one exposes the 'unspeakable underside of queer critique'.[44] The desire to find the homoerotic in the heart of the literary masterpiece, through a process of complex and sophisticated textual analysis, has undoubtedly meant that among literary critics there has been an undue emphasis on complex canonical texts. We should be aware that such an agenda may reflect rather too closely the polemical concerns of writers such as Foxe who would far rather we spend time reading the complex humanist letters of Careless and Philpot than asking difficult political questions or, even worse, becoming over-concerned with the words of artisans or workers.

NOTES
1 William Caxton, *Chronicle*, 1480 (Amsterdam: 1973), a4 (8V).
2 This chapter is exclusively concerned with male homosexuality. Despite the now common practice of collapsing male and female same-sex behaviour and desire into one category, it is clear that this move is inappropriate in terms of the early modern period.
3 Put this starkly, one can see why this debate over the status of homosexuality has a tendency to become rather heated. In particular, any claim that homosexuality is a historical phenomenon, and that it has not always existed, can feed, and indeed has fed, into homophobic constructions of homosexuality as modern, decadent and unnatural. In any discussion of this kind, one needs to be aware that all too many people in our culture share a homophobic fantasy of eradicating homosexuality and homosexuals.
4 In particular one needs to note the issues surrounding identification and subjecthood. For a discussion of these matters see Judith Butler, *The Psychic Life of Power: Theories in Subjection* (Stanford: 1997).
5 Alan Bray, 'Homosexuality and the Signs of Male Friendship in Elizabethan England', *History Workshop Journal* 29 (1990), pp. 1–19, 1.
6 Andrew Hadfield, *The English Renaissance 1500–1620* (Oxford: 2001), p. 45.

7 I will be using the term *papist* to refer to Bale's, and later John Foxe's, opponents. This is because for Bale his enemies were not Catholics – indeed he regarded himself as a Catholic. They were corrupters of the truth of God's teaching. Obviously, this is not my view of the people whom Bale wrote against.

8 On John Bale see Leslie P. Fairfield, *John Bale: Mythmaker of the English Reformation* (West Layafette, Indiana: 1976).

9 For the most authoritative recent discussion of Bale's use of sodomy in his polemical work see Alan Stewart, *Close Readers: Humanism and Sodomy in Early Modern England* (Princeton: 1997). See also Donald N. Mager, 'John Bale and Early Tudor Sodomy Discourse', in Jonathan Goldberg, ed., *Queering the Renaissance* (Durham, N.C.: 1994), pp. 141–61.

10 Garrett P. J. Epp comments that in Bale's play *Three Laws*, 'Sodomy is specifically male, an active force signifying illicit fleshly sexual activity'. Garrett P. J. Epp, '"Ito a Womannys Lyckenes": Bale's Personification of Idolatory: A Response to Alan Stewart', *Medieval English Theatre* 18 (1996), pp. 63–73, 66.

11 John Bale, *The First Two Partes of the Actes or Unchaste Examples of Englyshe Votaryes, gathered out of theyr owne legendes and Chronicles*, (London: 1560), STC 1274.

12 *Second Part*, Aii.

13 *First Part*, Lii.

14 *Ibid.*, Biv–Bii.

15 *Ibid.*, Bii.

16 It is also clear that for Bale this logic also applies to women.

17 Alan Stewart comments that 'In *Actes of Englysh Votaryes* ... Bale takes some popular and apparently innocuous stories and exposes (or creates) a sodomitical subtext'. Stewart, 1997, p. 42.

18 Bale, *Second Part*, Bii.

19 One can relate the textual effects of sodomy in Bale's text to Jonathan Goldberg's suggestion that sodomy in the Renaissance, and after, is in some ways inherently deconstructive since its protean nature and lack of stability means not only that its own meaning is precarious but also that it has a subversive effect on meaning itself. See Goldberg, *Sodometries: Renaissance Texts, Modern Sexualities* (Stanford: 1992), p 20.

20 Bale, *Second Part*, Bi–Biv.

21 The problem that Bale had defining sodomy was matched by similar problems when it came to defining the true church. For a discussion of this aspect of Bale's work see Claire McEachern, '"A whore at the first blush seemth only a woman": John Bale's *Image of Both Churches* and the Terms of Religious Difference in the Early English Reformation', *Journal of Medieval and Renaissance Studies* 25 (1995), pp. 243–69.

22 Although I shall refer to John Foxe as the author of *Acts and Monuments* it is important to note that this work is made up of a mass of other texts, letters, tracts, accounts of examinations, poems, etc. which Foxe assembled into one massive historical account of the English Church.

23 John Foxe, *Acts and Monuments* (London: 1570), p. 250.

24 *Ibid.*, pp. 250–1.

25 In these terms *Acts and Monuments* perfectly illustrates Bruce Smith's suggestion that 'homosexuality is not so much hidden *from* history as hidden *in* history'. Bruce Smith, *Homosexual Desire in Shakespeare's England: A Cultural Poetics* (Chicago: 1991), p. 12.

26 For a brief but interesting discussion of this picture see Diarmaid MacCulloch, *The Tudor Church Militant* (London: 1999), pp. 144–6.

27 For the woodcuts in Foxe's work see Margaret Aston and Elizabeth Ingram, 'The Iconography of the Acts and Monuments', in David Loades, ed., *John Foxe and the English Reformation* (Aldershot: 1997), pp. 66–142.

28 See J. F. Mozley, *John Foxe and His Book* (London: 1940), p. 131.

29 In these dramas Herod beats the messenger who informs him the wise men have left without telling him where Christ is. See Richard Beadle and Pamela King, eds, *York Mystery Plays: A Selection in Modern Spelling* (Oxford: 1991), pp. 65–97.

30 The violence in this picture performs a similar function to that of sodomitical desire; it encourages the reader to see Bonner as embodying characteristically cruel papist tendencies within a limited historical field of vision.

31 Foxe, 1570, p. 2243.

32 I am grateful to Diarmaid MacCulloch for pointing out to me that the possession of beards in Protestant Tudor polemics was a sign of Protestantism and masculinity.

33 Foxe, 1570, p. 2103.

34 *Ibid.*, p. 2103.

35 *Ibid.*, p. 2103.

36 *Ibid.*, p. 2005.

37 Jeffrey Marsten suggests that 'Renaissance friendship texts inscribe an erotics of similitude that goes far beyond the modern conception of mere sameness of sex'. Playing games with each other's names in the way that Philpot and Careless do seems a clear example of the kind of Marsten's 'erotics of similitude'. See Jeffrey Marsten, *Textual Intercourse: Collaboration, Authorship, and Sexualities in Renaissance Drama* (Cambridge: 1997), p. 35.

38 Alan Bray has commented on the tensions between images of the masculine friend and the sodomite. Bray writes that 'The reaction that these two images prompted was wildly different; the one was universally admired [the masculine friend], the other execrated and feared: and yet in their uncompromising symmetry they paralleled each other in an uncanny way'. Bray, 'Homosexuality and the Signs of Male Friendship', 1.

39 Stewart, 1997, p. 127.

40 One of the most important influences on Foxe's thought was the humanist Erasmus. Patrick Collinson has pointed out the influence of Erasmian humanism on the character portraits of Protestant martyrs in *Acts and Monuments*. ee Patrick Collinson, ' "A Magazine of Religious Patterns": An Erasmian Topic Transposed in English Protestantism', in Derek Baker, ed., *Renaissance and Renewal in Christian History* (Oxford: 1977), pp. 223–49.

41 Mark Breitenberg makes the point that Foxe's textual practices, in particular his reproduction of letters, documents, and documents has the effect of extending the meaning of *Acts and Monuments* into the wider Protestant community. Foxe's readers were implicitly being invited to take part and share in such exchanges as those that took place between Careless and Philpot. See Mark Breitenberg, 'The Flesh Made Word: Foxe's Acts and Monuments', *Renaissance and Reformation / Renaissance et Réforme* 15 (1989), pp. 381–407.

42 Stewart, 1997, p. xxix.

43 On Foxe's use of his sources and his editing practices see Patrick Collinson, 'Truth and Legend: The Veracity of John Foxe's Book of Martyrs', in *Elizabethan Essays* (London: 1994), pp. 151–77.

44 Rosemary Hennessy, 'Queer Visibility in Commodity Culture', *Cultural Critique* 29 (1995), pp. 31–76, 68.

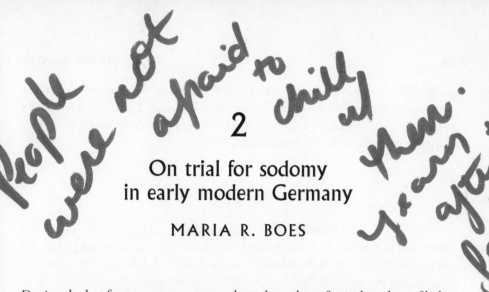

People not were not afraid to chill al then year are after fact.

2

On trial for sodomy in early modern Germany

MARIA R. BOES

During the last forty years an unprecedented number of suits have been filed in European and North American courts aimed at abolishing homosexual judicial and social exclusionary policies. Increasingly, acts of violence or harassment perpetrated against homosexuals enter the legal category of hate crimes. In this recent quest for emancipation and social justice, the courts can serve as liberating agents.[1] The opposite occurred in many parts of Europe during the early modern period.[2] Secular courts increasingly served as discriminating, and often eliminating, agents. Between 1459 and 1502 convictions for sodomy in Florence 'nearly quadrupled to a yearly average of 48'.[3] In Venice they jumped from eleven between 1348 and 1369 to 110 between 1448 and 1469.[4] In Aragon more than 150 men were sentenced to death during the period 1570 to 1630, and in Geneva fifteen received the same sentence during the period 1561 to 1610, while many others in these areas were subjected to severe corporal punishments.[5] Yet, while by the mid sixteenth century same-sex relations had become criminal in most European areas, this 'explosion of prosecutions' did not manifest itself uniformly.[6] In fact there were noticeable exceptions. One of them constituted the city of Frankfurt am Main, where only two men were sentenced between 1562 and 1696.[7]

It is the goal of this chapter to shed light on the underlying reasons behind this apparent divergent judicial norm by analysing the court records of Frankfurt's two trials. Several factors greatly facilitated this project. First, the nearly complete legal dossiers of the two cases. Located in Frankfurt's municipal archives, they contain statements by the suspects, witness accounts, detailed torture proceedings, legal opinions by the city's advocates, private pleas and summaries of the various judicial meetings.[8] The forty-seven-year time-span between the two sentences – 1598 to 1645 – proved to be advantageous for comparing and contrasting the various findings in the hopes of disclosing continuities and/or changes over time. Frankfurt's status as a free imperial city with political and judicial autonomy enhanced the objective of an

methods ←

in-depth socio-legal microanalysis such as this one and so did the city's hetero-
geneous religious composition. While predominantly Lutheran, Frankfurt's
community encompassed a Catholic minority and Jewish residents, as well as
Calvinist refugees from the Netherlands.

Judicial practices

Frankfurt's criminal jurisdiction lay in the hands of a city council, which was
composed of two-thirds patricians and one-third members of select guilds. All
councillors were men who belonged to the Lutheran Church. The council's
judicial powers extended over inhabitants and outsiders regardless of where
the crime had been committed. Its verdicts were final since there was no criminal court of appeal in the Holy Roman Empire. Similarly to that in most European areas, Frankfurt's criminal justice system operated without the help of an
independent or trained police force. The policing was done by the population.[9] The two cases under scrutiny thus do not only shed light on the city
council's judicial actions but also disclose insights into cultural interplays – or
the lack thereof – between Frankfurt's judiciary and its crime-reporting
agents: the people.

Frankfurt, like many other continental regions, had adopted inquisitorial
trial procedures. The *Constitutio Criminalis Carolina*, the criminal code promul-
gated by the Emperor Charles V in 1532, served as a guideline for the Holy
Roman Empire.[10] But free imperial cities such as Frankfurt and other
autonomous regions retained the right to diverge from the norm on the basis
of the Salvatory Clause. Inquisitorial procedures, heavily influenced by Roman
law, pivoted on the confession of the suspect, although two or three witnesses
could also bring about a conviction. If a guilty plea was not forthcoming, judicial torture could be applied and reapplied in order to elicit one. Both the witness interrogations and judicial tortures were carried out in seclusion in the
presence of only a few court members and not in front of an assembled court.
Witness accounts, given under oath, and statements elicited under torture
were written down and later read to the judiciary. Witnesses were never cross-
examined by the defence party. In fact, defence lawyers did not exist as yet.[11]
In contrast, the judiciary could and did consult legal advisers trained in Roman
law, the so-called advocates.

Hence, once a person became a suspect, he or she was in an isolated position. Without any legal assistance, suspects could rely only on their families
and friends or persons of higher social standing to plead with the judiciary on
their behalf.

Laws

The criminalisation process of same-sex relations is closely connected to the Roman Catholic Church, with its emphasis on the procreative purpose of sexual relations. Historians differ on the sentencing actions taken by the Church. John Boswell proposes a rather tolerant Church until the fourteenth century, despite restrictive ecclesiastical legislation, while others such as Warren Johansson and William A. Percy suggest the opposite. They stress the harshness of ecclesiastical actions from Pope Gregory the Great's legislation in the seventh century down to the Church's recommendation of death by burning during the Council of Nablus in 1120; of Thomas Aquinas' input in his *Summa Theologiae*; and Gregory IX's actions against heretics in southern France, which resulted in the correlation of same-sex relations to heresy, thus reinforcing death by fire.[12]

In contrast, secular legislation had a longer germination period. Germanic law codes, with three exceptions, did not cite same-sex relations as a felony.[13] Even the comprehensive *Sachsenspiegel* of 1230, one of the many regional codes of the Holy Roman Empire did not list any same-sex prohibitions.[14] However, with the reception of Roman law, the legal climate began to change, culminating two hundred years later in 1532 with Article 116 of the *Constitutio Criminalis Carolina* which criminalised such acts, including bestiality, as 'wider die natur', against nature, warranting death by burning.[15]

The contemporary term *sodomy* thus had a multiple meaning. Depending on the time and place, it also included sex between Christians and Jews, Turks and Saracens.[16] In Frankfurt's case the records use the term *sodomy* interchangeably for bestiality and same-sex relations. Although the city sentenced two men for sex with animals during this time frame, this chapter focuses on the two male-to-male sexual convictions only.[17] In compliance with contemporary practice, the term *sodomy* will be used throughout this chapter.

The case of Ludwig Boudin

Ludwig Boudin's case unfolded during the months of May to July 1598. Most curiously, the charge was launched by an individual who had no first-hand knowledge of his own allegations against the accused, namely sodomy, but based them on oral reports of others or on rumours in general. To make the case even more striking, the accuser, Thomas de Fuhr, was a French-speaking individual accusing another French-speaking person. Unfortunately the records do not disclose their place of origin, but it seems most likely that both belonged to the French-speaking group of Calvinist religious refugees from the

Netherlands whom the city of Frankfurt had allowed to settle locally.[18] The accused, a citizen of Frankfurt, was in fact a member of the local Reformed Church. Another common denominator between the accused and the accuser was their profession: they were both pastry bakers.

These common traits might have been purely accidental, but not according to the suspect. In a pre-trial summation he rebutted de Fuhr's charges of sodomy by proposing professional envy rather than sexual misconduct as the underlying reasons for the accuser's claim. In a lengthy and detailed statement the suspect recounted that several years previously de Fuhr's maid, after having been beaten by her employer, sought employment in his, Boudin's, household. To this he had agreed. As a consequence, the maid had diverted many customers from de Fuhr to her new employer. De Fuhr, greatly upset about this, had brought unfair practice charges against the suspect which were heard and consequently dismissed by the mayor. Boudin claimed that de Fuhr was very angry about the loss of his maid and customers and about the dismissed charges and had only two things in mind: to prevent him, Boudin, from continuing his trade and to have him removed from Frankfurt.[19] The suspect did, however, concede that he was aware that several years previously a *bös Geschrey*, a bad rumour, had circulated about him.

The accuser de Fuhr continued with his charges that a *bös Geschrey* had not only existed years ago but was, in fact, still making the rounds, and he pointed to various witnesses. He was successful with his claim because on 13 June, thirteen witnesses gave their rendition of the case. At first glance thirteen witnesses seem to be an impressive number of people with first-hand knowledge about the case. Upon closer analysis only six had experienced any direct contact with the accused while seven reported hearsay. They simply restated what other people, including the accuser, had told them. Yet they served as prosecuting witnesses.

This tendency to give credence to hearsay accounts obviously left the door wide open for judicial misuse. While this witness approach runs counter to modern notions of a fair trial, contemporaries seemed to be less inclined to think so, for Frankfurt's practices did not represent a judicial aberration. On the contrary, hearsay and rumour widely served as grounds for arrest. In a predominantly oral society, where people lived together in confined areas, and without an organised police force, rumour was used as a means for general and mutual surveillance.

Despite the apparent differences between the hearsay and contact witnesses, they shared common denominators. The time element stood out most conspicuously. In all instances the age of the witnesses was listed, as were the years of their encounters with the suspect. The witnesses ranged from eighteen to fifty years old at the time of the trial, and in many instances an extended period had elapsed between their experiences with the accused and the trial. A forty-six-year-old dated the incident to approximately twenty years ago; a forty-four-year-old cited a time frame of approximately four or five years; a thirty-year-old mentioned approximately six years. Only the two eighteen-year-olds cited a recent encounter with the accused, namely the previous 31 May.

These time elements are important for two reasons. First, the ages of the witnesses at the time of their experience with the suspect range from eighteen to over forty years. If we assume the accuracy of their statements, the suspect thus did not single out young men. This age distribution runs counter to findings from other areas, such as Florence, and Venice, where the 'classical, age-asymmetrical variant remained dominant' during the fifteenth century and where 'many of the male homosexual relations were pederastic'.[20] It also differs from findings for Aragon, for which E. William Monter asserts that 'as even the most sympathetic historian admits, the nearly invariable pattern of relationships was between older men and adolescents, between dominator and dominated'.[21] For Frankfurt this pattern could not be established in Boudin's case.

The second and arguably even more fascinating aspect of the time element is the prolonged time-span – over twenty years – between some of the witnesses' personal experiences with the accused (or, in the case of hearsay witnesses, their first learning about Boudin's alleged deeds) and the actual indictment. Moreover, it is safe to argue that more than thirteen people must have been aware of these innuendoes given Frankfurt's cramped topography and relatively small demographic size of only 17,000 to 19,000 inhabitants. In fact it is quite possible that the entire town knew about the rumours, especially considering Boudin's status as a fine pastry baker. The question thus arises how these rumours could circulate for such an extended period of time without any of Frankfurt's inhabitants taking recourse to an official indictment.

Witness accounts

Uninterrupted by any official questioning, the witnesses told their version of what had transpired. Three of the hearsay witnesses partly confirmed Boudin's rationale for his arrest, namely his competitor's anger at the loss of his maid resulting in financial distress. Strangely enough, they had heard this interpretation directly from the accuser de Fuhr. Two other hearsay witnesses stated that they had heard rumours about the suspect's alleged difficulties in his *Französiche Kirche* (French church), because he had touched boys. They also reported that they were familiar with the secular punishment for sodomy, death by fire.

Given the gossipy attitudes of early modern people, it is reasonably safe to conclude that, if two knew about this harsh penalty, many more were cognisant of it, including the suspect. Yet, for twenty years it did not deter Boudin from continuing his alleged same-sex pursuits; neither did it lead any of the locals to turn him in. The first clue to this riddle is provided by the following two witnesses.

A forty-six-year-old hearsay witness recounted that approximately twenty years previously a young boy had told him that Boudin had had dealings with another boy implying inappropriate sexual conduct. Rather than pursuing this rumour legally, the witness confronted Boudin directly, who refuted the charges by calling the boy a 'bad kid'. Another hearsay witness reported a similar verbal confrontational approach. Years ago, he had found a *pasquille*, a slanderous note, alluding to Boudin's sodomite behaviour. Instead of turning it over to the authorities for an investigation of the writer of this illegal note, and *ipso facto* alerting the authorities to rumours of Boudin's alleged sexual behaviour, he went directly to the suspect and showed him the letter. He admonished Boudin by telling him that he should be ashamed of himself. The suspect, according to the witness, seemed frightened but denied the allegations.

These hearsay witnesses thus preferred to deal with Boudin directly rather than have him legally prosecuted. It is also remarkable that they refrained from any threatening comments and physical assaults on the suspect. There remains, of course, the lingering doubt that these witnesses exhibited such a temperate approach while giving their renditions to the court. However, these reservations are offset by similar statements made by the contact witnesses.

A thirty-six-year-old recounted that approximately thirteen years previously on a late-night walk, he had met Boudin, who suggested he sleep over in his house, and he did. After he had fallen asleep, Boudin joined him in bed and started to touch him. But since he, the witness, turned around, nothing further could happen. In the morning Boudin got up and lay down beside his own wife – the first documented reference to the suspect's marital status. The witness's closing remarks, that *wisse sonsten nichts* (this was all he knew), exhibit a surprisingly matter-of-fact attitude on the part of a witness to sodomy, devoid of hatred, disgust or any other emotional reaction or value judgement.

An eighteen-year-old witness exhibited a similarly detached attitude. He stated that on 31 May, in the year of the indictment, Boudin, pretending to be drunk, had asked him to walk him home. On their way Boudin began to touch him, which he rejected by telling him that he, Boudin, had a wife. The next day the suspect asked him not to talk about the incident, claiming that when he had too much to drink he behaved strangely. To this the young witness simply replied that it did not bother him, it was none of his business – a rather nonchalant attitude for an eighteen-year-old, unless either the suspect or the issue itself appeared to be non-threatening to him.

A similar approach was evidenced by a twenty-two-year-old who stated that a couple of years previously he had been asked by his master to accompany Boudin to his home. Boudin, according to the witness, pretended to be drunk and touched him saying *er hab ihn gar lieb* (that he loved him). When the suspect repeated his emotional outburst and became sexually more demanding, the witness reproached him saying that he should be ashamed of himself and that he had a wife. Like the eighteen-year-old, this young man directed his seducer's sexual advances to his wife, in addition to using shame as a deterrent.

It is also remarkable that Boudin expressed his love for the young man. Not only did this declaration add a new dimension to a seemingly purely sexual trial, it also demonstrated that love between men existed and was verbally expressed.[22] Moreover, it says something about Frankfurt's general atmosphere about sodomy that Boudin felt free enough to express his innermost feelings despite the inherent judicial danger. It points to a divide between legal and popular sentiments towards sodomy.

Only one contact witness expressed anger at Boudin. A nineteen-year-old reported that, while the witness was drinking wine in Boudin's house, the suspect expressed his love for him and became sexually demanding. The witness angrily rejected his advances. His anger was, however, confined to a verbal outburst. A more sexually descriptive account was delivered by a thirty-year-old witness. He admitted that approximately six years previously, during his encounter with Boudin, both had engaged in sexual touching, which prompted Boudin to urge him to come home and sleep with him or 'he would get crazy'. The witness did not heed Boudin's request. He stated in his closing remarks that during the previous twelve years such intense rumours had spread around town that everyone became aware of Boudin's behaviour. The witness's apparent knowledge of the rumour, however, did not deter him from meeting with the suspect, let alone engaging in male-to-male sexual touching, unless, of course, he deliberately sought his company for these very reasons.

The statement of a thirty-one-year-old witness, referring to an episode of eight years previously, points in the same direction, namely that, despite such rumours, people were neither intimidated by nor frightened to associate with the suspect, or even to engage in close physical contact. The witness reported that one night he had met Boudin, who told him about a fight with his wife. As a consequence Boudin ended up staying in the witness's house, where they shared a bed for the night. Once in bed, Boudin touched the witness, who retorted that he should be ashamed and that 'such things belonged to women'. Similarly to previous witnesses, he brushed off Boudin's advances as sexual missteps, using guilt as the intimidator.

What prompted the witnesses and Frankfurt's people in general to exercise such restraint? The severe penalty for sodomy might have acted as a judicial

deterrent, especially since many seemed to have been aware of it. This interpretation, however, has to be seen against the backdrop of general sexual crime
sentencing. First, it increased dramatically towards the end of the sixteenth century, totalling 239 sentences during the 134-year period covered in this chapter.
Second, it also frequently entailed capital punishment.[23] A breakdown by category shows, however, that most of these sentences covered marriage-related
offences.[24] One thus has to expand the judicial deterrent argument to include
other factors such as the suspect's personality and the general local mentality
regarding sodomy.

It is reasonably safe to argue, on the basis of the witness accounts, that
Boudin was generally liked. Even the accuser's maid sought employment in the
suspect's house, and this despite the circulating rumours. She even enticed customers to switch from her previous employer to the suspect. In turn, had the
customers shown any abhorrent feelings against Boudin or sodomy, they would
surely not have bought his merchandise. Therefore, sodomy was not a deterrent. While the legislative and the judiciary, heavily influenced by Roman law,
took a very punitive stance, popular mentality was different though not indif-
ferent to the question of sodomy.

Judicial torture

After hearing the witness reports, the city council subjected Boudin to further
questioning. He was asked whether he knew why he was arrested, to which he
replied he did not. When his accuser de Fuhr was mentioned, the suspect
repeated his earlier allegations that de Fuhr was angry at him for employing his
maid and, as a consequence, started to talk badly about him. The suspect stated
that he knew the content of these talks, namely he was a sodomite. When the
interrogator referred to the various witness accounts alleging that he had had
contact with younger and older men, Boudin denied the accusations. While he
acknowledged knowing about the content of the slanderous note depicting him
as a sodomite, he countered that others were mentioned in that note as well.

Not satisfied with his answers, the councillors decided to subject him to
judicial torture. Initially Boudin was shown the torture instruments to intimi-
date him in the hopes of eliciting a confession. But since, again, he denied the
accusations, claiming they were based on hatred and jealousy, the interrogators
resorted to using the leg screw.

The first question posed under torture was an almost exact repetition
of a witness account, a pattern maintained throughout all consecutive torture
sessions regardless of whether the statements had been made by hearsay or contact witnesses. Boudin, under torture, replied that he would tell the truth if the

leg screw were removed, a request the interrogators granted. He now admitted that he had been touching one of the witnesses while lying in bed with him but he had been so drunk that he mistook him for his wife. He answered the second question in a similar fashion, saying that he had been too drunk even to remember the incident. Not satisfied, the interrogators reapplied the leg screw, more tightly than the first time, whereupon Boudin screamed in pain, begging to have it removed and saying he would tell them the truth. They complied, but Boudin again did not admit to any wrongdoing, repeatedly saying that he had been drunk and that when he was in this state he was a different person. He conceded, however, that occasionally he had been excessive in his dealings and he asked the city council for forgiveness. Since, again, the interrogators were not satisfied with his answers, Boudin was led to the rack and hoisted. But the suspect was persistent in his denial of sodomite behaviour.

Upon hearing Boudin's statements the following day, the city council decided to seek legal advice from its advocates. It was during the same session that the council listened to a plea from the suspect's wife to spare her husband from further torture. Ignoring the wife's plea, the advocates concluded, on the basis of the witness accounts and Boudin's own remark, that he was *genügsam überwiesen*, sufficiently proved guilty. Yet, they argued that, since the suspect had refused to confess under torture to any of the allegations, torture ought to be reapplied.

Two days later Boudin was informed that the city council had not been satisfied with his answers and that he was to be interrogated further. Again, he maintained his innocence. Questioned whether he had been ousted from the French church because he had had dealings with boys, he replied that these were false accusations; he did admit to having been refused communion.

After this exchange Boudin was hoisted on the rack. He screamed in pain maintaining his innocence. He was lowered from the rack and questioned further. But since he did not confess, he was hoisted again, and again he screamed in pain. This torturous procedure laced with intermittent questioning was carried out a further nine times, escalating the physical pain after each occurrence, so that all in all Boudin was subjected to eleven consecutive torture applications. Throughout Boudin was steadfast in denying most of the charges such as that he had sexually forced young boys. He repeated, however, that several times he had been under the influence of alcohol and when he was drunk he *sei ein armer Mensch* (was a pitiful person). Boudin at one point, screaming in pain, suggested that his accuser be questioned, and at another that if the city council wanted his life, so be it. It was only after he had become very weak that the interrogators had him removed from the rack.

One cannot help but ponder why the suspect was subjected to this extended series of excruciatingly painful judicial tortures, especially since they were conducted at the advice of Frankfurt's advocates, that is the same persons who, after Boudin had already been tortured three times, proclaimed the suspect to be guilty on the basis of witness accounts. This issue becomes even more puzzling when, later, Boudin's wife wanted copies of the various witnesses' and her husband's statements made under torture: the advocates refused to release the documents to her. Equally disconcerting is the fact that, despite Boudin's constant denial of a confession under torture, the advocates did not change their perceptions but reconfirmed their earlier findings of guilt. They based their assessment on six witness accounts yet they had subjected the suspect to torture on the basis of all thirteen. It is also troubling that there is no documentation disclosing the identity of the six witnesses upon whose accounts Boudin was to be convicted. One might attribute this omission to negligent recording were it not for other very detailed renditions of the case, including *nota benes* scribbled at the end of various documents referring to statements by the advocates.

Even the advocates' ensuing penal deliberations and decision seem perplexing. Conspicuously absent are any considerations of the accuser's motives for taking Boudin to court. Equally absent are deliberations with regard to the lack of proof of sexual bodily penetrations.[25] At best one can interpret Boudin's behaviour as unwanted touching or sexual overtures. While it is true that the advocates argued that, since the suspect had 'suffered a lot under torture', he should only be put in the public pillory and banished from Frankfurt for life at a distance of twenty miles, it is surprising that they consequently suggested that he should be subjected to further questioning.

While their consideration of Boudin's intense suffering under torture seems reassuring, one cannot help but wonder whether they did not use torture as an insidious punishment – a concept frequently applied to Jewish suspects – since they had already proclaimed the suspect guilty prior to the most intensive torture applications.[26] Also, why did they resort to this pattern of *ex post facto* questioning? A scribbled *nota bene* at the end of one of the documents furnishes an insight: one of the advocates had voiced a dissenting opinion proclaiming Boudin *de jure* innocent.

Yet this did not save Boudin from being exposed to additional verbal and visible judicial intimidations which included being led to the rack. Reasserting his earlier claims, he ended his deposition by asking a most revealing rhetorical question: 'why had all these witnesses been quiet for so many years – was it not their duty to report bad deeds to the authorities'?

Boudin's perceptive remarks, though most likely intended as a defence strategy, nevertheless confirm the proposition that the witnesses did not harbour a lot of resentment against him or his sodomite behaviour; otherwise they surely would not have bought his products, associated with him in private, even slept in his house and in his bed. It was only when de Fuhr, out of personal and financial motivations, resorted to officially indicting the suspect that the various people were legally obligated to speak out. And even then they demonstrated a remarkable restraint.

Frankfurt's population and thus popular opinion, while not necessarily in favour of sodomite behaviour, nevertheless seems to have been rather nonchalant about it. In fact, the suspect seems to have felt secure if not protected by the people's attitude for twenty years. Popular mentality served as a protective shield against judicial intrusion.

Forty-seven years later, this protective shield was still intact.

The case of Heinrich Krafft

Krafft's trial lasted from 10 March to 17 April 1645. The accused, a thirty-nine-year-old shopkeeper, was, like Boudin, a citizen and married. Unlike the previous suspect, however, his wife was pregnant and he had a son and daughter from a previous marriage. Apart from this, little else is known about him.

In Krafft's trial eleven witnesses were interrogated. As in the 1598 case, not all of these were contact witnesses. Two reported only hearsay accounts, which suggests that judicial procedures with regard to prosecuting witnesses had not changed during almost half a century. Unlike in the previous trial, however, none of the witnesses' ages was recorded in the documents. This does not mean that age was less important in this case than in the 1598; on the contrary. In Krafft's case the authorities stressed *Knabenschande* (seduction of boys) in their allegations.

Unfortunately the documents are vague as to what actually led to Krafft's indictment. It seems that a few possible suspects pointed to Krafft out of fear of being implicated. Apparently, rumours about Krafft's sodomite behaviour had been circulating for at least ten years according to the witness reports. Although the extended time-span from rumour to actual indictment resembled Boudin's case, most witness accounts exhibit a different tone, frequently stating resentment, anger, even fear of the suspect. A picture of victimisation emerges which had almost been absent in the 1598 case.

The question arises whether Krafft's behaviour was actually so provoking as to stir resentment or whether other, possibly judicial, factors were at work. Two witness records disclose, in fact, a different style of judicial questioning. In one instance the witness was asked whether he knew about Krafft's *Übelthat*, (criminal act), a suggestive inquiry which turned the suspect into a criminal before the verdict and thus left the door wide open for criminal innuendoes by the witness. In this particular case the witness reported that when on a

Saturday night he and Krafft went into the suspect's basement and drank wine, Krafft exposed himself and tried to sexually assault him. But since he screamed very loudly, Krafft had to let go of him.

The second suggestive question was even more targeted when a witness was asked outright whether the suspect had sexually assaulted him. Circumventing a direct reply, he described his encounter with Krafft from approximately five to six years previously. Similarly to the previous witness account, when he and the accused drank wine in Krafft's basement, the latter exposed himself and became sexually forceful with him. Once Krafft realised, according to the witness, that he could not achieve anything and that someone else had entered the basement, he let go of him. The witness, however, threatened that he would tell Krafft's wife about this incident. But whether he actually did was not disclosed in the documents. The witness finished his report by stating that he never had a drink with Krafft again.

Drinking wine in the suspect's basement emerged as a common theme. Six out of the eleven witnesses referred to it. One such was the witness who recounted his experience with Krafft from four years previously. While they were drinking wine in the suspect's basement, Krafft tried to sexually molest him during a three-hour period. Admitting to having been very scared, the witness asserted, however, that Krafft 'did not achieve what he wanted'. Closely connected to this account was the statement of one of the hearsay witnesses who disclosed that this witness, 'looking like death from fright', had come to his house, telling him what he just experienced in Krafft's basement.

The three additional witnesses who reported on wine-drinking in Krafft's basement differed, however, in their reactions to the suspect's overtures. One stated that he had told Krafft that his behaviour was dishonourable and dashed to the door, another recounted that he was 'shocked to death', and dashed to the door only to return the next day for a repeat scenario. The third such witness reported a similar repeat visit to Krafft's basement. On each occasion they drank wine and on each occasion the accused tried to sexually assault him. These two consecutive sexual molestations did not deter the witness from reassociating with Krafft. He reported that at a later date, when he and Krafft went for a walk, the suspect led him to another person's basement to drink wine. Again Krafft tried to sexually corner him, but he freed himself.

These last two witness accounts, while disclosing aggravated sexual assaults on the part of Krafft, seem, nevertheless, somewhat puzzling. The same two witnesses, after having experienced dramatic sexual assaults, returned and socialised with the suspect. Why would anyone, after having experienced unwanted sexual advances, go back to the same place seeking the company of the attacker? The question thus arises whether these witnesses did not greatly exaggerate their accounts under judicial scrutiny, either to cover up their own involvement and thus to appear above suspicion or to appease the judiciary since they had failed to report these incidents years previously.

It is equally remarkable that none of the witnesses, despite the frequent expression of anger in their testimonies, resorted to any personal physical retribution or revenge towards the suspect, nor did the local population, many of whom must have known about these incidents.

Judicial torture

Krafft now had to respond to these allegations. While, as in Boudin's case, many questions followed the witness accounts, the judiciary in Krafft's case diverged from these accounts by targeting sex with young boys and bestiality. The latter point has to be stressed because none of the witnesses had referred to, or uttered any insinuations tying Krafft to sex with animals.

Krafft vehemently denied these two charges. He also reversed some of the witness allegations, asserting that in one instance the witness had started with the physical exposure while in another it was the witness who initiated the sexual activities by talking about his previous male-to-male sexual encounters in other towns. Krafft, like Boudin, admitted, however, to having been drunk and that in this state he might have touched some of the men.

The excessive consumption of alcohol and Krafft's and Boudin's repeated references to drunkenness as a possible excuse for their behaviour, should not be interpreted as a sign of sodomite behaviour patterns.[27] Heavy drinking was a widespread contemporary cultural phenomenon, as demonstrated by the witnesses themselves.[28] In addition many of Frankfurt's criminal suspects used drunkenness as extenuating circumstances in the hopes of being acquitted or receiving a milder sentence.[29] Thus alcohol-related excuses were not unique to Boudin or Krafft.

Krafft asked the city council for forgiveness and pleaded to be released with a fine, citing his two children and the pregnancy of his present wife. He suggested donating the money to the poor. As in Boudin's case, an unmoved city council now sought the advice of its advocates. One of them, Jacob Schütz, stated that since the accused's confession was not complete and *mit Vieh aber will er nichts zu schaffen gehabt haben* (he did not admit to having had anything to do with animals), he should be interrogated further. It was in particular Krafft's denial of bestiality that seems to have irritated the advocates, for they now added four detailed bestiality-related questions: whether he did not keep goats at home and in the countryside, where he kept his animals in the countryside, whether he did not visit a peasant who had had something to do with goats, and the name of the peasant.

These suggestive questions exhibit a fundamental change among Frankfurt's judiciary. While it is true that Article 116 of the 1532 *Constitutio Criminalis Carolina* includes sex with animals in the same category as male-to-male sex, Frankfurt's 1598 charges and inquiries were confined to same-sex questions only. Forty-seven years later, however, at the explicit initiative of the advocates, the animal connection was heightened and male-to-male sex became closely correlated to bestiality. This development testifies to a transformation of the advocates' legal mentality, a change not reflected in the witnesses' attitude for none of them even alluded to bestiality.

A change in the judicial climate can also be observed from a scribbled *nota bene* at the end of the interrogation questionnaire. The advocates suggested keeping the witnesses' and suspect's statements secret, so that the common man and above all the young should not find out about it lest they be unduly influenced. Their reasoning for taking recourse to secrecy, in addition to their zealous attempts to equate same-sex relations with bestiality, testifies not only to an increasing influence of the legal profession over the treatment of sodomy, but also to their increasingly patronising if not condescending attitude towards the people. Both trends exhibit a widening gulf separating popular culture from the legal profession.

Krafft's wife, children and friends, also citing the effect of alcohol on the suspect, pleaded with the city council, as did Krafft himself, again stressing his frequently drunken state in addition to *gehässige Zeugenaussagen* (malicious witness accounts). In a follow-up letter he inquired about the content of the witness report, stating that several *so mir gehassig sind* (hate me). None of these pleas had any effect on the advocates or the city council, for Krafft was now interrogated under torture. He was subjected to the leg screw and hoisted on the rack. In line with the advocates' previous allegations, sex with young boys and goats formed the core of the interrogation. Again, the suspect categorically denied these charges. He also repeated his earlier statements that one of the witnesses had not objected to his sexual advances; on the contrary, he had *gern geschehen lassen* (enjoyed it), while another had actually initiated them. Even under excruciating pain, having been hoisted on the rack twice, Krafft did not confess to ever having committed sodomy with boys or men. He admitted, however, to having touched men sexually.

Under torture Krafft thus reconfirmed his earlier statement that he had had at least two willing accomplices. In Boudin's case a witness account could be interpreted similarly, which indicates that the two suspects were not the only ones in Frankfurt with male-to-male sexual or emotional desires and experiences. Unfortunately the records do not allow further deductions as to the existence of a local subculture.[30] It was also only in one instance that a witness in Boudin's case hinted at a special meeting place at the embankment of the local river Main.[31] The documents also disclose so little about the suspects' wives that it would be presumptuous to interpret the marital status of both suspects.

The city council, seemingly confused about Krafft, again took legal refuge in their advocates' advice, despite a third plea by the accused to spare him. As in Boudin's case, the advocates took Krafft's judicial torture and long incarceration into consideration for a milder sentence; yet they diverged from the previous case by stressing penal secrecy rather than public knowledge. In line with their previous argument, they considered public flogging to be unwise because of the local youth and suggested instead that Krafft be taken immediately from the prison to the city gates and banished for life at a distance of twenty miles. For once, the city council, heeding Krafft's request, interceded and allowed him an additional two weeks to conclude work-related arrangements.

The advocates' decision to conduct secret penal procedures represented not only a judicial divergence from contemporary penal practices where, with the exception of juveniles, criminals were punished in public, but also a decisive volte-face from the 1598 case where public exposure in the pillory was strongly advocated on the grounds *damit er bei jedermann ein abschewn gebe* (so that he should instil disgust in everyone).[32]

This policy reversal, replacing the intended evocation of disgust with secrecy, might be interpreted as a failure of the earlier policy to have the desired effect on the people. It also points to a growing judicial belief that sodomite behaviour was contagious. The people thought differently. They refrained from social stigmatisation even in the case of a more aggressive suspect such as Krafft. This reluctance might also explain why the *Häberfeldtreiben*, a form of German charivari, included male-to-male-sexual encounters as objectionable behaviour only after 1833.[33] It took centuries to change popular sensitivity towards male-to-male sex.

This reticence is difficult to explain, but the term *toleration* comes to mind. While it is frequently considered anathema or anachronistic to apply this word or even the concept to the early modern period, recent studies have shown its existence as far back as the twelfth century.[34] If the comportment of Frankfurt's population is an indication, by not attaching social stigmata to sodomy and refraining from condemning the suspects as socially aberrant despite official legislation, then the concept of sexual toleration seems to have been grounded in the people rather than in the so-called elite.[35]

The almost total absence of any religious remarks on the part of the witnesses furnishes an additional clue. Only one witness reported that he told Boudin he should be ashamed before God and the world. Quite obviously, many did not consider sodomy a terrible sin or 'the worst of sexual sins'.[36] It is, of course, tempting to reduce this to the general lack of pertinent comments by

German reformers including Martin Luther or assertions that 'Lutherans were more tolerant of popular traditions than Zwingli and Calvinists'.[37] But even years before Frankfurt converted to Lutheranism there were no local sodomy convictions, a possible argument against contentions that Catholic doctrine shaped 'popular consciousness'.[38] As these findings suggest, the common person seems to have been quite resilient and might have espoused a different moral mentality with regard to same-sex relations than many of their secular or religious leaders. References to the 'salient horror of homosexuality characteristic of the West since the fourteenth century', or 'the popular abhorrence for homosexuality', have thus to be regionally qualified.[39]

Conclusion

In Frankfurt's case one can assert that the population did not undergo a metamorphosis with regard to sodomy after the 1598 case, but that the advocates did.[40] Considering the absence of sodomite legal clauses in most Germanic laws, one might argue that, as protagonists of the new Roman law, they contributed to a tightening of sodomite prosecutions. In their quest to enhance and solidify their professional position, they became professional hard-liners. Their frequent, if not frivolous, recourse to judicial torture serves as one example. Their attitudinal shift towards secrecy in the 1645 case points to another, deliberately distancing their legal attitude from the common person, thereby widening the cultural divide between popular and legal mentalities. The prosecution of sodomy became an affair of the state, albeit of the legal profession and not the people. In the process, advocates turned not only into instruments but increasingly into the source of social control via their increased presence in the courts. This trend, with regard to sodomy, started to reverse itself only at the end of the twentieth century.

NOTES

This chapter is dedicated to the memory of my cousin Karl-Heinz Harnischfeger.

An abbreviated version of this chapter was presented during the 25th Anniversary Meeting of the Social Science History Association in Pittsburgh, 26–29 October 2000. My special thanks go to the members of the panel Hans Andersson, Tyge Krogh, Jutta Nowosadtkos and Magnus Perlestam. I am also grateful to Mary Beth Emmerichs, Joanne Klein and Gerald Soliday for their encouaging remarks, as well as to the audience for suggestive questions. I also want to express my gratitude to Susan F. Levine for her continued support.

1 The July 1969 Stonewall riot in Greenwich Village, New York, when gay people fought the police for two consecutive nights and days, turned into the most decisive impetus towards liberation.

2 John Boswell, *Christianity, Social Tolerance, and Homosexuality: Gay People in Western Europe from the Beginning of the Christian Era to the Fourteenth Century* (Chicago: 1980) and *Same-sex Unions in Premodern Europe* (New York: 1994); for England see David F. Greenberg, *The Construction of Homosexuality* (Chicago: 1988), p. 274.

3 Michael Rocke, *Forbidden Friendships Homosexuality and Male Culture in Renaissance Florence* (Oxford and New York: 1996), p. 60; see also pp. 4, 7, 26–7, 57.

4 Guido Ruggiero, *The Boundaries of Eros: Sex, Crime and Sexuality in Renaissance Venice* (Oxford and New York: 1985), p. 127.

5 E. William Monter, 'Frontiers of Heresy: The Spanish Inquisition from the Basque Lands to Sicily' reprinted as 'Sodomy: The Fateful Accident', in Wayne R. Dynes and Stephen Donaldson, eds, *History of Homosexuality in Europe and America* (New York 1992), pp. 192–215, 204–5, although a caveat must be added in that Monter's numbers might include bestiality cases; Monter, 'Sodomy and Heresy in Early Modern Switzerland', in S. J. Licata and R. P. Petersen, eds, *Historical Perspectives on Homosexuality: A Special Issue of The Journal of Homosexuality* 6: 1/2 (Autumn/Winter 1980–81), pp. 41–55; see also Mary Elizabeth Perry, *Gender and Disorder in Early Modern Seville* (Princeton: 1990), pp. 119, 123–4, who states that 'male homosexuality appeared so dangerous that men accused of it were isolated from others in the Royal Prison of Seville, their deviance regarded as a contagion that could easily infect others'. Randolph Trumbach, 'Sodomitical Subcultures, Sodomitical Roles, and the Gender Revolution of the Eighteenth Century: The Recent Historiography', in Dynes and Donaldson, 1992, p. 389.

6 Rocke, 1996, p. 27; Iwan Bloch, '*Die Homosexualität in Köln am Ende des 15. Jahrhunderts*', in Dynes and Donaldson, 1992, pp. 2–9, documents that in 1484 the city councillors decided not to prosecute; Richard van Dülmen, *Theater des Schreckens: Gerichtspraxis und Strafrituale in der frühen Neuzeit* (Munich: 1985), pp. 192–3, shows only two convictions for sodomy in Nuremberg between 1600 and 1692; Karl Wegert, *Popular Culture, Crime, and Social Control in 18th Century Württemberg* (Stuttgart: 1994), p. 189, asserts that 'only one case of actual sodomy (anal intercourse between males) was brought to trial in the eighteenth century'; Wolfgang Behringer, 'Mörder, Diebe, Ehebrecher: Verbrechen und Strafen in Kurbayern vom 16. bis 18. Jahrhundert', in Richard van Dülmen, ed., *Verbrechen: Strafen und soziale Kontrolle. Studien zur historischen Kulturforschung III* (Frankfurt am Main: 1990), p. 290 f85, documents only one case in 1603; for opposite assertions see Richard J. Evans, *Rituals of Retribution: Capital Punishment in Germany 1600–1987* (Oxford: 1996), p. 40; for England see Alan Bray, *Homosexuality in Renaissance England* (London: 1982), p. 74, who states that only 'isolated individuals [who] fell foul of the law'; J. M. Beattie, *Crime and the Courts in England. 1660–1800* (Princeton: 1986), p. 433, who documents only four executions in Surrey between 1660 and 1800, and even that number has to be assessed carefully, since the author does not differentiate between bestiality and same-sex crimes; for the Dutch Republic see Pieter Spierenburg, *The Spectacle of Suffering* (Cambridge: 1984), pp. 124–5, who states that 'around 1700 the authorities did not care about gay sex', whereas in 1730 a 'sudden proliferation of trials', occurred; for France, the picture is somewhat muddled: while Trumbach, 1992, p. 389, states that the Parlement of Paris executed 77 men between 1565 and 1640, Guy Poirier, *L'Homosexualité dans l'Lmaginaire de la Renaissance* (Paris: 1996), p. 48, indicates a more muted occurrence; see also Julius R. Ruff, *Crime, Justice and Public Order in Old Regime France*, (Dover, New Hampshire: 1984), p. 171, who does not list a single case for several regions in France; for Sweden see Jonas Liliequist, 'Peasants against Nature: Crossing the Boundaries Between Man and Animal in Eighteenth-century Sweden', in John C. Fout, ed., *Forbidden History: The State, Society and the Regulation of Sexuality in Modern Europe* (Chicago: 1992) pointing to the infrequent sentencing of male-to-male sexual behaviour.

7 Frankfurt's *Strafenbuch*, the book of punishments, which covers every sentenced criminal with his or her crime during the 1562 to 1696 period, served as the time frame for this data. It is located in Frankfurt's municipal archives.

8 Documented as *Criminalia*, pp. 378–9 and 1083, located in Frankfurt's municipal archives.

9 See Maria R. Boes, 'Public Appearance and Criminal Judicial Practices in Early Modern Germany', *Social Science History* 20: 2 (1996), pp. 259–79.

10 *Hals- oder Peinliche Gerichtsordnung Kaiser Carls V*, 8th edition by Johann Christoph Koch (Goldbach: 1966), hereafter referred to as the *Constitutio Criminalis Carolina*.

11 In contrast see Monter, 1992, p. 195, for Aragon, where 'all defendants were automatically given a court-appointed lawyer'.

12 Warren Johansson and William A. Percy, 'Homosexuality', in Vern L. Bullough and James A. Brundage, eds, *Handbook of Medieval Sexuality* (New York: 1996), pp. 165, 168 and 174.

13 Greenberg, 1988, pp. 250, 272–3, cites Visigothic Spain and the Old Norwegian Gulapingslog as exceptions; Helmut Blazek, *Rosa Zeiten für Rosa Liebe: Geschichte der Homosexualität* (Frankfurt am Main: 1996), p. 37, also includes the Frisian Codes.

14 Gunther Gollner, *Homosexualität* (Berlin: 1974), p. 152.

15 On the impact of Roman law see Michael Goodich, *The Unmentionable Vice: Homosexuality in the Later Medieval Period* (Santa Barbara, California: 1979), pp. 71, 86; *Constitutio Criminalis Carolina*, p. 58; article 116 was the precursor to the infamous paragraph 175 of the German penal code from 1871 to the 1960s which replaced the death penalty with imprisonment and loss of civil rights.

16 Greenberg, 1988, p. 275; for an explanation of the term *buggery* or *bougerie*, see Greenberg, 1988, p. 267; Brundale, 1996, p. 43; Ruggiero, 1985, p. 120; Poirier, 1996, pp. 11, 21, traces its linguistic connection to Bulgaria, the birthplace of the Albergensian heresy which, in the Church's interpretation, came to be closely associated with sodomy.

17 *Strafenbuch*, 25 August 1609 and 4 July 1617.

18 See also Monter, 1980–81, p. 44, documenting that in Geneva almost all defendants were religious refugees from France.

19 The importance of maids is amply documented by Merry E. Wiesner, 'Paternalism in Practice: The Control of Servants and Prostitutes in Early Modern German Cities', in Merry E. Wiesner, ed., *Gender, Church and State in Early Modern Germany* (London: 1998), p. 99; for France see James R. Farr, *Hands of Honour: Artisans and Their World in Dijon; 1550–1650* (Ithaca: 1988), p. 166.

20 Johansson and Percy, 1996, p. 159; Greenberg, 1988, pp. 309–10; Rocke, 1996, p. 13.

21 Monter, 1980–81, pp. 206, 290.

22 This also confirms Boswell's findings in *Same-sex Unions*, 1994, p. 38.

23 Nine were executed for incest alone, according to the *Strafenbuch*.

24 Frankfurt meted out 64 fornication, 61 adultery, but only 35 prostitution sentences. See also Jean-Louis Flandrin, *Le sexe and l'occident: évolution des attitudes and des comportments* (Paris: 1981), pp. 256–9, who documents similar findings.

25 See Gollner, 1974, pp. 153–4, on this legal point.

26 Maria R. Boes, 'Jews in the Criminal-justice System of Early Modern Germany', *The Journal of Interdisciplinary History* 30: 3 (1999), pp. 407–35.

27 Bray, 1982, p. 41.

28 Hasso Spode, *Die Macht der Trunkenheit: Kultur- und Sozialgeschichte des Alkohols in Deutschland* (Opladen: 1993).

29 In the following manslaughter prosecutions, drunkenness was advanced in the hopes for a milder punishment: *Strafenbuch* 10 August 1570; 16 June 1604; 8 June 1671; 30 April 1672; 30 August 1690.

30 Historians differ on the existence of a distinct subculture for this period. Among its proponents are Boswell's *Christianity* and *Same-sex Unions*; Ruggiero, 1985, pp. 135, 137–8, 144; Perry, 1990, p. 126; Monter, 1992, p. 42; arguing for its later appearance is Michael Foucault, *Histoire de la sexualité* (Paris: 1976–1984) 3 vols, esp. vol. 1; Randolph Trumbach, 'Erotic Fantasy and Male Libertinism in Enlightenment England', in Lynn Hunt, ed., *The Invention of Pornography: Obscenity and the Origins of Modernity, 1500–1800* (New York: 1993), pp. 252–82; see also his comments in 'Sodomitical Subcultures', 1992, pp. 388–97; Bryant T. Ragan Jr, 'The Enlightenment Confronts Homosexuality', in Jeffrey Merrick and Bryant T. Ragan Jr, eds, *Homosexuality in Modern France* (Oxford and New York: 1996), pp. 8–29, 12; Alan Bray, 'Homosexuality and the Signs of Male Friendship in Elizabethan England', in Jonathan Goldberg, ed., *Queering the Renaissance* (Durham, N.C.: 1994), p. 40; on linguistic interpretations of the term *subculture* see Greenberg, 1988, pp. 267, 31, and Poirier, 1996, pp. 12–22.

31 Bernd-Ulrich Hergemöller, *Sodom und Gomorrah: Zur Alltagswirklichkeit und Verfolgung Homosexueller im Mittelalter* (Hamburg: 1998), p. 55, cites the existence of special meeting places in many cities.

32 Juveniles were spared such public exposures for reformatory objectives: see Maria R. Boes, 'The Treatment of Juvenile Delinquents in Early Modern Germany: A Case Study', *Continuity and Change* 11: 1 (1996), pp. 43–60.

33 Ernst Hinrichs, 'Le Charivari et les usages de reprimand en Allemagne', in Jacques le Goff et Jean-Claude, eds, *Le Charivari* (Paris: 1981), pp. 297–306, 302.

34 Cary J. Nederman and John Christian Laursen, eds, *Difference and Dissent: Theories of Tolerance in Medieval and Early Modern Europe* (Lanham and New York: 1996); see also Ole Peter Grell and Bob Scribner, eds, *Tolerance and Intolerance in the European Reformation* (New York: 1996).

35 Communal restraint is also documented by Arthur E. Imhof, *Lost Worlds: How Our European Ancestors Coped with Everyday Life and Why Life is so Hard Today*, trans. Thomas Robisheux (Charlottesville: 1996), p. 56, but it applied to bestiality cases only; in contrast, also referring to bestiality cases, see Wegert, 1994, p. 189, and Liliequist, 1992, p. 61; see also Bray, 1982, p. 76, who seems to be arguing against the concept of tolerance.

36 Trumbach, 1992, p. 397; Monter, 1980–81, p. 45, found a strong religious correlation.

37 Blazek, 1996, pp. 48–9. Peter Burke, *Popular Culture in Early Modern Europe* (New York: 1978), pp. 216–18.

38 Ferdinand Rau, *Beiträge zum Kriminalrecht der Freien Reichsstadt Frankfurt am Main im Mittelalter bis 1532* (Potsdam: 1916) does not cite a single male-to-male conviction; Greenberg, 1988, p. 291; Boswell, 1994, p. 220.

39 Boswell, 1980, p. xxiii, and 1994, p. 262; Stephen Haliczer, *Sexuality in the Confessional: A Sacrament Profaned* (Oxford and New York: 1996), p. 168.

40 Poirier, 1996, p. 45, found similar attitudinal changes within the judiciary in France during the seventeenth century.

3

'The sovereign's vice begets the subject's error': the Duke of Buckingham, 'sodomy' and narratives of Edward II, 1622–28

DANIELLE CLARKE

In one of many scurrilous verses on the flagrant financial and political misappropriations of George Villiers, Duke of Buckingham, we find a rare example of a specific connection between sodomy and the Duke's circle, copied into a 1651 collection:

> Old Abbott Anthony
> *Thinkes hee hath well done,*
> *In leaving* Sodomy
> *To mary Sheldon,*
> *Shee hath a Buttocke plumpe,*
> *Keepe but thy [T]arse whole,*
> *She will hold upp her Rumpe,*
> *With her blacke Arse-hole*
> *These are they that* sway *in* Courte *and* City
> *Yet next Springe they will sing the* Cookold's Ditty[1]

This poem is an excellent instance of the segueing of sodomy into other discourses and of the cultural instability both of sodomy as act and of sodomy as discourse. Sir Anthony Ashley, 'who never loved any but Boyes', represents court corruption and much else besides in his sodomitical desire for anal sex, which in the reductive language of sex acts can be just as satisfactorily provided by Mary Sheldon as by boys.[2] Here it is the 'Arse-hole' that is desired, rather than the sexed body to which it belongs; distinctive sexualities are collapsed into one sex act. The emergent distinction between homosexual and heterosexual love is largely the product of the marginal commentary, which links sexual impropriety with financial corruption; the writer refers to

> this Peice of scandalous History, brought in by his giving an account of the many Matches that were made by the Nobility to chief Gentry, with the D. of Buckinghams kindred. But above all the miracle of those Times, old Sir Anthony Ashley, who never loved any but Boyes, yet he was snatch up for a kinswoman

as if there had beene a Concurrency [in] the kingdome that those that naturally
hated women, yet loved his kindred, as well as the king him. (f. 207)

Leaving aside the pointed joke that Buckingham even managed to marry off a
confirmed sodomite to one of his relatives (a joke that unsettles the widespread
denial of such a thing as a homosexual identity in the early modern period), the
comment sets up a series of important connections. It suggests a set of relationships between misogyny (understood as the repudiation of sexual relationships with women), kinship, and loyal allegiance with a scarcely veiled
implication that Buckingham's relationship with King James was an erotic one.
To put this differently, and in terms that infer the interrelationships (real or
imagined) of sexual dalliance and political, social and economic misdemeanours, we might designate the relationship described here sodomitical.[3]

The critical and historical consensus has been that, with the accession of
Charles I, Buckingham's relationship to his monarch underwent a significant
alteration, at least as far as purely sexual matters were concerned, although the
powerful patronage networks made possible by James's favour continued,
prompting much adverse comment, and, arguably, playing a direct role in the
assassination of Buckingham in 1628.[4] However, a closer look at the evidence
reveals powerful links between the two courts, not the least of which was
Buckingham himself, 'Eclypse of two wise princes'; Charles even adopted
James's affectionate nickname for Buckingham, 'Steenie'.[5] James I had actively
encouraged the strong friendship between his son Charles, Prince of Wales and
Buckingham, tacitly colluding in the masquerade which was the Spanish match,
as Bergeron's recent edition of their letters demonstrates. Whatever Buckingham's personal feelings towards Charles, he was smart enough to intuit where
his future interests lay; for the shy stammering Charles, Buckingham's prac-
tised ease and courtly knowledge must have been both comforting and attractive. After James's death Buckingham's influence, if anything, increased, much
to the consternation of commentators who had hoped that this potentially
dangerous and damaging force might be checked with the accession of a new
monarch. Republican commentators, looking back on the beginnings of the
reign from the perspective of the civil war, while acknowledging Charles's personal virtue, nevertheless used the suggestion of homoeroticism to infer the
King's fatal weakness and susceptibility to the influence of others, and to view
this as symptomatic of the corruption of the institution of monarchy itself:[6]

The face of the Court was much changed in the change of the king, for King
Charles was temperate, chaste, and serious; so that the fools and bawds, mimics
and catamites of the former court grew out of fashion and the nobility and
courtiers, who did not quite abandon their debaucheries, yet so reverenced the
king as to retire into corners to practice them.[7]

This transition, however, is one of degree rather than one of kind, and amounts to little more than a decrease in visibility. The republican writer Lucy Hutchinson conflates sexual disorder with notions of pretence and acting, summoning forth a generalised transgression which functions as a carefully coded metonymy for her own opposition to monarchy. It is clear from a range of witnesses and documents that the association of the court, and of Buckingham in particular, with sodomy, would not go away, predicated as it was in the case of both James and Charles on the fluid and potentially disruptive category of the favourite, which 'implies a special intimacy, including, but not restricted to, homoerotic desire'.[8]

The verses with which I opened this chapter are referred to, but not actually found, in Fairholt's nineteenth-century collection of poems relating to the fall of Buckingham, being excluded as 'much too coarse to print'.[9] Fairholt's squeamishness is absent from the manuscript copy and the marginal comments, and seems to confirm the nineteenth-century paradigm shift in discourses of sexuality which Foucault presents as the axiomatic model underlying homoerotic identities, formulated roughly as the act/identity dichotomy with which virtually all subsequent criticism on premodern sexualities has wrestled.[10] As many commentators have noted, 'that utterly confused category' can seem to be everywhere and nowhere at once in the early modern period, 'a way to encompass a multitude of sins with a minimum of signs'.[11] It is clear that sodomy rarely appears as itself, precisely because there is no single behaviour or set of behaviours to which it refers. This does not mean that homosexual love or desire is not experienced, nor that it is experienced in the ways that the regulatory languages of Church, state and law attempt to prescribe or proscribe.[12] By contrast, sodomy may function as a rhetorical trope which images a variety of disorders, transgressions and imbalances of power: '"Sodomy" is not a neutral term; it always signifies social disorder of a frightening magnitude.'[13] Contrary to the schematic Foucauldian model, the picture of sodomy that has been built up for the Renaissance period suggests a situation where discourses constantly subsume acts, deferring and relocating the physical and sexual experiences that give rise to the disturbingly imprecise areas and actions located within the term *sodomy*. In the case of the category of the favourite, the commentary, however critical, does also implicitly acknowledge that sodomy may represent a means to power for the socially inferior member of the partnership. This chapter builds upon the seminal work done on the complex relationships between sodomy, friendship, patronage and economics in the early modern period, as well as that undertaken in relation to representations of same-sex love.

These approaches are used in a new and largely unresearched context, namely the political and satirical use of sodomy to image various kinds of disorder in the body politic; specifically in the relationship of Buckingham to

James and then Charles. As Simon Shepherd argues, the favourite also presents a test to the monarch which challenges the boundaries set around sovereignty.[14] I am particularly interested in the use of historical discourses and the deployment of a Tacitean model of 'application' to suggest a sodomitical relationship, both sexual and economic; in turn, I hint at the possibility that sodomy functions discursively, and that in the case of Edward II narratives, it is the power of the story as a sodomitical discourse – barely contained by moral didacticism – that is the point, rather than sodomy as an act which usually remains unmarked where it leaves social and political relationships undisturbed; the only reason that Anthony Ashley's love of boys comes to the fore is that it images a larger disorder. I am concerned here with the rhetorical use of transgressions of morally acceptable and socially sanctioned male bonds in (primarily) historical texts linked to critiques of Buckingham. Sodomy rarely surfaces as an autonomous act in these texts, or appears *as itself*, but functions as an aspect of a series of anti-images of kingship and good rule based upon *orderly* male bonds; it is threatening precisely because they cannot be clearly demarcated or distinguished from good rule and proper male friendship. Lucy Hutchinson's coupling of 'mimics and catamites' is instructive here, as it is precisely the degree to which sodomites ape friendship, and favourites the powers of kings ('O King (no King) but shadow of a King', as Hubert writes of Gaveston)[15] which troubles the clear boundaries that the Edward II narratives insist are central to good rule.[16] In this way I wish to unsettle the acts/identities dichotomy and to suggest that the opposition that it sets up is anachronistic as a way to read non-heteronormative sex in this period – after all, heterosexual acts are also infrequently alluded to in direct terms unless other kinds of transgressions come into play, as the searches and testimonies gathered for the annulment of the third Earl of Essex's marriage attest.[17] The meanings of sex and sexualities are far more complex than Foucauldian paradigms will allow and as the representation of the relationships between Buckingham and the two Stuart kings in both 'popular' and 'high' culture illustrates. In short, my interest is in the signification, rather than the act, of sodomy; in the point at which sodomy becomes visible as a category within an applied historical discourse, and with how sodomy can be read and mobilised as a notion which is able to bear certain kinds of political meaning.

Edward II and the Duke of Buckingham

Dympna Callaghan has suggested that the narrative of Edward II seems to have been a source of 'perennial fascination' in the early modern period, but does not really tease out the historical specificity of this 'fascination'.[18] I am primarily concerned here with three Edward II texts and their development as narratives intended to be applied in the 1620s: Marlowe's *Edward II*, revived and reissued in 1622; Sir Francis Hubert's poem *The Historie of Edward II*, pirated in 1628 and reprinted in 1629; and Elizabeth Cary's historical narrative *The History of the Life, Reign, and Death of Edward II*, apparently written in 1627. Each uses similar material for the usual historical ends – using the past to instruct the present, and adopting Tacitean historiography to function as what D. R. Woolf terms 'crisis of counsel narratives'.[19] The story of Edward II is only one of the available narratives which address the various political and ethical issues raised by Buckingham's rise to power – others include Richard II and Sejanus – but, while these narratives also posit effeminacy and sexual excess as indices of tyrannical disorder (for example, Hayward's description of Richard II as 'a dastard, a meycocke'), the question of sodomy is most obviously adumbrated in the Edward II stories, as the weight of critical attention to Marlowe's version suggests.[20] Although each text conforms to both classical and early modern precepts regarding the utility of history, they use different generic frames: tragic drama, complaint poem, Tacitean prose history. These texts are less interested in evidence than in the means of its organisation and representation within a preestablished form or pattern which provide the taxonomies through which a reader makes the necessary identifications for the text to signify politically and didactically. Nowhere is this more true than with Tacitean history, with its setpiece orations, its distinctively aphoristic style, and its stress upon causality and the links between the 'private' man and his public conduct.[21]

In the functioning of the political didacticism of the Edward II narrative, sodomy has a pivotal role in the narrative of causality. Transgressive bonds with other men – political, sexual and financial – are produced as both cause *and* effect of Edward's profligacy, collapsed by most narratives into monetary expenditure, sexual licence, partisan patronage and verbal excess, but remaining shadowy and elusive within the texts themselves.[22] At the point at which sodomy might be disclosed, it is always located elsewhere, legible only through the signs of other discourses, in particular classical myth, the conventions of courtiership and the language of friendship, but also within a semantic field packed with overlapping and overdetermined nouns: minion, catamite, favourite, creature, ganymede, siren, damon, ingle, special friend. Nowhere is this sin or act named, even euphemistically, and the brutally suggestive imagery of Edward's death is confronted only by Marlowe. Sodomy as an originating act, as an ontology of bad and immoral rule, is something that the reader has to *assign* to the details presented in the narrative, via what Joseph Cady has called the 'practice of figurative denotation' and the drawing of historical analogies.[23] Chronicle histories, for example, generally enfold Edward's homosexuality into a general category of immorality that is less specific than these narratives become after Marlowe, in which Edward's bonds with men threaten, rather than coexist with, other kinds of sexual act. The transgression is sexual, certainly, but remains a generalised category: 'His Maners (being grossely corrupted by lewd and gracelesse companions) were so lascivious, and unbefitting the condition of the King, that hee became burthensome to his Nobility; and (almost) a scorne to his inferiour subjects.'[24] Never is sodomy unproblematically 'there' in the texts which treat Edward II; sodomy symbolises a collapse of distinctions rather than being a pure category (even in law) with limits and boundaries, but it does mark the limit of acceptable behaviour precisely by questioning where these peripheries might lie, and calling for the structural centre to reaffirm its relationship to the margins. It is notable that these texts, in line with their didactic character, conclude with a reaffirmation of the status quo and a reinstatement of moral and dynastic order.

The ground breaking work of Bray, Bredbeck and Goldberg, amongst others, has demonstrated that sexual disorder, epitomised by sodomy, seemingly that most plural of categories, images political, religious and economic disorder, and vice versa in certain instances.[25] As Bray suggests, 'homosexuality … was not part of the created order; rather it was part of its dissolution'.[26] Sodomy does not reserve a category of sexual acts to itself, rather it takes its place among a variety of deviant behaviours, not all of them concerned with choice of sexual object, an assertion which is borne out by the ballads excoriating the Duke of Buckingham's financial, sexual and sartorial excesses:[27]

> Nor shall you ever prove, by magick charmes
> I wrought the kings affection, or his harmes,
> Or that I need Lambes philters to incite
> Chast ladies to give my fowle lust delight.[28]

The terms in which Buckingham's misdemeanours are represented are almost exclusively those of heterosexual lust and over-indulgence: 'Venus' pavilions doe become thee beste, / Periwigs with helmets use not to be preste' and 'our Ladies / His absence greatly mourne; / And sweare they'll have noe babies / Untill he doth retourne'.[29] Such examples suggest Buckingham as effeminate, prone to the temptations of women and preferring the delights of Venus to those of Mars. It is only when the more specific matter of the extent of Buckingham's influence with James and then Charles is raised that his actions are given a sodomitical cast, in political rather than moral terms. 'Upon the Sodaine Death of the Great D. of B.' does not label Buckingham as performing an act of sodomy, but this inference is used to represent a transgressive version of a proper male bonds, the effects of which are distinctly political:

> He us'd the meanes: for with his darting eyes,
> (More then the basilisks or Babells spies,)
> Whatsoe're intended, or wheresoever meant,

Camelion-like, hee slilie would prevent,
The Brittaine crownetts and the clergie's bookes,
Were vail'd or burnt at's Ganimedian lookes.[30]

Buckingham exemplifies Hutchinson's doubled category of 'mimics and catamites' as he uses perversions of courtiership and the role of counsellor to advance his own interests, and his 'Camelion-like' willingness to change shape to suit the monarch's will (or his manipulative interpretation of it) is endemic to the favourite. The suspicion of a deviant sexuality hovers over many other accusations levelled at Buckingham. He is accused of 'over-great familiarity with the Prince': 'in all occurrences the Prince closed with him, and seemed to have him a large room in his heart'.[31] The deliberate pronoun confusions in one verse addressed to Buckingham indicate the extent to which the roles of king and courtier were perceived to be confused, resulting in a dangerous lack of accountability and a breach of prerogative: 'The king loves you, you him; / Both love the same; / You love the king, he you; / Both Buckingham. / Of sports the king loves games, / Of games the duke; / Of all men you; and you/ Solely, for your looke.'[32] The inversion of the proper power hierarchy between monarch and subject (however highly favoured) quickly finds expression in the inference of an eroticism not usually admitted to bonds between men, in the double entendres of 'sports' and 'games', 'loves' and 'looke'. When Rushworth, with tongue firmly in cheek, praises Buckingham as an 'Example rare in this Nation, to be the Favourite of two succeeding Princes', he raises the spectre of sodomy which marked Buckingham's relationship with James, while seeming to bear out the assertion that it is not so much the sexual act (or its absence) between men that is significant but the disturbance of power structures which such a relationship symbolises (whether between sodomites, favourites or friends).[33] What Buckingham does with James and/or Charles is not the issue in political terms; what such a relationship might represent definitely is.

One narrative through which such meanings were explored is that of Edward II, where a series of identifications have to be made by the reader with regard to the relationship between Edward and Gaveston, but also in the context of the possible application of this historical narrative in the 1620s. Elizabeth Cary's text, for example, insists that the monarch is a symbolic representation of the state, and a clear causal link is made between the private sphere and the public world: 'Your former errors, now continued, are no more yours, they are the king's, which will betray the kingdom. The sovereign's vice begets the subject's error, who practise good and ill by his example.'[34] The analogy presupposes that a distinct separation of the two spheres, public and private, is necessary to good rule. Indeed the problem for Edward II is precisely that the erotic *becomes* politically meaningful within the public sphere as desire is placed above duty, and a proper male bond – that between father and son, represented by Edward's oath to his dying father – is abandoned as Edward confesses his desire to the nobles:

> Temperately he lays before them the extremity of his inward trouble, which had so engrossed his private thoughts that he had been thereby enforced to estrange himself from them, and neglected the rights due to his crown and dignity. He lets them know the depth of his engagement, which had no aim repugnant to the public good, nor intention hurtful to their proper honours.[35]

Edward aims to integrate or reconcile his 'engagement' with the public sphere: 'Temperately' stresses the fact that his 'inward trouble' can be distinguished from the 'public good'. Yet at the same time as the separation of the erotic and the political is invoked, their connection is underlined as his 'inward trouble' has 'estrange[d]' Edward from his peers – a legitimate male or class bond is repudiated for an emotionally and socially illegitimate one – and led him to neglect his duties, which, as monarch, are uniquely and exclusively his, as the nobles are at pains to point out. Edward implies here that it is the absence of Gaveston that preoccupies him, leading to the neglect of his duties, but the rest of the text (like both Marlowe and Hubert) makes it clear that it is his presence (or that of his successor, Spencer) which is the true threat to political and moral order. While Gregory Bredbeck has argued that sodomy is 'a transition point' between the political and the personal, it becomes troublesome when it serves to blur these boundaries, and when, as with Edward, the desires of the body natural and the body politic become indistinguishable and are enacted in the same physical and conceptual space:[36]

> It is a very dangerous thing when the head is ill and all the members suffer by his infirmity. Kings are but men, and man is prone to error; yet if they manage their distempers with wisdom or discretion, so that they lie not open to public view and censure, they may be counted faults, but not predictions.[37]

Much of the language of both Cary's and, more famously, Marlowe's account of the Edward II narrative stresses mutuality, and the erosion of the difference in status between the king and his minion – an erosion made possible precisely by the relationship's homoerotic nature, unlike patriarchal marriage where sexuality serves to reinforce the proper hierarchy, concretised here by the endless movement of money, titles, and gifts down the social scale: 'the interview was accompanied with as many mutual expressions, as might flow from the tongues, eyes and hearts of long-divided lovers'.[38] Yet such an equality, reinforced in Marlowe's play by the use of an ambiguous rhetoric of kingship which simultaneously performs a kind of grammatical coupling: 'receive my seal; / Save or condemn, and in our name command' (I.i.167–8) – is a derogation from the hierarchy proper to patriarchal rule, which presupposes that the logic of heterosexual relationships will be reproduced within the homosocial world through social stratification and the distinctions of rank and station. As Edward peddles a language of parity ('Thy friend, thy self, another Gaveston', I.i.142), he contravenes the ideal of *arcana imperii* which is the exclusive domain of the reigning monarch, as Edward I points out on his deathbed: 'he unlocks the closet of his heart, and lays before him those same *arcana imperii* and secret mysteries of state, which are only proper to the royal operations, and lie not in the road of vulgar knowledge'.[39] The emphasis, in all three texts, upon Gaveston's low social status merely compounds Edward's profligate circulation of the secrets of state, as Lancaster remarks, 'That villain Gaveston is made an earl' (I.ii.11) where 'villain' is a term of social, as well as moral, insult. Edward thus undermines social order as surely as he depletes the exchequer by his disregard for the peers, their counsel and their privilege based upon birth: 'This mushroom must be cropped, or arms must right the king-dom' (Cary, p. 103). Edward's love for Gaveston demands equality of status, while his political role requires clear differentiation of their positions, result-ing in the production of an improper power relation, where Gaveston parodies the position of king (as does his successor as favourite, Spencer). In Marlowe's play Gaveston displaces the queen in the Chair Royal (I.iv.8–11), in the other accounts he mediates access to the king, controls decisions and advances friends and relations at will, becoming in the process the archetype of the over-pow-erful courtier, paralleling contemporaries' unease, disquiet and envy at Buck-ingham's power to advance his own interests through his influence with the king: 'Hee shall be king there, sitt in the kings throne, / Or els commaund the king, and that's all one.'[40]

The reader is required to differentiate the signs of male friendship from those of the transgressive behaviours which might be ascribed to the category of sodomy in order for the political import of these narratives and their figura-tion of the potential dangers of the relationship between Charles and Bucking-ham to be recognised and understood.[41] In other words it is necessary to posit Edward's bonds with men as a threat to a patriarchal order based upon homoso-cial exchanges of power *between* men, mediated by women.[42] What seems to happen in this narrative is that the relationship is deemed unacceptable, not because of any inherent quality that it possesses but because it violates the social and political rules governing the circulation of power, as Edward's constant admission that he is *subject* to his passions, and *subject* to Gaveston's charms (and thereby his influence), places him in a position of passivity, graphically and gruesomely undermined by the manner of his death, which is incompatible with the images buttressing patriarchal power.[43] As David Halperin has pointed out, irrespective of the gender identity of the participant, to be penetrated meant 'the voluntary abandonment of a "masculine" identity in favor of a "feminine" one'.[44] Erotic desire introduces a power relation of (feminine) passivity and (masculine) activity which cannot be tolerated within *either* the social hierarchy (where it effects a reversal of the proper movement of power) *or* within male friendship based upon equality. Edward's love for Gaveston, and then Spencer, introduces a troubling discontinuity into the troping of state and patriarchal family as homologous, because of the reproduction of heterosexual relationships of difference within an institution based upon homosociality: erotic desire turns up in the 'wrong' place (like Abbott's preference for arsehole over vagina), where it cannot produce anything other than a perversion of proper order.[45] The dynamic of erotic power, exercised over Edward, rather than by him, is antithetical in its direction to the functioning of the political hierarchy. Edward is subject to desire, itself a sign of weakness (and effeminacy in a male whose sexual object choice is female) in person and in rule, leading both to tyranny and to effeminization. Not only is Edward unable to govern his passions, his structural position in this narrative becomes that usually allotted to women in the scheme of homosocial reproduction of the patriarchal order – he mediates the rule of two good kings, guaranteeing the passage of the body politic from his father to his son.

It is not the case that Edward's relationships with men do not threaten or trouble the established patriarchal order – indeed, his neglect of the institution of heterosexual marriage is the thing which directly causes his downfall as Isabella turns her rejection to account, a point made explicitly by Cary: 'he hastens homewards, returning seized of a jewel, which not being rightly valued, wrought his ruin'.[46] Rather than power circulating between men by means of their marital bonds with women, privilege and wealth are prevented from further circulation by their investment in the favourite who becomes little more than a consumer, removed from social and political reciprocity and from the horizontal redistribution of power between men. If he bestows what he cannot consume, the favourite directs wealth and political capital away from the monarch and state and into the coffers of private individuals where it cannot be used for the common good. Wealth literally fails to circulate, as the accusations levelled at Buckingham clearly indicate: 'did not thy hand / Monopolize the glorie of this land? / Did not thy smiles or frownes make princes kneele?' The imagery of profligacy and excessive consumption spills into the associations built up between Buckingham, poisoning and witchcraft: 'That hee might mount, favorites honey tasted / Whilst others vitall power by poison wasted.'[47] In this narrative 'proper' male bonds, those between father and son, monarch and subject, are repudiated in favour of bonds which threaten these very structures, yet resemble them closely.

The boundaries of friendship in the court of Charles I

These narratives of Edward II aim to produce anti-images which didactically and contrastively reinforce 'proper' ideas of friendship and kingship – Marlowe is perhaps the exception, but neither Cary nor Hubert is ultimately subversive, wishing only for reform (by enforced deposition if necessary) of an existing insitution and social order. Hubert, for example, claims that he writes 'That (warn'd by theirs) Our Age like sins might shunne' (st. 8), at the same time making the contemporary resonances of his text explicit for those who wish to heed them. In the process of holding up the anti-image of power, however, both texts reveal the distinction they attempt to underline to be highly problematic: the male bonds that Hubert has in mind when he writes that 'Designes of Princes happiest prove / When their great Peeres do serve because they love' (p. 43) are intended to be distinct from those which pertain between Edward and his favourites, but such discriminations become increasingly difficult to sustain, precisely because of the language of male friendship in which the relationship between king and favourite is conventionally couched, as Goldberg notes: 'The peers, as much as the minion, want the king's love'.[48] Alan Bray has presented this problematic relationship as symptomatic of the slipperiness of early modern taxonomies regarding male sexual behaviour, in exploring 'the curious symmetry between the sodomite and the masculine friend'.[49] Montaigne's essay 'Of Friendship' demonstrates what Bruce R. Smith calls 'a *continuum* of erotic desire' at work in the bonds between men, which has its basis in the repudiation of sexual feeling, and the apparent incompatibility of true friendship, notions of ownership and the exchange of goods:[50]

> In this noble commerce, offices and benefits (nurses of other amities) deserve not so much as to bee accounted of ... the union of such friends, being truly perfect, makes them lose the feeling of such duties, and hate, and expell from one another these words of division, and difference; benefit, good deed, dutie, obligation, acknowledgement, prayer, thanks, and such their like.[51]

Commerce introduces inequality between friends, and it metamorphoses into something which resembles friendship: Montaigne's ideal is not available to Edward, only the imitative behaviours which ape it, and ultimately undermine it. As Bray has noted, in Marlowe's play 'the image we see is simultaneously both that of friendship and its caricature'.[52] Even within Montaigne's essay, which seems to make such crisp and precise distinctions, the line separating the ideal from its antithesis becomes unenforceable, because the two are interdependent:

> In true friendship, it is a generall and universall heat, all pleasure and smoothnes, that hath no pricking or stinging in it, which the more it is in lustfull love, the more is it but a ranging and mad desire in following that which flies

us ... As soone as it creepeth into the termes of friendship, that is to say, in the agreement of wils, it languisheth and vanisheth away: enjoying doth lose it, as having a corporall end, and subject to sacietie.[53]

The terms of this comparison imply the proximity of the prescribed and the pro-scribed, and it turns out that only the transgressive friendship makes itself visible by outward signs, recapitulating the classical distinction between platonic and erotic love:

this other Greeke licence is justly abhorred by our customes ... because accord-ing to use it had so necessarie a disparitie of ages, and difference of offices between lovers, did not more sufficiently answer the perfect union and agree-ment, which we here require ... [these desires] ... grounded upon an externall beauty; a false image of corporall generation ... if this furie did seize upon a base minded courage, the meanes of its pursuit, [were] riches, gifts, favour to the advancement of dignities, and such like vile merchandice.[54]

The things which break the bonds of male friendship and turn it towards sodomitical disorder – money, power and the erotic – are the very things which signify an imbalance of power between a king and his counsellors and make pri-vate desire a political issue. This is not to say that the sodomite and the favourite are one and the same, merely that they share the same discursive field in defin-ing (by symbolising its antithesis) proper male friendship. Whether cause or effect, expenditure without return, and honour without duty ('spend', 'expend, 'use' etc. having a sexual sense)[55] are indicative of a rupture in the bonds of exchange and duty which order the social structure, symbolised by the favourite and his continual exceeding of the limits of his role, in terms of wealth, status and influence. That this power is permitted to take hold is an indication of the weakness of the monarch, his poor conceptual grasp of his role, and his abnegation of good rule in privileging one kind of bond over another.

Alan Bray argues in his analysis of the links between Elizabethan friend-ship and sodomy that

the protecting conventions that ensure that [intimacy between men] was seen in an acceptable frame of reference were often absent by the end of the sixteenth century ... it provided a weapon that lay close to hand; and it left this intimacy more open and less secure in its meaning than the formal Elizabethan essays on friendship would have us believe.[56]

If this was so at the end of the sixteenth century, then by the 1620s the bound-aries seem to be even further confused. Francis Bacon's 1625 essay 'Of Friend-ship' in the volume dedicated to the Duke of Buckingham presents a marked contrast to Montaigne's struggle to set up and sustain distinctions between acceptable friendship and transgressive eroticism or materialism, a collapse which may have been based in Bacon's own experience.[57] The 1625 version is also notably at odds with the earlier version of this essay, which, rather like Montaigne, insists that '[i]t is friendship, when a man can say to himselfe, I love this man without respect of utility'.[58] The 1625 essay is a much longer and more complex undertaking; it is packed with precedents and authorities, and is much concerned with the dangers of solitude, especially for princes and rulers, as Bacon suggests that 'friends' provide ease for burdens, and can give useful counsel. He claims that there is 'no such *Flatterer*, as is a mans Selfe'.[59] In this formulation, friendship immediately has a utility, and the essay quickly moves towards a notion of friendship as a *political* category. In treating of the friendships of kings Bacon is undoubtedly attempting to circumvent and (in part) to justify his subject's problematic relationship to his dedicatee, and perhaps to justify Buckingham's continued habitation of the role of favourite:

> It is a Strange Thing to observe, how high a rate, Great Kings and Monarchs, do set upon this *Fruit* of *Friendship*, whereof we speake: So great, as they purchase it, many time, at the hazard of their owne Safety and Greatnesse. For Princes, in regard of the distance of their Fortune, from that of their Subjects and Servants, cannot gather this Fruit; Except ... they raise some Persons, to be as it were Companions, and almost Equals to themselves, which many times sorteth to Inconvenience. The Moderne Languages give unto such Persons, the Name of *Favorites*, or *Privadoes*; As if it were Matter of Grace or Conversation. But the Roman Name attaineth the true Use, and Cause thereof; Naming them *Participes Curarum* ... this hath been done, not by Weake and Passionate *Princes* onely, but by the Wisest, and most Politique that ever reigned.[60]

This account is hedged around with qualifications and slippery nomenclatures, as the notion of friendship slides inexorably into the politicised category of the favourite: the Latin term does not contradict this, it compounds it. The precedents and authorities that Bacon goes on to cite betray his own unease with the definitions he has tried to set up, and fly in the face of most contemporary interpretations of Sylla and Pompey, Tiberius and Sejanus. Bacon writes

> With *Tiberius Caesar*, *Sejanus* had ascended to that Height, as they Two were tearmed and reckoned, as a Paire of Frends. *Tiberius* in a Letter to him saith: [from Tacitus, *Annals*: 'on account of our friendship, I have not concealed these things']. And the whole Senate, dedicated an *Altar* to *Frendship* ... in respect of the great Dearenesse of *Frendship*, between them Two.[61]

Bacon, with his interest in Tacitus and the political usages of his work, could hardly have been unaware of the implications of this precedent, and the uses to which it might be put by Buckingham's detractors. Pierre Matthieu's 1628 *The Powerfull Favorite*, a loose translation of Tacitus, and interpreted as a 'satire on the Duke of Buckingham', suggests that the incident alluded to by Bacon marks the intrusion of private interests into the public government of the state – the contemporary resonances of this interpretation in 1628 are quite clear:

> not onely in private, but also in the Senate hee [Tiberius] called him companion of his labours, and commanded that his pourtrayture should be honoured together with his in the streets, respected in the Theaters, and carried in the standards of his armies. This is for the Prince to annihilate himselfe to please his servant; for it cannot goe well when the people perceive that favour transfereth soveraigne honours of superiours upon an inferiour, and that the Prince suffer-eth a companion in the kingdome to assist him to governe.[62]

Bacon's revisions and rewritings of the *Essays* for a new dedicatee in 1625 reveal the extent to which the categories of friend and favourite have been conflated – possibly to facilitate Bacon's own search for favour – but they do demonstrate the difficulty of drawing clear distinctions between different kinds of male bonds, and the ease with which one type might make itself known by means of another.[63] If sodomy is understood as a transgression of proper male bonds motivated by ambition, lust or greed, then it does seem to be summoned by the 1638 Latin translation of the passage in 'Of Ambition' where Bacon argues that the favourite is 'the best Remedy against Ambitious Great-Ones' where the term 'favourite' is rendered as *gratiosos et intimos*.[64]

There is thus a good deal of shared ground between the sodomite and the royal favourite, as the one is continually expressed by means of the other: both share the function of calling political power and status into question by dis-rupting hierarchical power structures, and by closely resembling that which they disorder. Just as sodomy is the inversion of friendship, so the favourite represents an improper relationship between king and subject indicative of a general corruption in rule, as the hierarchy goes into reverse: 'the Duke … sought to raise an opinion of his own greatness, and make the King grow less'.[65] Cary and Hubert both participate in the general critiques of favourites and their abuses of power in this period, criticising advancements based upon lack of talent and breeding, the usurpation of a power which should be the king's, and its manipulation to the favourite's own ends, culminating in the under-mining of the institution of monarchy itself, as it is mimicked and usurped by one who has no right to it:

> It is much in a king, that hath so great a charge delivered over to his care and cus-tody, to be himself dissolute, licentious, and ill-affected; but when he falls into a second error, making more delinquents kings, he brings all into disorder, and makes his kingdom rather a stage of oppression, than the theatre of justice, which opens the ready way to an ensuing misery.[66]

Such a multiplication of images opens up a worrying gap between signifier and signified, which enables the validity of kingship to be called into question, and the entire structure to spiral out of control. This abnegation of power is frequently grounded in the king's desire being identified with his will, which fails to check either his own excesses or those of his favourite, who becomes closely identified with him: 'it is oftentime as daungerous to a prince to have evil and odious adherents as to bee evill and odious himselfe'.[67] The placing of the monarch's will above the law, and thereby the abuse of his prerogative, marks the decline from absolute rule into tyranny, especially where the exercise of his will is seen to be guided by passion, and by the eroticised bond with the favourite. Hubert's Edward asserts that he is above the law:

> Kings made those lawes, and Kings may break them now.
> That pleas'd them then, and this now pleaseth you …
>   … There is not law
> Can bind a King but onely his desire.[68]

The slipperiness of the distinctions between these various male bonds is indicated by the favourites' aping of the functions of kingship, much as the outward signs of sodomy resemble those of friendship – indeed, the discourse of the favourite is intertwined with that of the sodomite on a number of levels. Cary reports that 'Nothing is concluded touching the government or royal prerogative, but by his [Gaveston's] consent and approbation … the king appeared so little himself, that the subjects thought him a royal shadow without a real substance'.[69] A whole set of social and political relationships depend, or appear to depend, on the need to keep sodomy in its 'place', to prevent it wandering from its acceptable and invisible place as one act amongst variant sexual behaviours to posing an overt threat to order. To put this differently, it must be prevented from signification. Accusations were repeatedly levelled at Buckingham in popular ballads and verses (not, we should note, at either Charles or James) which asserted that since the favourite held so much sway over the king, who was subject to his every whim, thus signifying as the passive partner in ways incompatible with his public role, that the crucial distinction between them had been fatally lost: 'Hee shall be king there, sitt in the kings throne, / Or els commaund the king, and that's all one'; 'I saw and searcht the royall cabbinett / Of secrets, and from his rich wisedomes myne / I digg'd those gems that made my actions shine'; 'did not thy hand/ Monopolize the glorie of this land? / Did not thy smiles or frownes make princes kneele?'[70] The antithesis of kingship mimics its actions and its place within a power structure. The usurpation of the functions of monarchy threaten to undermine the status of the institution itself, which becomes fundamentally unreadable, a set of unstable signs without a referent or a stable meaning, a disjunction between surface and meaning which itself functions to characterise bad rule and the descent into tyranny and disorder.

Conclusion

The Edward II narratives all deal with the slippery question of sodomy at a rhetorical level, using it as an exemplar to demonstrate the necessity of virtue in government, and of the need to maintain proper boundaries between the body natural and the body politic. Sodomy is the category which represents breaching of distinctions because it entails the incursion of desire into fields (friendship, politics, bonds between men) which are explicitly founded upon its repudiation. The sign(s) of sodomy works a radical disruption, troubling the heteronormative distinctions upon which order, hierarchy and patriarchal government are based, leading to the collapse of meaning into an endless play of signifiers, where, for example, the signs and behaviours by which a king might be discerned no longer signify unproblematically. This chapter has attempted to trace a relationship between the emergence of history and that of sodomy: as history becomes a discourse that tries to organise and taxonomise, sodomy is that which disrupts taxonomies (or conflates them). Both are discursively constructed from a textual field: sodomy is a set of discourses (law, theology, poetics) at the point of visibility. By contrast, sodomy is without a history, or a historical narrative, and is frequently understood only through the coded deployment of myths, sites of inscription, rather than 'evidence'. The narrative of Edward II is where these two discourses emerge, merge and trouble one another. For Foucault sodomy is an act without a discourse; in these texts it is a discourse without an act.

NOTES
1 British Library, London, Ms. Add. 10309, fol. 207. I am grateful to Janet Clare for transcribing this text for me. I would like to thank respondents at the Reading conference at which this paper was originally given, Alan Stewart for allowing me to read his unpublished essay, and Michael O'Rourke for his supply of references, comments and ideas.
2 Ibid., margin. The poem appears to have been transcribed in the 1650s from Sir Anthony Weldon's Court and Character of King James.
3 This view has been advanced most recently by David M. Bergeron, King James and Letters of Homoerotic Desire (Iowa City: 1999). 'By all sensible accounts, Buckingham became James's last and greatest lover', p. 98.
4 See Roger Lockyer, Buckingham: The Life and Political Career of George Villiers, First Duke of Buckingham, 1592–1628 (London: 1981) and Robert Wilcher, The Writing of Royalism, 1628–1660 (Cambridge: 2001), ch. 1.
5 Ms. Corpus Christi College, Oxford 328, fol. 102; Bergeron, King James, p. 125.
6 See Laurie A. Shannon, 'Monarchs, Minions, and "Soveraigne" Friendship', South Atlantic Quarterly 97.
7 Lucy Hutchinson, Memoirs of the Life of Colonel Hutchinson, Charles I's Puritan Nemesis, ed. N. H. Keeble, (London: 1995), p. 67.
8 Bergeron, 1999, p. vii.
9 F. W. Fairholt, ed., Poems and Songs on the Assassination of the Duke of Buckingham, in Early English Poetry, Ballads, vol. XXIX (London: 1851).
10 For a recent dissenting voice in relation to historical material see Allen J. Frantzen, Before the Closet: Same-Sex Love from Beowulf to Angels in America, (Chicago: 1998), esp. pp. 1–29.

11 Michel Foucault, *History of Sexuality*, vol. 1 (London: 1990) p. 101; Gregory Bredbeck, *Sodomy and Interpretation: Marlowe to Milton* (Ithaca: 1991), p. 13.

12 For quite different formulations of this view see Frantzen, 1998, and Mario di Gangi, *The Homoerotics of Early Modern Drama* (Cambridge: 1997), pp. 19–23.

13 Mario di Gangi, 'Asses and Wits: The Homoerotics of Mastery in Satiric Comedy', *English Literary Renaissance* 25 (1995), pp. 179–208, 182; see also Cynthia Herrup, 'The Patriarch at Home: The Trial of the 2nd Earl of Castlehaven for Rape and Sodomy', *History Workshop Journal* 41 (1996), pp. 1–18, 7.

14 Simon Shepherd, 'What's so funny abut Ladies' Tailors? A Survey of Some Male (Homo)sexual Types in the Renaissance', *Textual Practice* 6 (1992), pp. 17–30, p. 24.

15 Bernard Mellor, ed., *The Poems of Sir Francis Hubert* (Hong Kong: 1961), st. 230.

16 See Mario di Gangi's point about the way in which Edward II 'seems to confirm a modern ideology of doomed homosexual desire'. Di Gangi, 1997, p. 15.

17 See David Lindley, *The Trials of Frances Howard: Fact and Fiction at the Court of King James* (London: 1993).

18 Dympna Callaghan, 'The Terms of Gender: "Gay" and "Feminist" Edward II', in Valerie Traub, M. Lindsay Kaplan and Dympna Callaghan, eds, *Feminist Readings of Early Modern Cultre: Emerging Subjects* (Cambridge: 1996), pp. 275–301, 281–2.

19 D. R. Woolf, *The Idea of History in Early Stuart England: Erudition, Ideology and 'The Light of Truth' from the Accession of James I to the Civil War* (Toronto: 1990), p. 158.

20 Sir John Hayward, *The Life and Raigne of King Henrie IIII*, ed. John J. Manning, Camden Society, 4th series, 42 (London: 1991), p. 120.

21 See F. J. Levy, *Tudor Historical Thought* (San Marino: 1967), pp. 242–4, and Woolf, 1990, pp. 31, 143.

22 For a recent exploration of connections between economy and sodomy see Will Fisher, 'Queer Money', *English Literary History* 66 (1999), pp. 1–23.

23 Joseph Cady, '"Masculine Love", Renaissance Writing, and the "New Invention" of Homosexuality', in Claude J. Summers, ed., *Homosexuality in Renaissance and Enlightenment England: Literary Representations in Historical Context* (New York: 1992), pp. 9–40, 35, n. 13.

24 William Martyn, *The Historie and Lives, of the Kings of England* (London: 1628), p. 89. Probably written c. 1615.

25 See Alan Bray, *Homosexuality in Renaissance England* (London: 1982); Jonathan Goldberg, ed., *Queering the Renaissance* (Durham, North Carolina: 1994); David M. Halperin, 'One Hundred Years of Homosexuality', in his *One Hundred Years of Homosexuality and Other Essays on Greek Love* (London: 1990), pp. 15–40.

26 Bray, 1982, p. 30.

27 Jody Greene examines these connections in a different context in '"You must eat men": The Sodomitic Economy of Renaissance Patronage', *Gay and Lesbian Quarterly* 1 (1994), pp. 163–97.

28 Fairholt, 1851, p. 30.

29 Mary Anne Everett Green, ed., *Diary of John Rous*, Camden Society 66 (London: 1856), p. 22, and Fairholt, 1851, p. 14.

30 Fairholt, 1851, p. 49

31 John Rushworth, ed., *Historical Collections* (London: 1659), vol. I, p. 102.

32 Fairholt, 1851, p. 49.

33 Rushworth, 1659, I, p.167.

34 Elizabeth Cary, *The History of the Life, Reign and Death of Edward II*, in Diane Purkiss, ed., *Renaissance Women: The Plays of Elizabeth Cary, the Poems of Aemilia Lanyer* (London: 1994), p. 87.

35 *Ibid.*, pp. 96 –7.

36 Bredbeck, 1991, p. 50.

37 Cary, 1994, p. 123.

38 *Ibid.*, p. 99.

39 *Ibid.*, p. 84.

40 Fairholt, 1851, p. 35.

41 See Rushworth, 1659, p. 102, on the threat of the intimacy between Charles and Bucking-ham, and Richard Corbett's description of Buckingham as the King's 'darling Absolon', in Fairholt, 1851, p. 32.

42 My indebtedness to Eve Kosofsky Sedgwick's *Between Men: English Literature and Male Homoso-cial Desire* (New York: 1985) should be clear here.

43 For the purpose of my argument, the historical veracity of Edward's penetration by a red-hot poker is beside the point – it illustrates quite clearly symbolically the transgressions and discontinuities of a sodomised monarch.

44 Halperin, 'One Hundred Years', p. 23. I would question 'voluntary' in the case of Edward II's death; notably, he is 'sodomised' by his gaoler, in an instance where both act and the social status of the actor complete Edward's degradation by inverting the very terms in which Edward had placed his will above his kingship – to pursue sodomy is to forfeit kingship.

45 On the connections between sodomy (defined as anything other than legally sanctioned pro-creative sex) and other 'illegitimate' forms of reproduction, such as usury see Jody Greene, '"You must eat men"' and Will Fisher's 'Queer Money', which depends heavily on Greene, but adduces different examples.

46 Cary, 1994, p. 100.

47 Fairholt, 1851, pp. 47, 50. See also Rushworth's account of the Articles of the Earl of Bristol accusing Buckingham in May 1626 of sundry offences, including 'the imploying of his power … for the procuring of Favors and Offices which he bestowed upon base and unwor-thy persons for the recompense and heir of his lust' (p. 263) which he leaves to their Lord-ships' discretion, and of the Commons' impeachment against the Duke of Buckingham (1626), which includes the abuse of offices which 'have been ingrossed, bought and sold' (p. 304) and the debasement of nobility, honour and ancient titles into vulgar monetary reward, 'he hath enforced some that were rich … to purchase Honour' (p. 334).

48 Jonathan Goldberg, *Sodometries: Renaissance Texts, Modern Sexualities*, (Stanford: 1992), p. 119.

49 Alan Bray, 'Homosexuality and the Signs of Male Friendship in Elizabethan England', *History Workshop Journal* 29 (1990), pp. 1–19, 2.

50 Bruce Smith, *Homosexual Desire in Shakespeare's England: A Cultural Poetics* (Chicago: 1991), p. 55.

51 *The Essayes of Michael Lord of Montaigne*, trans. John Florio, intro. by Desmond MacCarthy (London: 1928), I, p. 203.

52 Bray, 1990, p. 10.

53 Montaigne, 1928, I, p. 198.

54 *Ibid*, I, p. 199–200.

55 See Fisher, 1999.

56 Bray, 1990, p. 15.

57 See Alan Stewart's essay, '"Ganimeds and favourites": Bribery, Buggery and the Fall of Fran-cis Bacon', unpublished paper.

58 Edward Arber, ed., *A Harmony of the Essays, etc. of Francis Bacon* (London: 1871), p. 162. The earlier version may be found in BL Harleian Ms. 5106, and is dated in the years 1607–12.

59 Bacon, 1871, p. 177

60 *Ibid.*, p. 167.

61 *Ibid.*, pp. 169–71.

62 Pierre Matthieu, *The Powerful Favorite, Or, The Life of Aelius Sejanus* (Paris: 1628), p. 5.

63 Lisa Jardine and Alan Stewart, *Hostage to Fortune: The Troubled Life of Francis Bacon* (London: 1999).

64 Bacon, 1871, p. 225. This passage appears first in the 1625 edition. Cassell's Latin dictio-nary defines *gratiosus* as 'enjoying favour, popularity, or influence', and *intimus* as '(Of friends) Most intimate, closest'.

65 Rushworth, 1659, I, p. 144.

66 Cary, 1994, p. 226
67 Hayward, *King Henrie*, p. 70.
68 Sts 56–7.
69 Cary, 1994, p. 101.
70 Fairholt, 1851, pp. 35, 39, 47.

4

Sodomy in early modern Venice

N. S. DAVIDSON

In 1632 William Lithgow published a collected edition of his travel memoirs under the enticing title *The Totall Discourse of the Rare Adventures and Painefull Peregrinations of Long Nineteene Yeares Travayles*. Lithgow was a Scot with a serious wanderlust. He had begun travelling away from his hometown of Lanark in his teens, possibly as a result of an assault in which his ears were cut off by four local men who found him with their sister. The *Totall Discourse* records three of 'Lugless Will's' subsequent journeys between 1609 and 1629, during which, according to his own estimate, he covered some 36,000 miles in all. One of his earliest destinations was Italy, and the first chapter of the book contains some fascinating observations on Rome, Naples, Florence, Venice and other cities. It ends with a ringing denunciation of the Italian penchant for sodomy: 'beastly Sodomy ... is as rife [in Padua] as in Rome, Naples, Florence, Bullogna, Venice, Ferrara, Genoa, Parma not being exempted, nor yet the smallest Village of Italy: a monstrous filthinesse, and yet to them a pleasant pastime, making songs and singing Sonets of the beauty and pleasure of their Bardassi, or embuggered boyes'.[1]

Placing sodomy in early modern Venice

The reputation of Venice in particular as a place of sexual licence was widespread in early modern Europe,[2] and it lasted well into the modern period: in the early twentieth century, the term 'Venetian' was still used by Gerald du Maurier's family as a synonym for 'lesbian'.[3] And for modern historians of sodomy the city of Venice remains an unusually worthwhile focus for study. Its archives and libraries do not offer the scale and consistency of documentation available in the records of the Ufficiali di notte of fifteenth-century Florence, exploited so carefully in recent years by Michael Rocke.[4] But they do contain enough information to enable us to reconstruct a local history of sodomy, and to understand some of the policies of the city's governing authorities and the response of its wider population. What makes Venice especially interesting in this context is its uniquely cosmopolitan population. By the later Middle Ages, and for centuries after, the city was host to communities of English and Germans, Dutch and Flemings, Bohemians, Poles and Hungarians, Slavs and Albanians, Arabs and Jews, Armenians, Persians and Turks. There were migrants from elsewhere in Italy, too, and from Venetian subject territories – from *Terraferma* cities such as Padua, Verona and Vicenza, and from Greek territories in the Mediterranean such as Cyprus and Crete. In 1468, in fact, the Greek scholar Cardinal Bessarion remarked that 'people from almost the entire world gather' in Venice. This openness to the outside world is one of the characteristic features of Venetian history in this period. As the French traveller Philippe de Commynes claimed, at the end of the fifteenth century, 'most of the people [in Venice] are foreigners'.[5]

Not all those who lived in Venice, therefore, were necessarily Venetian. And at times the use of the contemporary term 'sodomy' seems to have been almost equally capacious. The word appears frequently in the law codes of Italian cities in and after the Middle Ages as a rather loose label for sexual acts thought to be 'against nature'. Where further definition was given, its application was not always consistent. The statutes of the Republic of Lucca, for instance, issued in the mid fifteenth century and reissued in the 1530s, seem to restrict the term to sexual acts (including masturbation and oral sex) committed by men with each other. Venetian legislation of the same period, by contrast, used the word explicitly to include some sexual acts between men and women as well.[6] What linked these varied uses of the term was not so much the gender of the participants but the nature of their activities, none of which could lead to human procreation. As Lodovico Gabrielli argued in the later sixteenth century, sodomy 'is the gravest of all sexual sins because it violates nature and denies procreation'.[7]

It is sensible, therefore, to avoid making any automatic link between the sodomy that appears in our sources and more recent notions of homosexuality. But once that caution has been acknowledged, we are still left with the deeper question of the meaning of the acts described as 'sodomy' for the individuals involved. And here again the evidence available from Venice, literary as well as archival, may provide us with some insights.

In Venice, as elsewhere, the government's view of 'sodomy' was unremittingly hostile. In part this reflected the teaching of the Catholic Church. In the thirteenth century, for example, St Thomas Aquinas argued that God had created human sexual organs for the purpose of reproduction, and that their use for any act that did not issue in procreation was for that reason sinful, an offence against God and against nature, his creation. All non-procreative sexual acts were therefore to be condemned.[8] This thinking was echoed in the legislation of all Italian governments, which insisted that individuals found guilty of 'unnatural' sexual acts should normally be sentenced to death.[9] In addition, however, later medieval governments may have been motivated by anxiety about the drastic population decline caused by the Black Death in the mid fourteenth century, a decline that engagement in sodomy would do nothing to reverse. A combining of these preoccupations may be apparent in the widely published plea of the Franciscan Fra Cherubino da Siena, who begged wives in the later fifteenth century not to let their husbands use them sexually as if they were men.[10]

The religious and demographic arguments were further reinforced by a widespread belief that, if individual cases of sodomy were not punished, the wrath of God himself would be brought down on the whole community in the form of floods, droughts, famines, plagues or military defeats. This fear, and its attachment to sodomy, was made explicit in a bull of 1566 by Pope Pius V.[11] It appeared too in the diary of the Venetian patrician Girolamo Priuli, which explained that the Italian wars of the early sixteenth century had been God's punishment of the Italians for their sins, and in particular for their tolerance of male sodomy.[12]

Priuli's discussion provides us with a further clue to contemporary attitudes. For having condemned 'the vice against nature called sodomy' (an 'abominable and pernicious vice'), he then describes how young Venetian men had begun to use perfume, to dress themselves in beautiful clothes, open at the chest, and to act in ways designed to incite libidinous thoughts in other men. Because of this, he suggests, 'they can truly be called not young men, but women'.[13] Priuli thus linked sexual acts between men with a confusion of the genders – a confusion that is also apparent in the wording of Fra Cherubino's warning a few years before.[14]

The campaign against sodomy in Venice thus took place against the background of consistent official concern. And the government's pronouncements in the later Middle Ages suggest that sodomy was then seen as a growing problem. In 1421, for example, the Council of Ten declared that 'this abhorrent vice is increasing'; in 1500 the Ten again referred to 'the increase of such evils'. In 1511 the city's Patriarch announced that sodomy was now so prevalent that female prostitutes were going out of business.[15] The Republic's legislation therefore entrusted the investigation and punishment of offenders to its most powerful magistracies. In the fourteenth century the arrest and prosecution of sodomites had been the responsibility of the Signori di notte, an element in their obligation to maintain local order in the city. In 1406, however, after a particularly notorious trial involving some thirty-five individuals, both patricians and non-patricians, jurisdiction was transferred to the Council of Ten, a standing committee drawn from the Senate which was responsible for the security of the

state, and which exercised judicial authority over all offences considered threatening to the government. In 1418 the Ten established a special tribunal entitled
the Collegio dei sodomiti to investigate alleged offenders, and in 1448 a special
police force was created to patrol the city and arrest suspects.[16] And the punishments prescribed for those found guilty were fierce. From the fourteenth
century the law required that convicted sodomites should be burned alive, a
penalty that recalled the fiery destruction of the city of Sodom recorded in
Genesis 19. From the mid fifteenth century, however, the Republic's preferred
method of execution for this offence was decapitation, though the bodies of the
condemned were still subsequently consumed by flames.[17]

But while it is relatively easy to trace the fears of the authorities through
the surviving official documentation, recovering the history of sodomy itself
in the city is perhaps more problematic.[18] Most of our evidence comes from
the records of trials conducted by the Signori di notte (for the period before
the fifteenth century) and the Council of Ten – though some investigations conducted by the Avogadori di commun, the Quarantia criminal and the Inquisition provide us with further information. These records are not always
complete, and statistical trends derived from this evidence must therefore be
treated with caution. One unmistakable development, though, is the increase
in the scale of prosecution – and therefore of the evidence available to us – once
the Council of Ten had taken responsibility for investigations in the early fifteenth century. In the last quarter of the fourteenth century the Signori di notte
seem to have prosecuted only three individuals; in the following twenty-five
years, the Ten prosecuted 87, in 31 separate trials. In the fifteenth century as a
whole a total of 498 individuals seems to have been investigated by the Ten in
266 trials, the majority (two-thirds in fact) between 1451 and 1500. And the
increase continued into the sixteenth century: from an average of over three
trials each year in the second half of the fifteenth century to an average of over
five trials each year in the first half of the sixteenth century. By the seventeenth
century, however, the scale of prosecution was declining. Between 1590 and
1680 the Ten prosecuted a total of 273 individuals in 187 separate trials; but
the average fell from 3.2 trials each year in the 1610s to 1.7 trials each year in
the 1670s.[19]

A wide range of non-generative sexual acts is described in these trial
records,[20] and women as well as men appear as suspects. In August 1500, for
instance, Rada de Jadra was condemned to death by the Council of Ten for
employing young prostitutes in her brothel for sodomy – presumably, in this
case, anal intercourse – with their male clients. Two of the women involved, a
Greek called Angela Gaio and a Friulan named Ana, were exiled at the same
time, and a further investigation was begun against another woman, Marietta
del Beretino, named by Rada, on a similar charge, that 'in her house she had

run a school of sodomy for men with women'.[21] We do not know how old Angela and Ana were, but young girls were apparently valued as partners in sodomy of this kind, and a decree issued by the Council later in the same month states that some women kept girls as young as seven in their brothels for men who wanted anal intercourse with females.[22]

A man who enjoys anal intercourse with women or girls need not, of course, have any interest in sex with other men. But there is evidence to suggest that some men in early modern Venice found the prospect of a male sexual partner arousing, even when they were expecting to have sex with a woman. In 1578 the Council of Ten issued a decree in which it was claimed that the 'dishonesty and impudence of the courtesans and prostitutes of Venice has increased so much in recent times that, in order to attract and ensnare young men and to lead them astray, in addition to many other tricks, they have now taken to dressing themselves in male clothes ... and then ... when they find some young man, they excite him and provoke him, and so oblige him to go with them'. We know in fact that one celebrated prostitute in the sixteenth century, Giulia Lombardo, kept male clothes in her wardrobe, presumably for this purpose.[23] And the trial records do contain evidence of men who took both female and male sexual partners. In 1585, for example, a Perugian called Annibale was denounced by his landlady to the Venetian Inquisition for bringing both women and boys to his room for sex.[24] And in May 1619, a Genoese in his later thirties called Vincenzo Arnaldi was denounced in the Venetian subject city of Brescia for sodomy with both a fourteen-year-old boy from Tuscany called Romulo and an older youth from Milan, aged eighteen or nineteen, called Giovanni Pietro Cavanego. The evidence of witnesses, including Romulo himself, lent support to the suspicion that Arnaldi and Cavanego had a sexual relationship. But it also became clear during the investigation that Arnaldi was married to Cavanego's sister, and it was suggested too that he had some years before been guilty of abducting a young girl from her mother's house in Crema.[25]

These cases seem to indicate that sodomy with women was one of several different sexual practices a man might enjoy; sodomy with men was another. Evidence that a man had intercourse with another man should not therefore be taken as conclusive proof of an exclusively same-sex orientation. Indeed some historians have argued that involvement in same-sex sodomy was characteristic of a certain phase of a man's life between adolescence and marriage, no more than a stage in the usual process of growing up. This is Michael Rocke's conclusion in his study of the evidence in Florence, where the typical relationship involving two men was of an adult, unmarried male in his twenties or early thirties, and an adolescent, usually aged between fifteen and seventeen. The older partner took the 'active' role, perceived at the time as more properly 'masculine', while the younger adopted the 'passive', more 'feminine' position. Once married, however, men were expected to abandon same-sex activities.[26] The Venetian archives contain many similar cases. In the mid-1550s, for example, an employee at one of the government's tax offices, Francesco Camelli, was convicted and sentenced to perpetual imprisonment for sodomy with a minor called Marco from Padua, who had, it was emphasised, participated voluntarily.[27] In some cases the age difference was combined with a class difference. In 1486 the Venetian Ambassador in Rome, a patrician called Antonio Loredan, was found after investigation to have had a sodomitical relationship with a younger non-patrician from Verona called Bernardo Salerno. Bernardo confessed his involvement under torture, but only in what contemporaries termed the 'passive' role (*patiente* in the Latin).[28] Here again, we find a common pattern, in which the established hierarchy of status was preserved also in the sexual act.

But in Venice the differences of age and status were not always observed. In a fascinating case of 1464 involving thirteen males, both boys and adults (all patricians) were convicted of taking an active role in sodomy. And in 1516, the Ten expressed concern at information they had recently received of men in their thirties, forties, fifties or even sixties who were prepared to pay other men to penetrate them.[29] But such role reversals were not confined to the aristocracy: in 1608, for instance, a priest called Alessandro Rubilio was charged with maintaining a number of female prostitutes in his house in order to attract male clients with whom he could then have sex himself *come patiente*.[30] From time to time, indeed, evidence emerged of groups of men of all classes who engaged in sex with each other. In January 1545 the Mantuan Ambassador in Venice reported that attempts had recently been made by the government to arrest members of 'a sect of sodomites' in the city. Several *populani* and *citadini* had been successfully taken into custody, but the nobles involved had apparently been warned in advance and fled.[31]

Unfortunately, in many of these cases, the information provided about suspects investigated for sodomy is only brief and incomplete. But it is clear that not all men abandoned sexual activity with other men once they had married – Vincenzo Arnaldi, mentioned above, was certainly married when he was accused of sodomy with his brother-in-law, for example. And for some men at least, same-sex activities were clearly more than just an occasional pleasant alternative to sex with a women, before or after marriage. In 1500, for example, the Council of Ten tried a man called Vincenzo Sabolino, who confessed to a sexual relationship with Pasquale Catanio that had by then lasted for ten years.[32] In 1640 the Ten discovered that the patrician Giulio da Canal had also had a long-term relationship with another man; but in this case the couple had actually lived together for several years in the same house, and apparently slept together in the same bed. On many occasions, it was reported, Giulio had bought women's clothes for his partner.[33] What such cases seem to suggest is that, in Venice at least, some men did restrict their sexual activity solely to other men, and perhaps even to one other man in particular in a long-term and voluntary relationship.

Writing in praise of sodomy

We must of course be careful not to accept the veracity of our sources without question: we should be alert to the possibility of false evidence, from witnesses and defendants, and of mistaken convictions. In some cases the charge of sodomy might have been laid against individuals who were entirely innocent, and whose real offence (in the eyes of their accusers) lay elsewhere. This point has already been made by historians such as Cynthia Herrup, who has argued that in England – and especially in cases involving members of the elite – the charge of sodomy was often paired with other accusations simply to increase their effect.[34] But there are problems in exporting this sort of interpretation to the Venetian evidence, for cases of sodomy in the Republic only rarely involved individuals who were under investigation for other offences at the same time.[35] And in addition – despite the fierce opposition of both Church and state – the intellectual and social context in Venice was quite different to that in England.

Throughout the Renaissance, in fact, and well into the seventeenth century, there was a surprisingly self-confident literature available in Venice arguing that sexual preference was a matter of choice, not of law. One of the most fascinating examples is a book entitled *L'Alcibiade fanciullo a scola* (*Alcibiades the Schoolboy*), which was written in the city in about 1631 by a Conventual Franciscan called Antonio Rocco. The book tells the story of the successful sodomitical seduction of Alcibiades, an adolescent, by his teacher Filotimo. But what makes it especially significant for our purpose is the long and at times very witty debate that it records between its two characters. Filotimo takes a naturalist view of sexual desire: 'actions are natural when nature inclines us to them', he says. Sodomy cannot therefore be considered unnatural, for 'to call sodomy a vice against nature is ridiculous … that such a sweet delight should not be called "against nature" – and indeed is not "against nature" – is clearly demonstrated by the law of nature itself'. The sexual desire of one man for another is therefore natural, and should not be condemned by either Church or state. But not only are same-sex activities natural, and therefore morally the equivalent of a man's desire for a woman; they are also preferable. 'The delight one gets from women', says Filotimo, 'is bitterness, because of the fiery and poisonous effluent of their menstruation, a cause of putrefaction, ulcers, … sores and an infinite number of other ills.' Furthermore, sex with women results in pregnancy and childbirth, leading to a life of servitude for father and mother. 'Anyone can take a wife', Filotimo concludes, but 'those men who have a philosophical spirit have a full understanding of such matters' and therefore flee the bonds of sexual relationships with women. Rocco thus argues not just for the legitimacy of same-sex sodomy, but also for the deliberate selection by men of exclusively male sexual partners. And at the end of the story Alcibiades is brought to realise that 'he did not know what true delight was until he felt Filotimo's penis inside his anus [il cazzo nel culo]'. 'If this is the faith that leads to happiness', he says, 'where dwells the true god of love ... here [then] I consecrate myself to his service. If there are other Paradises, I willingly trade them for this one.'[36]

Rocco was born in the Abruzzi in central Italy in 1586. But after studying at the Universities of Rome and Perugia, he moved north to the University of Padua, and by about 1620 he was living in the parish of S. Moisè in Venice and working as a teacher of philosophy and rhetoric. He was well known in his lifetime for his publications on scientific and philosophical problems, which took as their starting-point the assumption that sense impressions provide the basis for all human knowledge, and which brought him offers of chairs at the Universities of Pisa and Padua. But he preferred to stay in Venice, where he died in the spring of 1653. For some twenty years after its composition the manuscript of the *Alcibiades* remained in the possession of a Venetian patrician called Giovan Francesco Loredan. It was published anonymously and with a false imprint, probably by Loredan and without Rocco's knowledge, in or just before January 1651. It quickly became notorious, and a second edition (on better paper) was soon issued.[37]

There seems to be no evidence to suggest that Rocco himself enjoyed sex with other men, and it is unclear, therefore, whether the arguments he presents in his book represent anything more than a purely intellectual commitment. His authorship of the book was by no means a close secret – Loredan mentioned it in his correspondence, for example[38] – and several denunciations were laid against Rocco in the Inquisition. In 1652, after the publication of the *Alcibiades*, one was even sent to the Congregation of the Holy Office in Rome, in which he was charged with 'living as an atheist'.[39] But Rocco received no punishment for his publications in Venice, and he continued to receive a pension from the government for his teaching after 1651. He was still a free man at his death in 1653.

As a work of literature the *Alcibiades* stands in an intriguing and subversive relationship with neo-platonism, not only in form but also in content. Rocco uses the debate between Filotimo and his pupil to reverse Ficino's allegorical interpretation of Platonic love as a chaste relationship between men which fuels the soul's ascent to ultimate beauty. Indeed, according to Alcibiades, it is precisely the physical consummation of their relationship, graphically described, that enables him to reach paradise.[40] But such literary allusions might be thought to cast doubt on the value of the *Alcibiades* as a source for the history of sodomy in Venice. To what extent can we take the arguments contained in a fictional work of this kind as a reliable expression of intellectual commitment on the part of its author? Italian literature of the Renaissance and early modern period was often characterized by a delight in parody and paradox, and Italian writers regularly published work that mocked the prevailing conventions of literary form. It could therefore be suggested that Rocco's report of the discussion between Filotimo and Alcibiades was nothing more than an amusing satire of the earnest debates about love that exercised the literati of the period. And if the work can be categorised as a provocative literary joke, then its arguments in favour of male sexual relations can be explained away as nothing more than clever self-advertisement.

But there is evidence that Rocco's rejection of traditional views on sexual morality went well beyond the confines of a literary game. Information presented to the local Inquisition in the 1630s and 1640s – well before the *Alcibiades* was published – suggests that he regularly repeated in private conversation some of the arguments presented in the book. Enrico Palladio, for example, questioned about his meetings with Rocco by the Inquisitor at Udine in 1648, recorded how, in conversation, 'Signor Rocco often used to ask us how long it had been since we last had sex, either naturally or against nature, and we would tell him what we had done. He would add, "You have done well, because that organ was made by nature, and we all have our own tastes and desires".'[41]

Furthermore, Rocco's assertions in the *Alcibiades* were by no means unique. One of the earliest Italian writers to discuss the legitimacy of sexual relations between men was a Sienese nobleman called Antonio Vignali in his dialogue *La Cazzaria*, written in the mid-1520s and first published in Naples in c. 1530. A Venetian edition appeared in 1531. The title of this work is difficult to translate into English satisfactorily, though later in the same century John Florio suggested that 'A Discourse of Pricks' might be suitable, since *cazzo* is the common Italian word for penis. The text is composed of a discussion between Arsiccio and his younger friend Sodo, the names by which Vignali himself and Marcantonio Piccolomini were known in the Sienese Accademia degli Intronati. The idea that anal intercourse is 'against nature' is, according to Arsiccio, 'unknown to nature herself. If nature had wanted men not to engage in buggery, she would not have made the experience so enjoyable; or she would have made it physiologically impossible … But in fact we see the opposite, for the anus receives the penis as easily as does the vagina.' In the course of the dialogue Vignali makes his *alter ego* declare that he prefers sex with men to any sexual activity with women, and the text ends with a description of sodomy between Arsiccio and Sodo – a remarkable conclusion given that the characters' real identities were so well known.[42] And the insistence that sexual desire is natural and morally neutral occurs also in the very funny *Corriero svaligiato*, written by a Piacentine nobleman called Ferrante Pallavicino who had settled in Venice after studying at the University of Padua: 'I do not understand with what justification the rigour of the law restricts the expressions of love permitted within marriage, nor those which are said to be contrary to nature in any other couplings.'[43]

The influence of these texts is of course hard to assess; but we do know that such books were widely read. In 1657, for example, a priest called Michele Brazzoni told the Inquisition in Udine that he had been given the *Alcibiades* by a Venetian patrician in one of the subject cities in Friuli, and that, after reading it, he had passed it on to an aristocratic neighbour.[44] And their arguments were certainly familiar to some of the men investigated by the Venetian authorities for sodomy. In 1550, for instance, an apostate Franciscan called Francesco Calcagno admitted to the Inquisition that he had said that he 'thought it was a vulgar thing [*cosa da plebei*] to have sex with any woman the natural way', and 'that he would rather worship a pretty little boy in the flesh than God' – a view he claimed to have taken directly from Vignali's *Cazzaria*.[45] Very similar comments were attributed in 1628 to Ortensio Barbieri, a priest who worked at Antonio Rocco's own parish church of S. Moisè in Venice. He was charged with saying that 'he did not know how to worship any other god than sodomy, from which he received greater happiness than the blessed in heaven', and with arguing that it was wrong to prohibit anal intercourse since God had obviously designed the human anus in such a way that its penetration was enjoyable.[46]

Interpreting the evidence

The implication of this Venetian evidence, then, both archival and literary, is that many of those involved believed that sodomy – 'unnatural' sex – was in fact entirely natural, and that it was reasonable to select one's sexual partners exclusively from one's own sex. In other words, they were able to resist or evade the normative expectations of both Church and the state. What is more, such beliefs seem to have been at the very least tolerated within the wider population of the city, for a striking feature of many of the trial records is the openness with which witnesses were prepared to report their knowledge of the suspects' offences and their failure to report that knowledge earlier to the authorities. The investigation of Ortensio Barbieri in 1628, for example, suggested that he had made no effort to conceal his sexual preferences locally, and that nobody had felt it necessary to denounce him previously. One witness informed the Inquisitor of a conversation with Barbieri in which the suspect had admitted his passion for Zanantonio Silvestri: the conversation had taken place some ten months before.[47]

It is also clear that, despite its public rhetoric against sodomy, the government often seemed to have little commitment to the strict enforcement of its own laws. As we have seen, the scale of prosecution declined after the first half of the sixteenth century. In 1553, in fact, the Ten reported that they now only rarely received denunciations for sodomy, and decided as a consequence to reduce the rewards offered to those whose accusations were upheld by the Council.[48] Even in cases where the suspects were found guilty – only ever a minority – the penalties were rarely imposed in full. The full rigour of the law was regularly invoked in cases that involved violence, especially against a minor. But where the sexual relationship was voluntary on both sides, the parties usually received a significantly reduced punishment. Vincenzo Sabolino, who confessed in 1500 to a ten-year sexual relationship with Pasquale Catanio, was sentenced by the Ten to just one year in prison, followed by exile. An alternative proposal to imprison him for life was defeated; and in the event he was released from prison after just eight months.[49] From the 1530s a short prison sentence or a period of galley service became the norm for sodomy, and the death penalty required in law was used less frequently. In 1580, for instance, after investigating the case of a priest called Paolo Torre, the Ten considered two alternative proposals: one calling for the application of the full legal penalty; the other that he should serve in the galleys for ten years. By a vote of twelve to three, he was sent to the galleys.[50] By the end of that century, government concern about the incidence of sodomy had reduced even further, and, even though the established laws were not revised, the death penalty was never subsequently used in sodomy cases.[51]

The contrast noted by William Lithgow in the 1630s between his view of sodomy as a 'monstrous filthiness' and that of many Italians who considered it merely a 'pleasant pastime' may therefore reflect some sort of reality in Venice. On the one hand we find a persistent religious hostility, bolstered by the laws of the state; on the other a pervasive social tolerance, endorsed (at least from the sixteenth century) by the tribunals of the state. How can this contrast be explained?

The most obvious theory would be that Italians no longer deferred to Catholic teaching. In a very few cases, that may well be true, though we obviously cannot say that everyone in Venice rejected religious doctrines in the thorough going way that (probably) Antonio Rocco did. But we might none the less still argue that many people, in and out of government, were prepared to accept a fracture between their society's stated religious ideology and its realised belief system. Perhaps they adopted a 'fingers-crossed' approach to Church teaching on sexual morality. Laws against sodomy thus remained on the statute book. But they did not engage the full support of the lay population, and they were only rarely enforced in full by the state, because it was assumed that the divine punishments threatened by the Church if the offence were tolerated would probably not materialise. When or if they did, of course, the laws could be quickly revived and the guilty punished.

Some historians have suggested that in these circumstances a self-conscious homosexual subculture emerged in the city. The suggestion is certainly attractive; but it is not at all clear that the individuals involved in sodomy really saw their activities in the recognisably modern way implied by such a phrase.[52] Neither the archive sources nor the literary evidence provide much information on the emotional component of same-sex and other sodomitical relationships in early modern Venice. Rocco's *Alcibiades* certainly makes no reference to anything other than the sensual pleasure of his two protagonists, and Rocco himself seems to have had a very cynical view of human feelings: 'everyone who loves, loves himself, not others', he once declared in one of his public discourses.[53] We cannot know whether the individuals involved in sodomy cases in Venice took as cool a view of their activities as Rocco, though the occasional glimpse of a long-term male relationships in the trial records might seem to suggest otherwise.[54] What we can extract from the evidence is some notion of contemporary expectations. While it is clear that the details reported in the trial records of conversations and actions may not always be wholly accurate, they do allow us to see how Venetians at the time thought, and what they considered was plausible. There was clearly no point in making an accusation that would simply not be believed by the authorities to whom it was delivered.

What is also clear is that an individual's decision to engage in unauthorised sexual practice was taken in full knowledge of the weight of official opposition to it. The openness of the city to migration from many parts of the world ensured that its population was continuously exposed to the reality of different beliefs and lifestyles; and the very existence of government laws that prohibited certain forms of behaviour might have served to make that behaviour seem even more attractive.[55] And there were pressures within Venetian society that worked against a wholehearted acceptance of traditional moral views. While it is clear that the demographic disaster of the Black Death in the fourteenth century initially encouraged governments to foster population growth, the population as a whole seems to have adopted policies that reduced pressure on resources by delaying marriage and thus reducing the size of their families.[56] In such circumstances, popular reactions to non-procreative sexual activities were likely to be milder than those of the state. And in Venice, where patrician males tended to marry late or not at all in order to prevent the fragmentation of the family estates, many men failed to conform to the established gender conventions governing marriage and the family anyway.[57] Alternative views on sexual behaviour would therefore perhaps seem less shocking in Venice, especially within the elite, than elsewhere.

Conclusion

This is not to argue that individuals had complete freedom, in early modern Venice or elsewhere, to form their own sexuality in any way they chose. They had to work within the intellectual and social constraints of the time. But they could play a part in shaping their own lifestyle, as they reacted to those constraints, and as new ideas and possibilities entered their consciousness and altered the way they behaved.[58] We should therefore be prepared to allow for a more variegated pattern of sexual conformity and dissent within Renaissance and early modern Venice than the legislation of the period might suggest. We should also be cautious of ascribing too great an authority within that society to the regulation of sexual behaviour by Church and state. Laws imposing what Goldberg has called 'a highly straitened form of procreative heteronormativity' certainly existed;[59] but in Venice, it seems, neither government nor their subjects were always keen to enforce them.

NOTES
Abbreviations

ASVa: Archivio Segreto, Vatican   f., ff.: folio, folios
ASVe: Archivio di Stato, Venice   reg.: *registro*
b.: *busta*   SU: ASVe, Santo Uffizio, Processi
CX: ASVe, Consiglio de' Dieci

1 W. Lithgow, *The Totall Discourse of the Rare Adventures and Painefull Peregrinations* (Glasgow: 1906), p. 38. The first edition of the book was published in London.
2 See for example L. J. Abray, *The People's Reformation: Magistrates, Clergy, and Commons in Strasbourg, 1500–1598* (Oxford: 1985), p. 191: 'Venice was a symbol of debauchery to the Alsatians.'
3 M. Forster, *Daphne du Maurier* (London: 1993), p. 28.
4 See especially M. Rocke, *Forbidden Friendships: Homosexuality and Male Culture in Renaissance Florence* (Oxford and New York: 1996).
5 Bessarion, letter to Doge Cristoforo Moro and the Senate of Venice, 31 May 1468, printed in H. Omont, 'Inventaire des Manuscrits grecs et latins donnés à Saint-Marc de Venise par le Cardinal Bessarion (1468)', *Revue des Bibliothèques* 4 (1894), p. 139; *Mémoires de Philippe de Commynes*, ed. B. de Mandrot (Paris, 1901–3), vol. II, p. 213. Cf. N. S. Davidson, '"As much for its culture as for its arms": The Cultural Relations of Venice and its Dependent Cities, 1400–1700', in A. Cowan, ed., *Mediterranean Urban Culture, 1400–1700* (Exeter, 2000), pp. 199–202.
6 *Statuta lucensia* (Lucca, 1490), liber 4, cap. 91, and the long text of 21 July 1458 printed in the 'Additiones quarti libri' (unpaginated); *Gli statuti della città di Lucca* (Lucca, 1539), pp. 216v ('*Evvì anchora unaltra sorte di stupro detestabile, il quale si dice contra natura farsi nel maschio, loquale chiamano Sodomia*'), 221r; CX, Misti, reg. 28, 105r–6v, proposed decree of Council of Ten, 27 August 1500: '*et quoniam pro quanto intelligitur et congnoscitur hic detestandum actus non modo inter mares cum maribus, verum etiam ad masculos et feminis*', printed in *Leggi e memorie*

venete sulla prostituzione fino alla caduta della Republica (Venice: 1870–72), pp. 86–8; cf. also p. 94.

7 L. Gabrielli, *Metodo di confessione, cioè arte, over ragione, & una certa brieue vie di confessarsi* (Venice: 1572), quoted by R. M. Bell, *How To Do It: Guides to Good Living for Renaissance Italians* (Chicago and London: 1999), p. 193. Cf. *Leggi e memorie venete*, p. 75, order of Council of Ten, 13 June 1492: '*adhibenda sunt omnia studia et remedia possibilia ut nefandissimum et horendum vitium et crimen sodomie in hac civitate extinguatur et deleatur, quod est contra propagationem humani generis*'.

8 Thomas Aquinas, *Summa theologiae*, 1a2ae.31, 7; cf. also 2a2ae.154, 11–12. Merry Wiesner-Hanks dates the first definition of sodomy as a crime against nature to the mid thirteenth century: *Christianity and Sexuality in the Early Modern World: Regulating Desire, Reforming Practice* (London: 2000), p. 261. For a sixteenth-century restatement of the Thomist line see B. Fumi, *Summa quae Aurea Armilia inscribitur* (Venice: 1554), pp. 249v–50r (a text first published in Piacenza in 1550).

9 For Italian legislation against sodomy see N. S. Davidson, 'Theology, Nature and the Law: Sexual Sin and Sexual Crime in Italy from the Fourteenth to the Seventeenth Century', in T. Dean and K. J. P. Lowe, eds, *Crime, Society and the Law in Renaissance Italy* (Cambridge: 1994), pp. 86–90.

10 Cherubino da Siena, *Regole della vita matrimoniale*, ed. F. Zambrini and C. Negroni (Bologna, 1888), pp. 72–5. Cherubino died in 1484; his tract was printed about twenty-one times before 1500.

11 *Bullarium diplomatum et privilegiorum sanctorum romanorum pontificum* (Turin: 1857–72), vol. 7, p. 437 ('Cum primum', 1 April 1566): cap. 11 requires that all sodomites should be released for punishment to the secular authorities, in a phrase that was used conventionally to refer to the death penalty.

12 G. Priuli, *I diarii*, ed. A. Segre and R. Cessi (Bologna: 1912–38), vol. 4, pp. 30, 33–6. Other sins mentioned by Priuli include uncontrolled sexual licence in nunneries and the violation of virgins in church buildings. The long-established fear of divine wrath in response to sodomy was still present in Protestant England in the seventeenth century: see C. B. Herrup, *A House in Gross Disorder: Sex, Law, and the Second Earl of Castlehaven* (Oxford: 1999), p. 83.

13 Priuli, *Diarii*, p. 35: '*veramente non juvenes, sed mulieres vocari possunt … de homeni diventavanno femine*'.

14 Cf. also the condemnation of sodomy in the tract, possibly produced in the Veneto and attributed to the founder of the Capuchins, printed by Melchiorre da Pobladura, 'La "Severa riprensione" di fra Matteo da Bascio' (1495?–1552)', *Archivio Italiano per la Storia della Pietà*, 3 (1962), p. 30.

15 P. G. Brunet, *Les Courtisanes et la police des moeurs à Venise* (Sauveterre: 1886), p. 17; *Leggi e memorie*, p. 87; M. Sanuto, *I diarii* (Venice: 1879–1903), vol. 12, col. 84.

16 The decrees of 1418 are printed in *Leggi e memorie*, pp. 186–8; the tribunal appears in Latin in the documents with the title 'Collegium contra sodomitas'. For a clear summary of the administrative history and further references see S. Chojnacki, *Women and Men in Renaissance Venice: Twelve Essays on Patrician Society* (Baltimore and London: 2000), p. 35. The case of 1406 is discussed at length by G. Ruggiero, *The Boundaries of Eros: Sex Crimes and Sexuality in Renaissance Venice* (Oxford and New York: 1985), pp. 127–33.

17 Venetian legislation is summarized by M. Ferro, *Dizionario del diritto comune, e veneta* (Venice: 1778–81), vol. 10, pp. 72–3; the Council of Ten's 1445 debate on the proper punishment for sodomites is discussed by P. H. Labalme, 'Sodomy and Venetian Justice in the Renaissance', *The Legal History Review* 52 (1984), pp. 241–2.

18 Several excellent studies of the archival sources for the history of sodomy in Venice have been published in recent years, and I gladly acknowledge my use of their findings in the following paragraphs: E. Pavan, 'Police des moeurs, société et politique à Venise à la fin du Moyen Age', *Revue Historique* 536 (1980), pp. 241–88, and, more recently, E. Crouzet-Pavan, '*Sopra le acque salse*': espaces, pouvoir et société à Venise à la fin du moyen âge (Rome:

1992), especially vol. 2, pp. 837–45; Labalme, 1984; Ruggiero, 1987, especially ch. 6; and G. Martini, *Il 'vitio nefando' nella Venezia del Seicento: aspetti sociale e repressione di giustizia* (Rome: 1988). Useful overviews are also provided in G. Scarabello, 'Devianza sessuale ed interventi di giustizia a Venezia nella prima metà del XVI secolo', in *Tiziano e Venezia: Convegno internazionale di studi, Venezia, 1976* (Vicenza: 1980), pp. 75–84; R. Canosa, *La restaurazione sessuale: per una storia della sessualità tra Cinquecento e Settecento* (Milan: 1993); and Chojnacki, 2000, esp. p. 35.

19 Ruggiero, 1987, pp. 126–35; Scarabello, 1980, p. 81; Martini, 1988, tables I–II, pp. 132–3.

20 Although sex with animals was included within the contemporary definition of sodomy, cases of bestiality were rare in Venice itself – not surprisingly, since large domestic animals were not normally kept in the city. For the case of Simone, however, a butcher's boy from Friuli who was investigated in 1365 on a charge of having committed 'the abhorrent sin against nature' with one of his master's goats, see L. Münster, 'Un processo per sodomia a Venezia e una perizia medica relativa ad esso', in *Fracastoro: studi e memorie nel IV centenario* (Verona: 1954), pp. 82–4, who prints the summary of the trial from the records of the Signori di notte. The case is also discussed by Ruggiero, 1987, pp. 114–15.

21 CX, Misti, reg. 28, fols 101*v*,105*r*–6*v*. On 4 August of the same year a boatman called Bernardino had been sentenced to two years in prison, followed by five years in exile, for sodomy with a woman named Menega who was apparently German: fol. 101*v*.

22 CX, Misti, reg. 28, fol. 107*v*.

23 CX, Comune, reg. 33, fols 167*r*–*v*; Cathy Santore, 'Julia Lombardo, "somtuosa meretrize": A Portrait by Property', *Renaissance Quarterly* 41 (1988), pp. 44–83, p. 57. Cf. also Pietro Aretino's *Dialogo nel quale la Nanna insegna a la Pippa*, published in Venice (under a false imprint) in 1536, in which the old prostitute Nanna advises her daughter Pippa to dress in male clothes if she wants to entice well-heeled clients: for a modern edition see P. Aretino, *Sei giornate*, ed. G. Aquilecchia (Bari: 1969), p. 168.

24 SU, b. 55, 'Annibale da Perugia': 'tutta la vita sua è desonestamente usar con putti et teneoli disonestamente come fa le donne …'. Fellow soldiers also reportedly criticised him for his sexual activity with boys.

25 ASVe, Quarantia criminal, b. 133, 'Vincenzo Amadi [*sic*]'. Another literary dialogue from the early sixteenth century, often attributed to Pietro Aretino, the *Dialogo di Giulia e di Maddalena*, depicts the same male characters in anal intercourse with women and with men, as well as in reproductive intercourse with women: see G. Galderisi, ed., *Il piacevol ragionamento de l'Aretino* (Rome: 1987). Aretino spent the last thirty years of his life in Venice (from 1527 to 1556); one of his enemies accused him of enjoying sex with both males and females: see the *Vita di Pietro Aretino del Berni*, (London: 1819), pp. 24, 28–9, 34–43. This text is probably the work of Nicolò Franco. See also D. O. Frantz, *Festum Voluptatis: A Study of Renaissance Erotica* (Columbus, Ohio: 1989), pp. 110–11.

26 See Rocke, 1996, pp. 88–9, 94–105, 115–18, 126–9, 243–6; cf. also Ruggiero, 1987, pp. 116–18, 121–5. Italian men tended to marry only in their late twenties or early thirties: C. F. Black, *Early Modern Italy: A Social History* (London: 2001), p. 22.

27 CX, Criminali, reg. 8, fols 119*r*–*v*. Francesco escaped from prison in February 1570 and took refuge in a church: CX, Criminali, reg. 11, fol. 71*r*.

28 CX, Misti, reg. 23, fols 44*r*, 50*r*, 53*v*, 72*v*–3*r*. At the same time the Council of Ten investigated Loredan's chancellor, also called Bernardo, for sodomy with an adolescent called Marco: fol. 73*r*. On the Loredan case see Labalme, 1984, p. 235.

29 Ruggiero, 1987, p. 124; *Leggi e memorie*, pp. 95–6. Girolamo Priuli also complained in his diary that some older patricians had become so accustomed to sodomy that they were prepared to pay younger men to take the active role with them: *I diarii*, p. 36. Cf. also the remarkable confession of Pellegrina Donà to the Venetian Inquisition in 1647, in which she described an outing some eleven or twelve years earlier of a large group of patrician men and women to a house in Murano, where they found a life-size statue of a man with an erect penis on which several women and two of the men pleasured themselves: SU, b. 103, 'Caravagio

Salvatore [*et al.*]', spontaneous confession of Pellegrina Donà, 3 May 1647; G. Spini, *Ricerca dei libertini: la teoria dell'impostura delle religioni nel Seicento italiano* (Florence: 1983), p. 166, n. 16; G. Scarabello, in *Storia della cultura veneta* (Vicenza: 1984), vol. 4, part II, pp. 360–1.

30 Martini, 1988, p. 113.

31 Archivio di Stato, Mantua, Arch. Gonz., b. 1477, letter of Benedetto Agnello to Sabino Calandra, castellan of Mantua, Venice, 29 January 1545. I am most grateful to Dr David Chambers for providing me with this reference.The terms *populani* and *citadini* are used loosely by Agnello to refer to non-citizens and citizens.

32 CX, Misti, reg. 28, fol. 102r: Vincenzo was apparently the passive partner, despite his 'grandi etate'.

33 CX, Criminali, reg. 57, ff. 88r–9r, 95r–v: Giulio was condemned to perpetual exile in his absence.

34 C. Herrup, 'The Patriarch at Home: the Trial of the Second Earl of Castlehaven for Rape and Sodomy', *History Workshop Journal* 41 (1996), pp. 1–18; and more recently her *House in Gross Disorder*, 1999, pp. 32–3, 37.

35 One case that might be thought to match the English model is that of the patrician Zuanne Memmo, investigated at the end of the sixteenth century: see J. Walker, *Honour and the Culture of Male Venetian Nobles, c. 1500–1650* (unpublished Ph.D. thesis, University of Cambridge: 1998), pp. 109, 210–18.

36 A. Rocco, *L'Alcibiade fanciullo a scola* ('Oranges', '1652'). Copies of the seventeenth-century editions of this text are now very rare. There is a good modern edition edited by L. Coci, *Antonio Rocco: L'Alcibiade fanciullo a scola* (Rome: 1988).

37 For further information on Rocco's life and the history of the text see Spini, 1983, pp. 161–6; and L. Coci, '"L'Alcibiade fanciullo a scola": nota bibliografica', *Studi Secenteschi* 26 (1985), pp. 301–32.

38 Coci, '"L'Alcibiade"', p. 304.

39 SU, b. 103, 'Caravagio Salvatore (*et al.*)', anonymous letter to Roman Inquisition from Venice, 20 July 1652.

40 For a very helpful survey of the use of the theory of Platonic love in Italian literature of this period see J. Kraye, 'The Transformation of Platonic Love in the Italian Renaissance', in A. Baldwin and S. Hutton, eds, *Platonism and the English Imagination* (London: 1994), pp. 76–85. Other texts mentioned by Kraye which may also have helped to shape the *Alcibiades* include Leone Ebreo's *Dialoghi d'amore*, published in Rome in 1535 and in Venice in several editions from 1541, which includes an erudite and flirtatious dialogue between Sofia and her male admirer Filone; and Bruno's *Eroici furori* of 1585, which expresses a fierce hostility to the female body in terms similar to those used by Rocco.

41 SU, b. 103, 'Caravagio Salvatore (*et al.*)', deposition in Udine on 23 November 1648.

42 I translate from the first modern edition of E. Cléder, ed., *Arsiccio Intronato: La Cazzaria* ('Cosmopoli', actually Brussels: 1863), p. 35. The most recent edition is P. Stoppelli, ed., *Antonio Vignali: La Cazzaria* (Rome: 1984).

43 F. Pallavicino, *Il Corriero svaligiato*, ed. A. Marchi (Parma, 1984), letter XXXIX. The book was first published in 1641. A manuscript in praise of sodomy was reportedly found among Pallavicino's possessions when he was arrested in Avignon at the beginning of 1643. He denied composing it himself: it may perhaps have been a copy of the *Alcibiades*. See ASVa, Barb. Lat. 6157, fols 10r, 36r–v, 65r–v, and Barb. Lat. 9746, fols 53v, 78v. I am most grateful to the Revd Dr Dermot Fenlon for helping to secure a microfilm of these documents.

44 Brazzoni's testimony appears in the Archivio della Curia Arcivescovile, Udine, Santo Uffizio, b. 41, and has been printed in E. Kermol, *La rete di Vulcano: inquisizione, libri proibiti e libertini nel Friuli del Seicento* (Trieste: 1990), p. 147.

45 SU, b. 8, 'Fra Francesco Calcagno', interrogation in Brescia of 15 July 1550. Calcagno was found guilty of repeated offences against local minors, and was executed in Venice on 23 December of the same year.

46 SU, b. 86, 'Frigerio fra Vincenzo (*et al.*)', denunciation of 9 September 1628. Evidence presented to the Inquisition suggested that Barbieri had had a number of male sexual partners,

some of whom were identified by name.

47 SU, b. 86, 'Frigerio fra Vincenzo (*et al.*)', deposition of Giovanni Battista de Zanchi, 20 September 1628.

48 *Volumen statutorum legum, ac iurium DD. Venetorum* (Venice: 1665), p. 277v: decree of 26 June 1553.

49 CX, Misti, reg. 28, fol. 102r, 7 August 1500. The law at that date required that older males who allowed themselves to be sodomised should be whipped and then sentenced to between five and ten years in prison for severe or repeated offences: Pavan, 1980, p. 278. Only three weeks later, on 27 August, it was decided that older males who allowed themselves to be sodomized should be executed: CX, Misti, reg. 28, fols 105r–6v (printed in *Leggi e memorie*, pp. 87–8).

50 CX, Criminali, reg. 13, fols 4v–6r, 5 August 1580. Three other suspects were sentenced on the same day – Antonio Trigestin and another priest called Zuanne Cagnoleto were sent to the galleys for two and four years respectively; Nicolò Cremonese, 'retento per patiente di sodomitico' was whipped and then exiled for five years. Nicolò's age is not given.

51 Cf. Labalme, 1987, pp. 243, 246, 251–2, Martini, 1988, pp. 68–9.

52 See Ruggiero, 1987, pp. 135–45, 159–61; and cf. the observations of Ian Hacking, *The Social Construction of What?* (Cambridge, Massachusetts, and London: 1999), pp. 17, 27–8.

53 Antonio Rocco, 'Amore é un puro interesse', in the *Discorsi Academici de' Signori Incogniti, Havuti in Venetia Nell'Academia dell'Illustrissimo Signor Giovanni Francesco Loredano* (Venice: 1635), p. 165.

54 It may also be worth considering the unpublished manuscripts of Felice Feliciano, a fifteenth-century cleric and notary from Verona, who spent part of his career in the service of the Venetian patrician Angelo Adriano. These contain a number of poems which exploit the conventional forms of Petrarchan love poetry to praise the sculptor Cristoforo Geremia, making use also of some entertaining double meanings. Other poems in the collection record Feliciano's unrequited love for a woman, Pellegrina da Campo. See L. Pratilli, 'Felice Feliciano alla luce di suoi codici', *Atti del R. Istituto veneto di Scienze Lettere ed Arti* 99 (1939–40), pp. 33–105.

55 Cf. Chojnacki, 2000, pp. 34–5; cf. also J. Butler, *Bodies that Matter: On the Discursive Limits of 'Sex'* (London and New York: 1993), pp. 96–7; L. Roper, *Oedipus and the Devil: Witchcraft, Sexuality and Religion in Early Modern Europe* (London: 1994), p. 150.

56 D. Herlihy, *The Black Death and the Transformation of the West* (Cambridge, Massachusetts, and London: 1997).

57 Chojnacki, 2000, pp. 180–2, 186–200, 205, 244–5.

58 Cf. Butler, 1993, pp. 93–5; Anthony Giddens's idea of the 'essential recursiveness of social life' in his *Central Problems in Social Theory: Action, Structure and Contradiction in Social Analysis* (Basingstoke: 1979), pp. 73–81; and Ian Hacking's idea of 'looping' in his *Social Construction of What?*, 1999, pp. 104–5.

59 J. Goldberg, *Reclaiming Sodom* (New York and London: 1994), p. 1.

5

'Wild, filthie, execrabill, detestabill, and unnatural sin': bestiality in early modern Scotland

P. G. MAXWELL-STUART

When the Jesuit Martín del Rio published an anecdote about a cow which gave birth to a physically normal child who later gave evidence of bovine tendencies, he added, 'What is one to think of this?' It was a question deep in the consideration of theologians throughout the premodern period, who discussed over and over again in fascinated detail the appearance of monsters, deformed creatures both human and bestial, changelings and the ability or non-ability of evil spirits to engender offspring upon willing or unwilling women.[1] These prodigies were difficult to interpret. Were they and the actions which led to them *contra naturam*; or diabolical in origin; or signs sent or permitted by God as coded messages concerning his will and human fate? Were they caused by natural physical deficiencies or superfluities or accidents; or were they, like so many other extraordinary objects contained in *cabinets* and *Kunstkammers*, evidences of the occult multiplicity of God's universe?

There is, however, a linguistic problem pertaining (although not, of course, exclusively) to Scots and English, which bedevils discussion of this and related sexual phenomena, at least in the earlier period: namely, the definition of 'sodomy' and 'buggery'. In 1570, for example, two men were convicted before the High Court of Justiciary in Edinburgh of the 'wild, filthie, execrabill, detestabill, and unnatural sin of sodomy, otherwise named bougarie, abusand of their bodies with utheris, in contrare the laws of God, and all other human laws'. This seems clear enough until we read elsewhere of John Jack alias Scott, who was convicted in 1605 of 'sodomie' with a mare; and of Andrew Taylor who was tried for 'sodomy' in Aberdeen in March 1709, his offence turning out, according to other more detailed records of the court, to be bestiality with cows. The word 'buggery', too, is regularly used of offenders clearly accused of bestiality, in cases ranging from 1619 to the beginning of the eighteenth century, and in consequence we have to beware of making any assumption about the character of sexual actions so designated.[2] Not even James VI, whose bisexuality is often taken for granted, offers the historian an unequivocal bugger or sodomite. Peculiarities noticed in his behaviour, such as leaning upon men's shoulders or constantly fiddling about his codpiece, are susceptible of other explanation; for they may equally well point to mild cerebral palsy, with attendant athetoid features and a possible touch of spasticity.[3] In consequence we cannot be sure that there is any clear-cut evidence of what would now be called 'homosexual anal intercourse' in premodern Scotland, since the cases of buggery or sodomy which appear in court records, at least, point to sexual intercourse with animals and not with human beings of the same sex.[4]

Bestiality was not an uncommon occurrence in earlier societies. A Bronze Age rock painting from Sweden shows a man buggering a quadruped; various Greek vase paintings show Satyrs or their leader Silenos mounting animals; the Hittite legal code prescribed different penalties for the act, depending on the animal involved;[5] and the Bible issues an explicit prohibition against it. 'Neither shalt thou lie with any beast to defile thyself therewith ... and if a man lie with a beast, he shall surely be put to death', Leviticus 18.23; 20.15. In Scotland the earlier surviving records are patchy, but one can trace the offence throughout the seventeenth and eighteenth centuries, although there seems to have been an agglomeration of cases during the late 1650s, a point to which I shall return later. What is most notable here is that there does not appear to have been statutory warrant for them. England had its statutes of 1533 and 1548 against 'buggery', but there is no equivalent in Scottish law; so anyone accused of the offence was, in effect, being prosecuted on the strength of the prohibition found in Leviticus.[6] Not surprisingly, perhaps, we find that many of these cases had come first before the kirk or presbytery sessions, meetings of ministers and elders held regularly once a week to deal with parish or presbytery matters of all kinds, but especially those relating to moral discipline.

On trial for bestiality in early modern Scotland

Typical is the record of John Muir, who appeared before the session of Lanark on 17 July 1654.[7] Present were two of the ministers in Lanark, the baillies of the burgh (local or district officials appointed to hold local courts for the administration of justice and to assist ministers of the kirk in executing ecclesiastical acts and statutes), and four elders, one of whom acted as clerk. Accused of 'the scandell of bowgerie', Muir confessed as follows:

> That since the terme of Beltane last,[8] he haith sex [six] severall tymes committit the land defyleing sin of bestiallitie[9] fyve tymes in the oppin feilds befoir the sicht of the sune and once within the hous under nicht, the first act being committit upon the second day of July instant, being the Saboth day, and deprehendit by one

Agnes Hamiltoun, ane member of our congregation, which was the meane the Lord was pleasit to discover it by.

Obviously the fact that Muir had broken the Sabbath in such a spectacular fashion would have exacerbated his offence in the ears of those listening to his confession. Similar Sabbath-breaking appears in other cases,[10] but it evoked no additional indignation in the written record, perhaps because the offence was regarded as vice enough of itself. Certainly the language of the documents expresses an extremity of abhorrence. Incest, for example, attracted no more than the phrase 'abominable cryme', with the occasional variants 'vyl and scandalous carriage', 'scandall', or 'horridde sine of incest'.[11] Bestiality, on the other hand, is a 'maist detaistabill, odious, and abhominabill' crime, 'a vyild and filthie cryme', 'horrid wickednes and unnaturalnes', 'a vyle sinne', 'a gross abomination', and a 'fearefull and unnaturall acte of beastlynes'.[12] Hence, no doubt, the reaction of Katharine Tack who claimed to have seen Archibald Mader *in flagrante* with a cow, and 'wes suddenly affrighted, and her eyes dazelled and blinded, and her legges did trimble under hir, and shoe said to hir selff, "The Lord save me! What is that?"'[13] Katharine was a mature woman of forty at the time and, like Mader, lived in the countryside. She was therefore in no position to plead innocence of such things, and it seems to have been the repulsiveness rather than the unexpectedness of the event which overtook her.

Witnesses were either women or men (gender does not seem to have played a significant role here), and were usually eye-witnesses to the act, although in the case of John Brown from Fife witnesses deduced the offence from the marks of his wooden leg they saw in and around a byre where a cow was giving signs of having been sexually molested.[14] The witnesses were often servants, as one might expect, but a casual traveller, a soldier, and even, in the case of John Hamilton, the accused's own brother, can be found among the depositions.[15] Witnesses were usually quick to report what they claimed to have seen, and to denounce the offender. Alexander Robertson was reported only three days later, but this was perhaps unusually fast. William MacAdam and William Lindsay found themselves accused within two weeks of their offence, John Rob within three, George Brown within four or six.[16] John Tannahill was accused in the same month as he committed the act, although the full list of his offences stretched back two and a half years.[17]

Between about two and nine months was common,[18] but perhaps more interesting are those cases which appear to have remained unreported for several years. William Balloch from Baldernock in Stirlingshire stood accused in 1656 for 'the horrid cryme of bestialitie comittit be yow with ane kow upon the aught day of July 1646 yeires upon the hie way that leids from Glasgow to Kilsyth', an extraordinary interval which makes one wonder whether '46' is a scribal error.[19] He may have fled, of course, as did Thomas MacHaffie, delated in 1647 and re-accused in 1655 after he returned from Ireland, or one Hall (his forename is missing in the record), who was accused in 1708 'in sua farr as about seven years agoe or therby he was found in that abhominable fact on a Sunday morning and a mare, whairupon he immediatly fled and never since seen, but said to be in Teviotdale'.[20] On the other hand, witnesses were not always forthcoming, and that caused a delay. Thomas Milner was accused in 1652 and fled at some point between then and 1655 when his indictment for 'bowgrie comitted be yow with ane meir' was drawn up. The following year, however, there was no one available to prosecute him and no witness to give evidence, and although Hamilton was indicted on 20 August 1654 his name still appears for the same offence in 1657.[21] Sometimes the accused were held in confinement for varying periods of time. David Johnston complained of being locked up in the Tolbooth of Edinburgh 'a considerable tym', and John MacLurg 'confest to severall gentlemen of the paroch about a year agoe or therby, ffor which he was putt into the prisone of Kirkcudbright and therafter transported to Edinburgh wher it is beleived he yet remains'.[22] The chilling 'it is beleived' signals how easy it was for people to be lost in the judicial system before they even came to trial, and a letter from Robert Nisbet to the justiciaries in Edinburgh shows how desperate conditions could be for those in ward.

> Your peititioner hes now beine prissoner this 14 weikes in greit meissary ffor the alledged crym off beastiallity quhilk [which] your peititioner is inocent off, neither can it ever be maid upe by any one or uthers that ever your honors peititioner did committ the lyke; and seeing by my long restrante ffrom any handy labor my wholl meins is exaused [exhausted], so that I have nothing to live wpon bot is lyke to sterve, and your peititioners wyff and chyld going a-begging.[23]

The majority of those accused confessed, either to the witnesses or to the kirk or presbytery session or to the court – sometimes, indeed, to all three in successive interrogations. But some flatly denied an accusation, such as William Young in 1622, William Balloch in 1656, Peter Colquhoun in 1658 and Archibald Mader in 1659, while in 1694 John MacWat took his principal witness against him, Janet Scot, before the presbytery, accusing her of malice and calumny – perhaps a risky strategy, since he himself was summoned before the presbytery two years later 'anent the old scandal of bestiality'.[24] Others prevaricated. John Fraser, confronted by his neighbour, exclaimed, 'Why? What did I doe?' David Malcolm, caught in the act by James Grey, 'fell upon his knees to the ground and cryed for Gods sake to give him mercie'. Grey replied that this was not the first time he had committed such an offence, but Malcolm protested that it was and said that although he had often been tempted before, and indeed had tried to accomplish the act, he had never been able to do so until this one occasion on which he had been caught.[25] The indictment addressed to John Rennie, on the other hand, said

> [yow] did acknouledge it with seeming sorrow and said yow wou'd not again committ that horrid wickedness; but upon bad advice from your mother and others, yow have added this aggravation to yowr former guilt, impudently to deny the crime in presence of those who saw yow committ it, altho by the confusion yow appeared in, it was evident yowr conscience convicted yow of yowr guilt.[26]

By contrast, Thomas Gib, who faced the Presbytery of Stirling on 18 April 1593, denied the offence but was then subjected to pressure from his minister, Mr Gavin Donaldson, to confess that he was guilty. Thomas had been arrested, put in irons, and confined in Castle Campbell whither the minister came to see him, 'and baid him say that he did the said fault; and upon his words, [Thomas] confessis he said as he baid him'. Once brought before the presbytery, however, Thomas reverted to his former denial, thereby leaving the brethren in something of a quandary. They decided to postpone the matter for further investigation and to release Thomas on caution (bail) of £100 (whether Scots or English is not stated: it was probably the former). Thomas thereafter disappears from the records.[27]

During David Malcolm's admission that he was tempted, he blamed Satan for gaining power over him, and this was a stratagem (whether genuinely believed or not makes no difference to the claim) employed by more than one person accused of bestiality. William MacHaffie, his presbytery alleged, 'withdrew himselff from the cumpany of his wyff for a long tym and lay in the barne besyde his mare'. This MacHaffie denied, as he also denied making a confession to the minister of his parish, saying to the session 'it was not trew, bot only the Devill that tempted him to say such a thing', and to a neighbour that 'he saw the Devill in the cloud'. William Lindsay, too, admitted that on 15 April 1657 he was busy harrowing with a grey mare, a black stallion, and a black mare nearby, when 'the Devill entrit and intysed him to have lying with the said black mear', although (presumbly because of the presence of the stallion) it was not until two days later that he was presented with a convenient opportunity to have sex with her.[28] Satan was also offered to James Davie by one of his accusers as an explanation for his conduct. '"Did yow see the Devill?" said [Katharine Bayne's husband] to him. "No", said James bot shed some tears.'[29] There is no evidence, however, that either the ecclesiastical or the criminal courts took much notice of any hint that the offence was committed under diabolical inspiration. Nor did the courts have much time for claims that the accused was mad at the time. Thomas MacHaffie 'alledged that he was distracted in his wittes when he confessed and was phrenatick; but the presbitrie thought it was bot a schift, and that it was trew which he had declared to his minister'.[30]

The mechanics of the offence to which these men were confessing, or of which they were accused, are made clear in various testimonies. In addition we are sometimes given details which tend to answer our tacit questions. John Rob, for example, stood on some turf, holding the mare steady by her tail and halter, and when she moved he brought her back to the spot which was convenient for him. John Muir, on the other hand, hobbled the animal until he had finished, while John Fraser almost mounted the mare's back.[31] Most accused seem to have kept themselves more or less fully clothed during the act. John Aikman is unusual in being almost naked.[32] The animals most frequently abused were mares and cows, although in 1702 Thomas Fotheringham was also accused of having sex with a sow, and John Rennie in 1718 with a ewe;[33] and it seems as though the act was most often perpetrated in the morning – on one recorded occasion, very early, 'when all the houshold wes in bed'.[34]

Where ages are given in the records, there often appears to be quite a discrepancy between those of the offenders and those of the witnesses against them. John Aikman was fourteen, Robert Stewart eighteen, David Hogg not yet twenty, James Easton about twenty; William Young is described as 'a boy', and William MacAdam as 'a young man'. Of the eighteen witnesses throughout the records whose ages are given, only six are under thirty. The rest fall mainly between forty and fifty, with one aged thirty-one and two aged sixty. In the case of Archibald Mader, one of the two recorded witnesses, William Warnock, was only twelve. It might be thought his evidence would be inadmissible on the grounds of his nonage, but David Hume informs us that in certain circumstances the normal objections would be overruled.

> On special occasions, where, from the nature of the charge, persons of earlier years are necessary witnesses, and are capable also of understanding the matters in which there is need of their evidence, the Court may and do take their examinations without an oath, *ut prosint ad veritatem indagandum* (so that they may be of use in tracking down the truth).[35]

Bestiality was a capital crime, and therefore those who were found guilty of it were executed according to the mode usually employed in Scotland. Thus, John Muir and William MacAdam heard the following:

> It is fund be ane assyse [jury] that John Moore and William MacAdam ar guiltie of the crymes of bestialitie contenit in ther severall dittays [*indictments*], and therfore the commissioners and I in ther name ordeane and adjudge thame to be tane upone Wodinsday nixt the 9 of this instant to the Castellhill of Edinburgh betuix tuo and foure hours in the afternoon, and ther to be stranglit at a stake till they be dead, and ther bodies burnt to ashes, and their gudes escheat [confiscated] for the use of the commonwealth.[36]

Of the fifteen recorded sentences, nine were executions. Two trials, those of Patrick Bartilmo and John Rennie, were abandoned. A commission against Bartilmo says he had 'lyin long under the scandall of the horrid cryme of bugurie' and called for his arrest and examination, and the assembling of witnesses' statements against him. Since the case never came to court, one may presume the commission was not successful in at least one of its aims.[37] The remaining four accused, Archibald Mader, James Davie, Alexander Neill and David Oliphant, were found not guilty, the last after considerable legal argument by his advocate on his behalf, leading to a unanimous acquittal.[38]

But why did these men commit a crime which carried so heavy a weight of communal disapproval and, in many instances, horror and repulsion? In part, the answer may lie with the relatively tender ages of many of the accused. A considerable number of opportunities was offered to boys and young men removed for long stretches of time from female company. Boys often slept in the byre next to the animals or spent the most part of their working day out in the fields, tending their father's or master's farm animals. They saw the creatures mount one another openly, without guilt or hesitation, and were inspired to imitate what they saw. Two or more boys together would both teach and help each other, one often urging his companion to commit the act before or after him.[39] Should opportunity and time continue while the boys grew into their teens or early twenties, it is not surprising that what had begun as sexual experimentation and imitation might turn into a habit to be continued as long as the individual remained undiscovered, or at any rate unreported, and perhaps until he married, at which time the urgency of his lust could be directed into socially acceptable directions. Imitation was certainly the excuse offered by Robert Nisbet.

> The said Robert being examined did declare that upon Monday befor, being most part of the day in Mr. Jhonstones meadow and being com hoam, he turned over som wheatt. After turning the wheatt, he and the men with him drank 3 or 4 pints of aill. Afterward he was desired be Mr. Jhonestone to keep the Governor of Berwick his horse that night in the meadow ... and that night, about midnight, the cowser [stallion] began to bray and to leap the mear once or tuice; and at the same tym, having seen the couser, he [i.e. Nisbet] had intentioun to the mear.[40]

Occasionally other, criminal circumstances were attendant upon the charge of bestiality. John Hamilton, who was reported to the authorities by his brother, came from a somewhat sinister family. His father had been arrested at some point for witchcraft and his wife 'made ane drink for him that had ended his dayes to prevent his burning'. Poisoning, it seems, ran in the family because when John's wife became ill his two sisters, Janet and Alison, suggested to him that he should 'let them give his wife a drink which, they said, should end her dayes becaus (they said) shee was useles for him', adding that he would then be able to get a more profitable wife; after which they urged him to go to John Hoggart in Stitchel in Roxburghshire and commission him to make a coffin and dig a grave for her.[41] Such a background should have been deeply prejudicial to his case, yet he appears again, as I noted earlier, charged with bestiality, in a list of cases for trial in 1657. Whether this means he was acquitted in 1654, or became a fugitive only to be re-arrested, or offended once more the same way, the surviving evidence does not allow us to say.

There remains the apparent oddity of a cluster of cases in the late 1650s needing comment. Of the seventy-seven cases between 1570 and 1734, which I have been able to examine – and I do not pretend that this is an exhaustive list – thirty-seven (nearly 50 per cent) were tried between 1654 and 1659.[42] One must make due allowance for possible gaps in the surviving records, of course, and for the incompleteness of the survey. Even so, the apparent remarkable increase in numbers of prosecutions during a specific period may be significant and therefore require explanation. Scotland during this period was under military occupation, a process which was completed in 1652, and the 'Protectorate' did not come to an end until 1659. Throughout the Protectorate there were attempts to unify Scots and English law – Cromwell disbanded all the courts and prohibited all jurisdictions other than those authorised by the English Parliament. Justices of the Peace, who had been established in Scotland by James VI in 1609, were reintroduced in 1656 and immediately began to take over much of the responsibility for prosecuting cases of immoral behaviour, which before had been the preserve of the kirk and presbytery sessions.[43] Once again the kirk, whose tendency had always been to fissiparousness rather than unity in spite of its tacit hopes and declared intentions and was now being exacerbated by the conflicting claims of episcopacy and presbytery, was left divided in itself and at odds with the judicial pretensions of the state.

Conclusion

It may not be a coincidence that pressure to try other social deviants seems to have increased at this same time. There had been a lull in applications to try witches, for example, during the first half of the decade, but from 1657 the number of applications for such trials began to grow rapidly. Over a hundred cases were tried in 1658 and 1659 and forty persons were executed.[44] But, as Larner points out, these cases tend to be concentrated in particular areas where local pressures upon the justices may have been especially strong.[45] Trials for bestiality show no such concentration. The accused came from various, dispersed regions within Scotland (mainly, it must be said, the Lowlands: but this could well be a feature of the judicial records we have), and in consequence one must look to a more general sense of moral perturbation within the populace to explain the clustering. A country militarily occupied by a foreign power and subject to assaults upon its national church and legal system, of course, has all the excuse it needs for such agitation.[46]

NOTES

Abbreviations

APS = *Acts of the Parliamentl of Scotland* (Edinburgh, 1844–75)
CH 2/424/4 = Dalkeith Presbytery Records
CH 2/722/2 = Stirling Presbytery Records
JC = Records of the High Court of Justiciary in Edinburgh
RPC = *Register of the Privy Council of Scotland* (Edinburgh, 1877–98)

1 Del Rio, *Disquisitiones magicae* (Louvain: 1599–1600), Book 2, question 14. Cf. Ambroise Paré, *Opera chirurgica* (Frankfurt-am-Main: 1594), Book 24. Pierre Boaistuau, *Histoires prodigieuses* (Paris: 1560). See also J. J. Cohen, *Of Giants: Sex, Monsters, and the Middle Ages* (Minneapolis: 1999) and L. Daston and K. Park, *Wonders and the Order of Nature* (New York: 1998). E. Fudge, 'Monstrous Acts: Bestiality in Early Modern England', *History Today* 50 (August 2000), pp. 20–5.

2 R. Pitcairn, ed, *Criminal Trials in Scotland*, 3 vols in 4 (Edinburgh: 1833), 2, p. 491 and note. *JC* 16/1 (p. 50). *JC* 26/89/D386. For other examples of 'buggery' = 'bestiality' see *RPC* 12.77, pp. 174, 641. *JC* 26/15, *JC* 26/18, *JC* 26/19/5, *JC* 26/20/2.

3 A. W. Beasley: 'The disability of James VI and I', *The Seventeenth Century* 10 (1995), pp. 152–62. Attempts to show that James's affectionate letters to Esmé Stuart and George Villiers are informed by homoeroticism (D. M. Bergeron, *King James and Letters of Homoerotic Desire* (Iowa City: 1999)), founder upon a misunderstanding of the King's psychology and of the expression of male friendship during this period.

4 As with the 1570 case, there is room for a question mark over Gavin Bell, against whom a commission was issued on 8 December 1645 'for tryeing, processing, and judgeing [him] anent the committing of the vyild and filthie cryme of buggurie', *APS* 6.1.482, since the exact nature of the buggery is not specified in the record. It may be worth noting, however, that premodern Scotland is not the only country to use 'sodomy' as a term for bestiality. The New York legal code apparently still employs that particular word to refer to sexual intercourse between a human and any animal or bird (M. Dekkers: *Dearest Pet: On Bestiality* (London: 1994), pp. 118–19). The case of Paul Methven, referred to by Madeleine Bingham, *Scotland Under Mary Stuart* (London: 1971), p. 229, as one of homosexuality was in fact an offence of adultery, as is made clear by Knox in his *Historie of the Reformation of Religion in the Realm of Scotland* (Edinburgh: 1644), pp. 353–4. 'The servand woman of the said Paul had betwixt that and Christmas left his house, she had borne a child, no father to it could she finde, but alleadged her self to have been suppressed late in an Evening.' Cf. *Booke of the Universall Kirk*, Part 1 pp. 55–6.

5 Dekkers, 1994, pp. 12, 15, 72, 118. Modern societies are no less affected. An analysis of court proceedings in Austria between 1923 and 1965 uncovered a rate of approximately fifty people per annum accused of bestiality; and Kinsey's investigations into American sexual experiences in the 1940s suggested that up to 50 per cent of young men in the countryside had had sex with animals on at least one occasion. Dekkers,1994, p. 135. A. C. Kinsey and W. B. Pomeroy, *Sexual Behaviour in the Human Male* (Philadelphia: 1948), pp. 667–78.

6 The 1533 English statute was intended to punish 'the detestable and abominable Vice of Buggery committed with mankind or beast', and apparently had no counterpart anywhere else in Europe. The sixteenth century, at least, tended to identify buggery with bestiality, whether that meant sexual intercourse with animals or with humans regarded as little better

than beasts, because sexual actions *contra naturam* were regarded as worthy only of animals. See R. Davenport-Hines, *Sex, Death, and Punishment* (London: 1990), pp. 59–60. William Taylor was prosecuted in May 1710, his indictment beginning, 'Yow are indited and accused that, where by the law of God exprest in the 20 chapter of Leviticus, laws of this and all other well governed realms', etc, *JC* 26/93/D655. The reference to criminal laws other than the Biblical may be vague because there was no relevant statute in Scotland. On the other hand this case was tried after the Act of Union and in consequence the drafter may have been thinking of the existence of English statutes.

7 *JC* 26/16.

8 1 or 3 May, or possibly 21 June. The date varied in different parts of Scotland.

9 Called 'bugury' on a separate document in this case.

10 John Fraser, 1656: *JC* 26/20/3. Adam Wilson, 1656: *JC* 26/20/2. David Hogg, 1699 *JC* 3/1 (p. 119). David Wilkie, 1658, offended 'at Whitsounday last or thairby': *JC* 26/24.

11 'Abominable cryme': *JC* 26/19/1; *JC* 26/19/8, *JC* 26/20/2, *JC*26/21/2/2, *JC* 26/20/1, *JC* 26/21/4/2, *JC* 26/21/1, *JC* 26/22/3/23. 'Vyl etc.', *CH* 2/424/4, 'Scandall' and 'Horridde sine':*JC* 26/26.

12 *RPC* 12.77, *APS* 6.1.482, *JC* 26/18B, *JC* 26/20/2, *JC* 26/24, *JC* 26/23 and *JC*26/24/2/12.

13 *JC* 26/26: 22 March 1659. The evidence refers to 1658.

14 *JC* 26/20/7: 10 July 1656.

15 *RPC* 12.641, *JC* 26/20/2, *JC* 26/17, *JC* 26/20/7, *JC*26/21/5/1 and*JC* 26/16.

16 *JC* 26/24/2/13, *JC*26/16, *JC*26/22/2/13, *JC* 26/15 and *JC* 26/94/D691.

17 *JC* 26/24: 21 June, 1658.

18 Muir, *JC* 26/16, Colquhoun, *JC* 26/26, Hogg, *JC* 3/1 (p. 118). Wilkie, *JC* 26/24.

19 *JC* 26/21/5/1.

20 *JC*26/18B, *JC*26/86/D250. Cf. David Malcolm who was alleged, by two witnesses, to have committed bestiality with a mare five years before, *JC* 26/23; and William MacHaffie, who declared that his own minister had advised him to run away to Ireland, *JC* 26/18B. Robert Nisbet 'did secretle absent him self and hid him amongst the corne: who after long at much searching be many of our nighbours was ffound and carried to prisson', *JC* 27/17.

21 *JC* 26/18 and *JC* 26/19/5. *JC* 26/16 and *JC* 26/22/1/1.

22 *JC*2/13 and *JC* 26/86/D250. Prison was not always available locally for offenders. John Falconer had to be farmed out to private houses because there was nowhere else to keep him in ward in Stonehaven, and a letter to the clerk to the justice in Edinburgh makes it clear that the authorities in Stonehaven did not have much confidence in their ability to prevent him from escaping, *JC* 26/26. Shifting prisoners from place to place was fairly common. Cf. James Brewhouse, accused of bestiality in August 1657 concerning whom a letter was dispatched from Brechin to Edinburgh, making it obvious that the local authorities wanted him off their hands as soon as possible. 'I will earnestly intreat you acording to your promise that ye will cause retane the prisoner and dispatch the honest men [the witnesses] becaus of the time of harvest. Iff the pannell [accused] be remitted bak to Suster whair he sinned, ye will be pleased to move the judges to send him to Montroise wher he will be within ane quarter of ane myll wher he comitted that horrid fact, and it will be from ws ffyve myles at least', *JC*26/23.

23 *JC* 26/17: 7 November 1655. He may have been reduced to this state after only four months, for the first document relating to his offence is dated 3 July.

24 *RPC* 12.641, *JC* 26/21/5/1 and *JC* 26/26. *Registers of the Presbytery of Lanark*, pp. 118, 125.

25 *JC* 26/20/3 and *JC* 26/23. John Aikman, too, at first said he had intended to commit the deed but could not manage it, and then confessed in full to the minister, *JC* 26/20/2.

26 *JC* 26/101/D1027: 19 December 1718.

27 *CH* 2/722/2. Castle Campbell was a feudal fortalice in the parish of Dollar of which Gavin Donaldson became minister on 4 April 1589.

28 *JC* 26/18B and *JC* 26/22/2/13. Cf. Robert Stewart, *JC* 26/20/7. In the record relating to Lindsay, the word 'bowgrie' is crossed out at one point in the text and 'bestiallitie' substituted. On the cover of the document, however, the offence is designated as 'buggerie'.

29 *JC* 26/26. Satan appears in this same role in bestiality cases elsewhere in Europe. See, for example, P. Sörlin, *Wicked Arts: Witchcraft and Magic Trials in Southern Sweden, 1635–1754* (Leiden: 1999), p. 34 relating to Sweden. Similarly, Conrad Heller from Rottweil and Thongi Schenzlin from Schwenningen blamed the Devil, who in both cases appeared to them in physical form, for making them have sexual intercourse with animals, State Archives of Rottweil, Archivalien II, Abteilung I, Lade III, Faszikel 4, nos 3 and 9. I am grateful to Dr J. Nye for supplying me with these German references and texts. In a modern case of lycanthropy, the subject explained that the Devil would enter her and turn her into a wolf, urging her to acts of bestiality and lesbianism H. A. Rosenstock and K. R. Vincent: 'A Case of Lycanthropy', *American Journal of Psychiatry* 134 (1977), pp. 1147–9. John Muir, by way of contrast, blamed God who, he said, had provoked him to this sin as a punishment for his disobedience to his parents and for his breaking the Sabbath, *JC* 26/16.

30 *JC* 26/18B: noted in the commission issued for his trial, 31 March 1647.

31 *JC* 26/15. Cf. William Balloch, who stood upon a stone at the roadside and held on to the cow's tail with one hand, *JC* 26/20/7, *JC* 26/16 and *JC* 26/20/3. Scottish cattle and horses were rather small during the seventeenth century. See I. Whyte, *Agriculture and Society in Seventeenth-century Scotland* (Edinburgh: 1979), pp. 80–1.

32 *JC* 26/20/2.

33 *JC* 3/1, and *JC*26/101/D1027.

34 John Muir, between 8 am and 9 am, *JC* 26/16. John Fraser, between 10 am and 11 am, *JC* 26/20/3. William Lindsay, 11 am, *JC* 26/22/2/13. Cf. Archibald Mader, 'before noon', *JC* 26/26. The quotation related to Adam Wilson, *JC* 26/20/2. John Muir also committed one act at night, within the house; Robert Stewart at 6 pm, *JC* 26/20/7; and Robert Nisbet at midnight, *JC* 26/17. In the case of Andrew Taylor, one of the witnesses could not recollect whether the act took place during the day or the night, even though the indictment was issued a maximum of six months and a minimum of three months from the date of the alleged offence, *JC* 16/1 (p. 50).

35 D. Hume: *Commentaries on the Law of Scotland*, 2nd ed., 2 vols (Edinburgh: 1797), 2, pp. 138–41, quotation from p. 139. Hume goes on to give examples of witnesses of both sexes aged between ten and thirteen.

36 *JC* 26/16: 1 August 1659. This sentence also called for the execution of the cow which had been abused. Similarly, in the cases of John Jack (17 September 1605) and Peter Colquhoun (before 1 April 1659), the animals involved were executed as well, Pitcairn, 1833, 2.491. *JC* 26/26. On the subject of animals' fates in cases of bestiality see further E. P. Evans, *Criminal Prosecution and Capital Punishment of Animals* (London: 1906). According to D. Hume, James Mitchell was executed by drowning on 1 March 1675, *Commentaries*, 2, p. 364. He indicates, however, that this was unusual.

37 *JC* 26/20/3 and *JC* 26/19/2. *JC* 26/101/D1027.

38 *JC* 26/26, *JC* 26/97/D790, *JC* 3/1 (pp. 760–3, 788–92) and *JC* 3/19 (pp. 1–3).

39 Dekkers, 1994, pp. 133–5.

40 *JC* 26/17: 4 July 1655. The evidence of all the Scottish cases I have examined suggests that bestiality was particularly a crime committed in the countryside rather than in the town. Early modern towns do not seem very often to have provided the requisite ambience for bestial sex. In sixteenth-century Venice, for example, it was quite a rare offence. See G. Ruggiero, *The Boundaries of Eros* (Oxford and New York: 1985), pp. 114, 120. In modern towns, by contrast, the situation may well be conducive to it: Dekkers, 1994, pp. 137–41.

41 *JC*26/16: 20 August 1654.

42 The number of cases in individual years is as follows: 1654 = 3, 1655 = 4, 1656 = 11, 1657 = 8, 1658 = 8, 1659 = 4.

43 See J. Findlay, *All Manner of People: The History of the Justices of the Peace in Scotland* (Edinburgh: 2000), pp. 39, 41.

44 C. Larner, *Enemies of God: The Witch-hunt In Scotland* (Oxford: 1981), pp. 75–6. A roughly similar pattern can be seen in data from the Home Circuit Assizes in England. There is a

notable rise in the number of witchcraft cases between 1640 and 1649, with only a slight falling off between 1650 and 1659, and then a major fall from 1660 onwards. J. Sharpe, *Instruments of Darkness* (London: 1996), p. 109. The rise is associated with the activities of the witch-pricker Matthew Hopkins in East Anglia.

45 Similar localised pressures may well have influenced the many executions for bestiality in Sweden during the second half of the seventeenth century and the first half of the eighteenth century, Sörlin, 1999, p. 81.

46 Further research is needed. It would be instructive, for example, to see what was the pattern, if any, of trials for incest during the Protectorate in particular and the whole period reviewed here in general. More detailed work would also have to be done on bestiality to fill in possible gaps and to study the sociology of the participants, both accused and accusers.

6

Sodomy in early modern Geneva: various definitions, diverse verdicts

WILLIAM NAPHY

Few would doubt that morality, especially sexual morality, was a great concern to ministers, magistrates and individuals in the sixteenth century in both Protestant and Catholic societies. However, this interest in sexual mores did not always manifest itself consistently. For example Calvin, the Company of Pastors, the Consistory and the magistrates on Geneva's various councils were concerned with different types of sexual misconduct.[1] One obvious example can suffice – adultery. Kingdon made this point when he wrote that 'adultery, however, was regarded as not only grounds for divorce but also as a crime'.[2] The state became involved because adultery involved the breaking of the marriage contract, thereby forcing the magistrates to exercise their 'responsibility for the maintenance of rules for keeping public order and controlling property'.[3] However, despite this obvious incentive for state intervention in this area of sexual mores, we know from any number of Calvin's sermons that he thought the government did not take immorality, especially sexual immorality, seriously.[4]

The question that arises, therefore, is what sort of immorality interested both magistrates and ministers and which did not? In other words, did they evidence differing attitudes towards sexual misconduct? Adultery was clearly an example of a sexual act which concerned both Church and state. It violated marriage vows made before God and property contracts made before notaries. Adultery caused both scandal and interfamilial conflict. Therefore, the state took an interest because of issues of property and the possible consequences for public order. The Church, on the other hand, was more concerned about the act itself as a violation of God's highest law and an occasion for gross scandal amongst believers. Were all sexual acts as likely to attract the attention of both state and Church?

One might suggest plotting sexual misconduct on a continuum between church and state. From Calvin's comments and the surviving trial records as well as the council records, it seems clear that one form of sexual behaviour fell almost wholly on the Church side: premarital sex.[5] By this I mean not promiscuity or prostitution but sex, usually between individuals who might well be intent on marriage or indeed already engaged. The Consistory thought this a serious matter and regularly held couples to account. Usually this was when the (unmarried) woman became pregnant and the immorality came to light. Pregnancy was not always the only sign. Geneva, after all, was a fairly small city and the elders became increasingly good at sniffing out immorality. However, much to the annoyance of the Company of Pastors, the magistrates seemed to give scant regard to this matter. This is hardly surprising. There was no reason to make such behaviour a crime since the state could rely on societal mechanisms, the shotgun (or perhaps one should say, the arquebus) wedding, to solve the problem and regularise the situation.[6] Hence, although fornication, to use the more common terminology, was frequently condemned by the Consistory, the secular courts dealt with it in a perfunctory manner.[7]

However, fornication did concern the state when it shaded into promiscuity and prostitution. Not surprisingly though, in a small city, neither of these was ever that significant a problem. The state-sanctioned brothel had closed with the Reformation, and prostitution seems not to have been a significant problem thereafter.[8] Promiscuity, especially when it involved a woman with a large number of young men of prominent families, did concern the state.[9] When the promiscuity involved one woman and a group of men at the same time, the magistracy focused its attention on the behaviour of the men (who might have been involved in mutual, unnatural acts while waiting their turn). If the woman had sex with a number of men in succession, the official interest was in punishing the woman.[10]

So far this hypothetical continuum has looked at those sexual acts which make numerous appearances in the records of the Consistory. One must also consider sexual crimes which were relatively frequent in the records of the councils and courts but rarely brought before the ministers and elders. The crimes one might include at the magisterial end of the continuum were sexual assault (whether against men or women), child molestation, bestiality and same-sex acts. These were capital crimes and, as such, were not brought before the Consistory. Why, then, did the court, rather than the Church, handle these crimes? Is it perhaps because fornication, promiscuity, and prostitution were the incorrect application of something which was socially acceptable – 'natural' sex (heterosexuality)? The defendants were misusing their sexuality and needed correction so that they would channel their behaviour into 'natural' usage, that is, within the bonds of marriage.[11] When an individual strayed into areas that were more than simple misuse, for example adultery (which upset public order) or prostitution and appeared to be engaged in determined and calculated sexual conduct, the state was drawn into the matter. Repeated misuse and stubborn wilfulness in sexual immorality (even 'natural' sexuality) demonstrated a deeper problem, which the Consistory could not correct and which, therefore, concerned the state.

If this interpretation is correct or rather helpful, then those sexual acts that primarily interested the state were ones that were perceived to be not the misapplication of acceptable sexual conduct but sexual conduct which was unacceptable full stop. In other words, was there any correction or admonition which would alter the behaviour of someone who raped, or attempted to rape, of someone who molested children or, finally, someone who indulged in same-sex acts or bestiality? If this were the case, then it might imply that the early modern mind understood child molestation, same-sex acts and bestiality as more than just a misdirection of normative sexual interest. If these sex acts were seen as indicative of a preference or predilection, then Consistorial admonition would not have been warranted or useful but criminal prosecution would have been necessary and indeed the only reasonable course of action.[12]

Prosecuting sodomy in early modern Geneva

The best place to pursue this thesis is the trial records themselves. One must begin by saying that bestiality was almost unknown in Geneva. After all, the republic was overwhelmingly urbanised and possessed few rural holdings. Also, only two cases of lesbianism survive.[13] The judges were so shocked by these two cases that the public verdicts read out at the defendants' execution were intentionally vague and gave almost no idea of what the actual crime was. If Queen Victoria could not conceive of lesbianism, then Geneva's magistrates could not bring themselves to speak of it even when presented with a living, breathing example. Same-sex trials involving men were, on the other hand, quite lurid and the public summations were specific and detailed.

Male same-sex trials are what remain for examination. Monter has considered them twice before in the context of a wider statistical study of Genevan sodomy trials.[14] From his work one learns how many dossiers remain (over fifty), the number of people prosecuted (over a hundred), and when the last executions occurred (mid seventeenth century). What is missing is a detailed discussion of the information contained in the cases themselves. In general, some interesting points arise from such a consideration. Sodomy was the label that seems to been used for a range of crimes, for example, all of the pae-dophilia cases involving boys (the molestation of young girls was called rape). Also sodomy included sexual assaults against men by men, and, as one might expect, cases of consensual acts between men.

One might take the view that the use of one term shows an inability or unwillingness on the part of the judges of early modern Genevan society to

differentiate. Superficially that is true. However, any careful reading of the tran-
scripts shows that this is not the case. Trials in Geneva generated more or less
standardised lists of questions for any given crime. However, sodomy trials had
more than one list. For example, in paedophilia cases the judges were concerned
to discover if the accused had been involved in sodomitical activities from an
early age. Torture was used quickly and repeatedly. Doctors were asked to give
forensic evidence; one case was abandoned because the medical report failed to
support the charge.[15] Conviction and execution occur in almost all cases.

The sexual assault of adult males produced another judicial approach to
the cases. The identification of previous accusations and the number of eye-
witnesses were the distinguishing features of the investigations in these cases.
Torture was only used if the defendant varied his testimony.[16] Despite significant hearsay testimony, convictions usually came only if the defendant had a
history of prosecutions for the crime. However, previous accusations normally
only allowed the court to torture. If the accused managed to resist the torture
and never varied his testimony then an acquittal was a distinct possibility. For
the most part, though, the cases ended with a 'not-proven' verdict and a sentence of banishment 'to God's judgement'.

Cases involving consensual sex presented a wholly different set of features. For obvious reasons there were usually no witnesses to the sex itself. The
crimes attracted the attention of the state because of things overheard in
moments either of passion or anger. That is, the relationship was uncovered
rather than a sexual act being observed. The age of the parties was very important; the younger the defendants, the more likely the case would end short of
death. Finally, proof of previous sexual relations with a woman and, especially,
successful procreation were advanced as evidence that the defendant was
unlikely to be guilty of the charge.

Rather than reiterating the excellent statistics marshalled by Monter, the
discussion below will focus on specific aspects of the testimony preserved in
some of the dossiers in an effort to discover some idea of the views on sexual
deviance held by magistrates, witnesses, and (most importantly) the defendants (see Table 1). For the purposes of this chapter, I have chosen to confine
my remarks to a small case study based on the sodomy trials that occurred
during Calvin's ministry. The end of the chapter will also consider a few trials
from the years thereafter. Although complex both individually and collectively,
these trials can be discussed in brief.

The first two dossiers are fragmentary and refer initially to a couple of
cases which encapsulated two prominent features of these trials: the use of torture and the willingness of defendants to confess to some acts while steadfastly
denying others. The most interesting point in the Myvioz trial is that he was
acquitted on the more serious charge.[17] Sadly all that survives from the second

Table 1 Genevan sodomy trials during Calvin's ministry (1535–64)

Name(s) of accused sources	Trial dates	Charged with	Torture	Convicted of	Sentence	Source	Additional
Jean Myvioz	24–5 Jan. 1542	Fornication & sodomy		Unknown	Perpetual banishment	PC2: 529	
Unknown	1545/6	Sodomy	Excessive	Unknown	Unknown	PC2: 681	
Lambert Le Blanc	7–16 Mar. 1554	Sodomy & solicitation	Probable	Sodomy	Executed	PC1: 502	
Five unnamed youths	27 Dec. 1554	Sodomy	No	Sodomy	Beaten	RC48: 169	Roset, 363; Calvini opera, 15: 69
Mathieu Durand	7–23 Jan. 1555	Paedophilia	Definite	Paedophilia	Executed	PC1: 517	
Jean Levet & Gabriel Pattu	26 Dec. 1555	Paedophilia	Unknown	Sodomy	Beaten	PC2: 1073	
Guillaume Collin	27 Jan.–12 Feb. 1556	Sexual assault	Not required	Sexual assault	Executed	PC1: 561	
Thomas de Reancourt & Jacques Beudant	4 June–11 July 1561	Sodomy	Definite	Sodomy	Banished	PC1: 957	
Guillaume Branlard & Balthasar Ramel	17–21 Aug. 1561	Sodomy	Unknown	Sodomy	Branlard, executed; Ramel, banished	PC1: 971	
Pierre Jobert & Thibaud Lespligny	3–16 Nov. 1562	Sodomy	Definite	Sodomy	Executed	PC1: 1078	
Hozias Lamotte	29–31 Dec. 1563	Paedophilia	Unknown	Paedophilia	Executed	PC1: 1167	PC1: 1168
Simon Chastel, Pierre Roquet & Mathieu De Convenir	4–7 Jan. 1564	Sodomy	No	Sodomy	Beaten	PC1: 1168	

trial is a legal evaluation of the torture employed in the case. The lawyer advised that the torture had been overly zealous and, therefore, the confession was probably unreliable.[18]

The case of Lambert Le Blanc is much more interesting and warrants a more detailed evaluation.[19] The most famous aspect of the case is Calvin's legal opinion. Calvin's nineteenth-century editors ascribed the advice to this case.[20] This association is incorrect. As can be seen from the letter itself (see Appendix 1), the legal advice related to a case involving five youths, two of whom were very young, and three older boys. In the opinion Calvin and his three colleagues recommend that the younger boys should be caned privately and the three older boys executed. One can infer from their further comments that they expected the Senate to reject this latter advice and settle for a more lenient sentence. The advisors then dutifully suggested an alternative. Because of the way Calvin's nineteenth-century editors treated this opinion in the *Calvini opera*, it has been assumed that this advice related to Le Blanc, who was a religious refugee (and, presumably, four others), and that Calvin was recommending a harsh sentence while implying that the Senate might prefer to sweep the case under the carpet. Since Le Blanc was subsequently burned, the assumption in the historiography has been that the advisers were successful in swaying a morally wavering Senate.

In fact this is completely mistaken.[21] As one can see, the next case, from December of the same year, related to five unnamed youths. According to Roset (a contemporary chronicler), 'in December, a certain number of children attending the school committed some evil and detestable acts with one another. The younger ones were caned and the older ones burned in effigy and beaten.'[22] This is the sentence recorded in the council records as well.[23] It is also the account that most closely matches the situation outlined in the legal opinion. Why has the opinion been misattributed? It would appear that, originally, all court records relating to a given year were included in the back of the volume of minutes for that year. At some point in the nineteenth century the trial dossiers and senatorial correspondence were extracted and organised into separate archival files. In the register for 1554 the extractors found a sodomy case and a legal opinion on a sodomy case. They placed them together presumably because they had overlooked the brief paragraph relating to the youths' case in the minutes themselves.

The important point for us, though, is that Calvin's opinion relates not to a religious refugee but to the five young scions of local Genevan families. The case was so sensitive that, despite the legal advice, no record was kept and the names were not recorded in the minutes. The assumption that leniency would be shown was, therefore, not necessarily a comment on any general moral laxity on the part of the Senate but an astute awareness of the socio-political realities of the situation. The advisers, including Calvin, were perfectly aware that there was almost no chance that the Senate would order the execution of the three older youths. Thus they contented themselves with trying to avoid a potential cover-up. In that they were successful.

If the Le Blanc case is no longer significant because of the attachment of Calvin's name, is there anything of interest left? In the course of the interrogations, which appear not to have involved torture, Le Blanc confessed that he had committed sodomy in Turin, Lyon and Geneva and had got a woman pregnant as well. He had seen some sodomites burned in Paris and he knew that his actions were sinful. Also one of his two Genevan lovers had been trying to blackmail him. He related that he had had sex in city streets as well as country fields and that his repeated attempts at solicitation had sometimes been successful and sometimes rejected. The judges commented on his 'brutal and disorderly appetite'. Thus, the most interesting feature of this case is the matter-of-fact acceptance – by all the participants – that Le Blanc's behaviour was normative for him.

Durand's case was wholly different.[24] He worked for Jean Revery, a bookseller, and had previously been employed by Jean Crespin and Jean Girard, both prominent printers in Geneva. He was accused of using a pet bird to entice his master's seven-year-old son into his loft, where he assaulted him. A number of witnesses from the household, including the child, Jean, testified against him – face to face – and the weight of circumstantial evidence was sufficient to allow the court to use torture. He quickly confessed to his 'disorderly and brutal desire and appetite'. The court seems to have been concerned that Durand might not have realised that his actions and the crime of sodomy were one and the same thing. However, he admitted that there had been considerable casual conversation, *chez* Crespin, about buggery as a result of the punishment of the three youths the month before (see above). Further, he testified that he was well aware that *bougrie* was *sodomie*. The judges were consistently keen to ensure that defendants were aware that the two things were one and the same. Presumably they were aware that the technical term, *sodomie*, differed from the colloquial, *bougrie*. Moreover, the natural reticence of the magistrates and ministers about discussing or describing the crime in detail meant that there was the possibility of a plea of ignorance. In addition to this desire to associate the common terminology with the legal, this case also involved opinions from lawyers (including the same Colladon who co-signed the opinion from Calvin; see Appendix 1) and a forensic report from two *barbiers* (doctors), assuring the court that the boy had indeed been forced.[25]

The case of Levet is fragmentary and very confused.[26] All that remains is a deposition by a certain Gabriel Pattu against Levet. As the result of this, someone (probably Pattu) was beaten. It may be that Pattu was only a witness or he may have been a defendant giving evidence against his sexual partner. The most likely explanation is that the case involved yet another attempted sexual assault against a 'bed-mate' at the school. There is simply not enough information to decide what was actually being investigated. In addition the dossier strongly suggests that Pattu was relatively young. If one accepts his youth and combines that with the location of the events (the school), then one can present a plausible reconstruction of the case. Pattu and Levet were schoolmates who were accused of sexual experimentation. This interpretation agrees with the seemingly lenient sentence (beating).[27]

More information survives in Collin's case.[28] Le Blanc had been accused of consensual sex and solicitation, Durand of child abuse. Collin was charged with attempting to assault a grown man who was sharing his bed in an inn.

Again, the court asked whether the defendant had ever heard the crime of sodomy referred to as buggery. Collin said that he did not know that the two were the same. The inn's hostess, his bed companion and various other guests at the inn all related that in the middle of the night there had been a commotion when Estienne Phillipon of Limoges awoke to find himself being molested by Collin. He pushed Collin out of bed and struck him on the head with a piece of stone prised from the wall. Collin admitted that there had been a disturbance and that he had been attacked but claimed it was all a misunderstanding resulting from his attempts to snuggle up to Estienne for warmth. Again, legal advice was sought. Not surprisingly, the three lawyers (again, including Colladon) advised that there was enough proof to stop the trial without any recourse to torture. Collin's evasions and alterations and the witnesses's statements all pointed to his guilt. The court dutifully convicted and executed him.

With the case of Reancourt and Beudant we return, or so it might seem, to consensual adult sex.[29] In fact this case deeply troubled both the judges and the legal advisers. There is no doubt that Reancourt suffered from some mental problem. Numerous witnesses told of his exhibitionism and repeated attempts to fondle them. He seemed wont to molest Geneva's worthies in church. Diverse legal opinions, including one by Colladon and a fascinating one which has had the signature(s) cut out, all accepted that Reancourt was guilty but advised against his execution (presumably on the grounds of diminished responsibility). The court and the advisers all stressed that Reancourt was married and had two children.[30] Moreover, the case was further complicated by Beudant's role. It appears that some of Geneva's leading citizens had tired of Reancourt's antics and had organised a sting operation.[31] They persuaded Beudant to go along with Reancourt's advances and then broke into the room to catch him in flagrante. Needless to say, the judges did not like this approach and thought it very suspicious that Beudant had even been willing to tolerate the charade for a moment.[32] In the end they banished both men after dunking Reancourt three times. Their excuse for leniency was the addled mind of Reancourt and, surprisingly, the youth of Beudant (though he was eighteen).[33]

The next case involved Branlard and a youth, Ramel.[34] The interesting feature of this case was that, yet again, one of the defendants, Ramel, received a reduced sentence because of his youth. Nevertheless, he was beaten and banished for allowing Branlard's attentions.[35] However, Branlard was convicted not only for his involvement with Ramel but also because he admitted to having been involved with a certain Jean Fontaine who had been executed for sodomy in 1554 or 1555.[36] Also the records and legal advice stressed the fact that Branlard had never been with a woman.

Unlike the parties in trials discussed thus far, Jobert and Lespligny appear to have been a long-standing couple.[37] They confessed to having taken active and passive roles in turn.[38] Age was never raised as an issue in the case. How had they been discovered? After dinner one night in their inn they had got into a violent argument in the course of which there had been some name-calling.[39] The fight had been heard by a number of people, and this testimony formed the basis of the prosecution. The evidence suggested that their relationship had been long-standing and, until tortured, they were unwilling to implicate one another. They were both drowned. Sadly, beyond the fact that they travelled together, the only other information preserved in the case is that Jobert had specifically returned to Lespligny in Geneva after a business trip.

The last two cases during Calvin's ministry can be treated together as Lamotte was mentioned in both. In the first case Lamotte, a private tutor, was accused by his pupil of beating him and, aroused by the violence, molesting him.[40] The child, Jean Cherubim, broke down at the dinner table and told his parents.[41] Even without the accusation of paedophilia, Lamotte would have been in trouble since the father had explicitly forbidden Lamotte from striking his child. This is not surprising as private and public teachers in Geneva and indeed throughout France were usually forbidden by contract from corporal punishment; they could only nominate children to be beaten by their own parents.[42]

For their part the judges were most interested is discovering the root of Lamotte's desires. He confessed that he had been abused by two of his cousins in Anduze on a number of occasions. Although he had told his aunt about the abuse, it had not been stopped. Lamotte, poignantly, confessed that he knew that the Bible forbade sodomy and that he was well aware of what God had done to Sodom and Gomorrah. He testified that he had fled to Geneva because of his faith and, because of that same faith, he admitted his guilt and called upon the court to punish him as he deserved. They obliged.

Lamotte was also mentioned in the next case.[43] It appears that in addition to his assault on the young Cherubim he had also molested Simon, who then introduced this novel behaviour to his friends, Pierre and Mathieu. As with the earlier case involving very young children, they were beaten in private. They were also made to place a faggot of wood on a blazing fire as a vivid reminder of the fate that awaited them should they re-offend. Finally their parents were instructed to ensure that the boys did not see one another again until they were grown up. It appears that the boys were sent into the countryside.

This has been a rather hasty examination of the cases that occurred during Calvin's ministry in the city. Do they have any features in common? Unlike any other category of crime in Geneva, almost every sodomy prosecution required legal advice. Also, the questioning by the judges demonstrated a very subtle and detailed understanding of human nature, sexual development and individual psychology. It is also clear that people not only committed buggery but were also labelled buggers. There were constant references to 'brutal and disorderly

appetites'. The stress laid upon heterosexual activity or lack thereof was enor-
mous. Previous arrests and prosecutions for sexual immorality, especially of an
'unnatural' variety, were important. All these features suggest that the judges
were trying to identify a pattern and that they expected that such a pattern
could be identified. Two salient features of this pattern were clearly the lack of
any previous sexual contact with women or having been abused as a child. This
implies that the judges had a normative pattern in mind for the various types of
sodomitical activity: this is both instructive and illuminating. That is, the judges
assumed that child abusers were more than likely to have been introduced to
the behaviour (i.e. abused) at a young age and that sodomites involved in sexual
activities with adults of the same sex were unlikely to have had sexual relations
with members of the opposite sex. Finally, the constant and crucial involvement of lawyers only serves to highlight the almost total lack of involvement
by the ministers. Even when ministers were consulted, it was primarily
because they had legal training. The emphasis seems to be upon the appetite
and character of the perpetrators rather than upon the immorality of fornication and even adultery. The assumption was that the accused were given over
to an appetite (preference) and that magisterial punishment not ministerial
admonition was required.

'For pleasure': denying and confessing sodomy

Although the foregoing discussion gives some idea of the content of the trials,
it does not do justice to the defendants. The emphasis, thus far, has been on the
views and interpretations of the judges. However, the great value of the
Genevan trials is the survival of the verbatim records of the interrogations and
the extensive number of depositions taken from others by the examining magistrate. These should allow one to get some idea of how the defendants viewed
their own behaviour. Some of this has already come through the discussion, for
example, Lamotte's appeal for punishment for his sins. Let us turn, finally, to
three minor cases and one spectacular case.

In 1566 Bartholomy Tecia was arrested at the Academy.[44] This case is
fascinating because of the number of depositions from other students who were
sharing accommodation (and beds). These included the testimony of Theodore
Agrippa d'Aubigné who later became a prominent figure in French Protestantism.[45] However, this was more than a deposition as d'Aubigné and Garnier
(another student) were initially arrested along with Tecia. They were quickly
exonerated and became witnesses against Tecia.[46] For his part Tecia had repeatedly tried to entice his room-mates into sexual acts while studying or wrestling
(nude) with them late at night. He also made passes at those with whom he

shared a bed – most notably d'Aubigné. The latter claimed that one night he awoke to find himself being forced and turned to rebuke Tecia for his behaviour. His presence of mind was such that he managed this in Latin. One can surely see a great Calvinist writer in the making. More seriously it may also imply that there was an insurmountable language barrier between Tecia from Piedmont and d'Aubigné from Gascony.

Eventually Tecia admitted the offences. He had stripped off his clothes one night while studying and pressed his affections on another student while trying to incite him with lewd language. He had also tried to force d'Aubigné one night in bed, d'Aubigné clearly did not repel these advances as forcefully and as quickly as he tried to claim. The court thought his account dubious and eventually reduced him to tears. He confessed his fault in not acting quickly to expose Tecia and begged for mercy (which was granted). Tecia stressed that nothing actually happened though he did know that he was doing wrong (like Lamotte, he mentioned Sodom and Gomorrah). The court also discovered that he had been raped when he was ten by an Italian nobleman and then repeatedly abused in return for presents. Colladon, in his legal advice, declared that one could not use Tecia's youth and ignorance as an excuse; it was clear that he was knowingly guilty of the crime. Hence, Tecia was drowned. The court and its legal adviser seem to have made a distinction between uneducated youths guilty of sexual experimentation and educated ones who were, with malice afore-thought, engaging in something they knew to be a capital crime and manipula-tively trying to seduce others into the same.

The next trial, that of Du Four and Brilat, gives some fascinating insight into the views of families and neighbours on same-sex acts.[47] Du Four was the son of a prominent Genevan who had land-holdings in the rural hinterland. Brilat, a cowherd, had boasted of his affair with the socially and economically prominent Du Four at least five weeks before the actual trial, though this had not been reported to the authorities or the local minister. Brilat had received grain and money from Du Four and appears to have had access to some special pasturage rights on Du Four's land. Eventually the relationship foundered when a dispute over grazing land (Du Four was trying either to reclaim the land or to use his relationship to extend his family's holdings – the situation is unclear) led to a fist-fight. Brilat was badly beaten and ran back to his village in tears accusing Du Four of being a bugger – not of having committed buggery, but of being a bugger.

Various female servants who were doing some washing overheard this accusation. Renauld, a fourteen-year-old cowherd, had witnessed the argu-ment, seen the fight and heard the same accusation. One of Brilat's female rel-atives dressed his wounds but, when he confessed that the insult was based on personal experience, she had told him to keep quiet. The court called eigh-teen witnesses. Most of his village must have known about the fight and the name-calling. However, it was the local minister and Du Four's father who had heard of the accusation and then initiated the investigation, not the local villagers. Indeed, it emerged that *père* Du Four and the minister had been trying to discover the basis of the relationship for some time.

It is clear from this case that the villagers did not want to attract undue attention to themselves or Brilat. They may well have found the relationship socio-economically advantageous. In any case they certainly wanted to protect Brilat. The court had little trouble in getting him to confess. Du Four claimed not only that he was innocent but also that he was unlikely to have had been tempted to commit sodomy since he had had sex with a woman. He said that his father knew about his fornication and that this further strengthened his case. The court was less than impressed and tortured Du Four. In the end he would only admit to active buggery and denied ever being the passive partner despite Brilat's testimony that they had exchanged roles. Also Du Four never claimed ignorance of the crime while Brilat gave an impassioned plea for mercy when the enormity of his sin was explained to him. In the end, both were drowned – Du Four's plea, as a *citoyen*, to the Conseil des Deux Cents failed to save him.

The case of Jean de la Rue, although very brief, was equally fascinating.[48] He was an eighty-year-old who was arrested for making a pass at a foreign student in an inn. The student raced to the authorities. De la Rue confessed, quite freely, that for many years he had been given over to this crime and had committed sodomy with many people in Geneva and elsewhere. When asked why he had been doing this he replied that it was for 'pleasure, for grain and for poverty'.[49] He went on to emphasise 'pleasure'.[50] After a very speedy trial – comprising only this single interrogation – he was executed.

The last area for discussion is a clutch of trials involving over a dozen men.[51] The way in which sodomy became part of a trial arising from a charge of spying is all that need concern the reader here. Pierre Canal was a prominent citizen, the factor or steward (*saultier*) of the Senate. In the paranoid aftermath of a failed Savoyard attempt to retake the city, he was accused of seditious contacts with a Savoyard nobleman. He was a spy; a charge he made no attempt to deny. The Senate acted quickly to round up all his known associates. However, when they did, they were struck by what they discovered. Canal had an extensive range of friends drawn from very diverse socio-economic strata in Genevan society. In addition he was in the habit of entertaining these people, often as a group, to dinner at his house. The authorities considered this suspicious in itself. They feared that this group was an extensive spy network. In fact they had arrested Canal's sexual partners.

One of the more amazing aspects of the trial was the admission in a deposition that Canal had been publicly called and known as a bugger for the previous eight years. The magistrates even received reports from Zürich that

Canal had been involved there with two youths in 1602 though the city had taken no action (presumably because of Canal's prominence in Geneva's ruling elite). Under torture he admitted that he had been passive and active with numerous men and that he had given and received money in exchange for sex. He also admitted to oral sex, which particularly upset the court. The result was an extensive list of contacts including a lively trade in students at the Academy, the premier training ground of Reformed ministers. Even more galling for the magistrates, many of these liaisons took place in the Hôtel-de-Ville – city hall. In a Clintonesque touch, they admitted 'eating' one another but denied that they had ejaculated. All the defendants admitted that they were aware that their behaviour was both sinful and criminal.

Conclusion

While the number of trials under examination in this chapter is relatively small, the cases present some interesting and consistent features. First, the judges use a single technical term, *sodomie*, to refer to a variety of sexual activities that are actually very different from one another. However, the use of a single term cannot be taken to mean that the courts were incapable of making distinctions between the crimes before them. The methodologies used in the trials themselves show that a distinction was being made. Cases of child abuse relied heavily on forensic medical evidence and almost invariably resulted in a conviction. The judges tried to discover at what age the defendant had been introduced to the activity. They were also keen to try to uncover a motive for the assault since they seemed unable to understand why anyone would continue in an action so obviously painful and harmful to a child. In cases of sexual assault, the focus of the judiciary differed dramatically. The court was keen to uncover a pattern of behaviour consistent with the charge. The age of the defendant was important but not the age at which the activity commenced. Sexual assault was difficult to prove and usually resulted in banishment. Consensual sex was even more difficult to prove since those involved were unlikely to implicate one another. In these trials the age of the defendants was important only at the end of the investigation when the court was trying to settle upon an appropriate punishment. In general the magistrates seemed to have taken the view that youth was a mitigating factor well into late adolescence. Just as importantly, everyone seems to have expected that someone who had engaged in heterosexual acts was very unlikely to have committed sodomy. The corollary was that sodomites were people who had given themselves (by choice) over to their own appetites (tastes). In addition the judges and lawyers never showed any sign of thinking that these appetites were universally 'latent' in all men. The sodomites before them were individuals who had chosen to give in to desires specific to them-selves. Taken together, the primary conclusion arising from these trials is that Geneva's magistrates and ministers had well-formed views on sexual develop-ment and responsibility. They seem to have had some notion that child abusers had often themselves been abused. What is also certain is that the use of a single term did not imply an inability to distinguish between the crimes. In the eyes of Geneva's rulers there were various types of sodomy and these warranted diverse investigative methods and strikingly different results.

Appendix 1: To the Senate

We (the undersigned) have witnessed the confessions of, and depositions against, the five young boys prosecuted in the presence of our magnificent Lord Syndics and our-selves touching the crime of sodomy and have paid careful attention to the informa-tion. We have also considered, examined and conferred amongst ourselves.

This is our opinion: the crime against the respective youths has been sufficiently proved. Further, this crime is one of the most atrocious and abominable that there is. It is clearly punished by the Holy Scriptures and the law[52]. Nevertheless, we think there is a difference in the crime of the youths and [therefore] the punishment due them. The two youngest were only passive in the crime and, because of their extreme youth, they did not easily understand the horror and atrociousness of the crime while the elder three did. Despite this, they should not escape punishment since they already have some discernment and ability to reason.

Therefore, so that they might fully comprehend and remember their crime and to prevent their re-offending, it seems best to advise that they be beaten privately in the presence of our Lord [Magistrates] and members of their family. This punishment in the presence of their family should give them a [suitable] fright and render them more receptive to their fate and [subsequent] admonitions so that they will more fully comprehend the mercy they have been shown as well as the true scale of their crime. [To this end] it would be good to represent to them death at the stake by burning some wood in front of them and threatening them with the same [fate] if they re-offend. A complete record of the [trial and its results] should be kept.

As to the three older boys, we have considered their ages and find them guilty of the said crime. Special consideration has been given to their behaviour as well as their physical and mental development. In the past, this crime has been explained to them frequently and at length. Moreover, they witnessed the execution at the stake of the last sodomite. In addition, they have given further proof of their guilt in the course of the examination when two of them confessed they had previously fornicated with two small girls. For these reasons we have not decided that their age cannot exempt them from the punishment due this crime.

Although legal precedence excuses the crimes of youth, there are express rules laid down. Some youths are not mentally mature; they do not completely understand what they have done. However, some are pubescent or prepubescent[53] and they are capable of [sexual crimes] since they are physically able to commit and perpetrate such crimes. Despite the suggestions of the law,[54] we find that they merit death. Nevertheless, [they might not merit] a punishment as harsh as they would get if older; they might not get [normal] punishment corresponding to this crime. Thus, they merit some leniency and perhaps can be drowned [rather than burned].

However, if it pleases your Excellencies to show them mercy it still seems that they cannot be excused from a public and exemplary physical punishment. Hiding this crime is impossible. There is a greater danger and scandal in not punishing the crime – or hiding the punishment – than in a public and exemplary punishment. Also, one should consider that one is ignoring God in covering up such a crime and allowing the guilty to go unpunished There is the danger that the Saviour will inflect a very terrible punishment on the type of men who want to hide this crime and that His wrath will fall upon many others [more generally].

Therefore [as a compromise], we suggest that the three older boys should be beaten publicly in the city's streets with a rope around their necks. In some of the places where they are beaten a fire should be lit to show them the punishment that such a crime merits. They should be threatened with the same if they re-offend. After the beating, they should be left in terror for some time, publicly chained up wherever you think best. Later they should be gaoled on bread and water and, if you think best, their relatives can guard them warning them about what will happen [if they re-offend].

Germain Colladon [lawyer]   Jehan Calvin [lawyer & minister]
Francoys Chevallier [lawyer]   Abel Poupin [minister]

NOTES

1 The Company of Pastors comprised all the Republic's ministers while the Consistory was the Company plus twelve magistrates (one syndic and two senators along with about three from the Council of Sixty and six from the Council of Two Hundred). The supreme governing body of the city was the Senate (or Petit Conseil) with about 25 members including four ruling syndics, a secretary, treasurer, factor/steward and then the remaining 18 (or so) senators. Only native-born Genevans could serve on the senate. The senate was joined by an additional 40 (or so) magistrates (both native-born and naturalised) to form the Council of Sixty, which considered mostly foreign policy issues. This larger council, when augmented by approximately another 135 magistrates, formed the Council of Two Hundred which was the final court of appeal for citizens and was the main body for validating senatorial decisions of the previous year. Elections were held every February for most magisterial posts (the city's prosecuting magistrate, the Lieutenant, and his four assistants, elected in November, were the exception). The populace was comprised of *citoyens* (native-born citizens), *bourgeois* (naturalised citizens), *habitants* (resident aliens) and *natifs* (mostly rural locals with no civic status or rights).

2 R. Kingdon, *Adultery & Divorce in Calvin's Geneva* (London: 1995), p. 5.

3 Kingdon, *Adultery*, p. 10.

4 For the role and subject matter of sermons in Geneva see W. G. Naphy, *Calvin and the Consolidation of the Genevan Reformation* (Manchester: 1994), pp. 153–62, 173, 189.

5 The best available published source on this is R. M. Kingdon, T. A. Lambert and I. M. Watt, eds, and M. W. McDonald, trans., *Registers of the Consistory of Geneva in the Time of Calvin*, vol. 1: 1542–1544 (Grand Rapids: 2000).

6 The 'anticipation' of the wedding ceremony during the engagement period as well as the

seduction of women under the promise of marriage were serious concerns for ministers and magistrates no less than for parents. Cf., but one example from many, Archives d'État de Genève [AEG], Procès Criminels [PC, série]: 551 (14–30 October 1555): Case against Guillaume Guyon for seducing Etiennette DuPuis under the pretence of marriage.

7   The bulk of the fornication cases resulted in the defendants being gaoled for a few days on bread and water. In some few cases the individuals were expected to marry or, at least, the father was forced to acknowledge and support the child.

8   See chapter 1 in W. G. Naphy, *Plagues, Poisons & Potions: Plague Spreading Conspiracies in the Western Alps, c. 1530–1640* (Manchester: 2002).

9   For example AEG, PC1: 1517 (28 January–1 February 1569) where Claude Chrestien and Jaques Molliez were prosecuted for an evening of group sex (in turn) with a chambermaid that also involved three other men including the son of a member of the local gentry, Sieur de Veygiez.

10 Cf. AEG, PC1: 1340 (23 March–3 April 1566): François Malva, Guillaume Delafin, Charles Goula, François Clerc, Jean Losserand, Jehanton Dubois, Jacques Delonnex, Louis Curtet, Guillaume Messier, Jean Saultier and Claude Blanchet were all prosecuted for fornicating (separately) with Louise Maistre. The men were sentenced to incarceration on bread and water for six to nine days while Maistre was executed (for adultery). The men were all native-born or naturalised citizens. Maistre had accepted food and money from the men.

11 See Naphy, 'Reasonable Doubt: Defences Advanced in Early Modern Sodomy Trials in Geneva', in B. Pullan, ed., *The Trial in History* (Manchester: forthcoming).

12 This very quandary forms the basis for much of the modern dispute about the best way to punish, correct and rehabilitate sex offenders.

13 AEG, PC1: 862 (12–24 October 1559): Jaquema Gonet, a serving girl, was drowned for sex with her master's young daughter, Esther Bodineau (aged fifteen) and Esther's younger brother, Nicolas (aged eight or nine). Also, PC1: 1465 (16–31 March 1568): Françoise Morel was drowned for a sexual assault against a girl with whom she was sharing a bed and for lesbian acts in the past that she confessed under torture. For more on these cases see Naphy, 'Reasonable Doubt'.

14 E. W. Monter, 'La Sodomie à l'époque moderne en Suisse romande', *Annales* 4 (1974), pp. 1023–33 and his 'Sodomy and Heresy in Early Modern Switzerland', *Journal of Homo-sexuality* 6 (1980–81), pp. 41–55. For a more general discussion on the topic see K. Gerard, *Pursuit of Sodomy: Male Homosexuality in Renaissance and Enlightenment Europe* (arrington Park, Pennsylvania: 1987) and M. Goodrich, *The Unmentionable Vice: Homosexuality in the Later Medieval Period* (Santa Barbara: 1979). It is also possible to consider a comparison of the response to sodomy in Geneva with another city by considering G. Ruggiero, *The Boundaries of Eros: Sex, Crime, and Sexuality in Renaissance Venice* (Oxford and New York: 1985) or M. Rocke, *Forbidden Friendships: Homosexuality and Male Culture and Renaissance Florence* (Oxford and New York: 1996).

15 AEG, PC2: 1813 (13 December 1595): Jean, the thirteen-year-old son of Simon Picavet (from Chaumont near Chateau-Porcien-en-Champagne), was accused of allowing himself to be sodomised by a certain Bernardin in a local village. The medical report by Simon Tuffé found no sign of dilation or violence 'autre comme naturelle disposition'.

16 On judicial torture see J. H. Langbein, *Torture and the Law of Proof: Europe and England in the Ancient Regime* (Chicago: 1977). Cf. J. Heath, *Torture and the English Law: An Administrative and Legal History from the Plantagenets to the Stuarts* (Westport: 1982).

17 AEG, PC2: 529 (24–5 January 1542). He was accused of sodomy and fornication. It appears that the sodomy charge involved the sodomising of his wife rather than a same-sex act. He confessed to fornication, frequenting prostitutes, beating his wife and having abandoned her for seven years but he steadfastly refused any 'unnatural' acts.

18 AEG, PC2: 681 (1545?). The anonymous lawyer recommended that the case be abandoned and the unknown defendant be banished because 'en tout de p[ro]ces je trouve que a este excede de la torture plus de troys foys [the limit under Genevan Law] sur mesmes

judices selon intellege[n]ce et interp[re]tation des loy car aultrements nauvoir jamays fin de torture'.

19 AEG, PC1: 502 (7–16 March 1554).

20 G. Baum, E. Cunitz and E. Reuss, eds, *Calvini opera*, in *Corpus Reformatorum* (Brunswick and Berlin: 1863–1900), vol. 15, col. 69–70. The heading to the letter reads: 'Calvin au sénat de Genève. Chargé avec quelques autres personnes de donner son avis sur la peine à infliger à cinq garçons impliqués dans le procès de Lambert Le Blanc, il s'acquitte de cette commission'. The note (5) dates the trial (and opinion) to 7–15 March 1554.

21 Le Blanc eventually confessed (without torture) to sex with both men and women in France and Italy for money and pleasure.

22 Michel Roset, *Les Chroniques de Genève*, ed. H. Fazy (Geneva: 1894), p. 363.

23 AEG, *Registres du Conseil* [RG, volume] 48, fos 169–169v (27 December 1554).

24 AEG, PC1: 517 (7–23 January 1555): Mathieu, son of Jean Durand, print-worker from Clermont-en-Auvergne.

25 See 9 January 1555 (the dossiers are unfoliated but broadly chronological so reference is made to the dates): 'houteuses mesmes au fondeudz de cul lequel il trouvent p[ar] leurs bonne foy estre aulcunement macule & corrupmus a lentrer'.

26 AEG, PC2: 1078 (26 December 1555): Gabriel, son of Thivent Pattu.

27 Although a further complication, there is the possibility that this is the sole surviving fragment relating to the five youths mentioned in Calvin's legal opinion. Pattu's case is dated to 1555 on the day after Christmas. Christmas Day was frequently the date on which Genevan notaries changed the date of the year. The *Registres du Conseil* has 1554 but this trial 1555. Thus there is the chance that the two relate to the same date (December 1554) while seeming to be separated by a year. Sadly there is no way to prove this.

28 AEG, PC1: 561 (27 January–12 February 1556): Guillaume, son of Thomas Collin, from Anjou.

29 AEG, PC1: 957 (4 June–11 July 1561): Thomas, son of Michel Reancourt from Tournai-en-Normandie, goldsmith, and Jacques, son of Pierre Beudant, from Nîmes, tailor's servant, aged eighteen. Both men were registered aliens (*habitants*).

30 For example Colladon mentioned the 'grand aage dud Thomas et quil a femme et enfans'. A second opinion said 'en p[re]mier lieu et sans aucun doubte q[ue] led Thomas estat en aage dhom[m]e p[ar]faict ay[n]t femme et enfans'.

31 Jacques Fabri a merchant citizen was in serious trouble for having discussed Reancourt's previous passes at Beudant and having advised Beudant to be an *agent provocateur* rather than reporting the events immediately. Beza, Calvin's successor, seems also to have been involved in the plot to catch Reancourt.

32 Especially as they had progressed as far as intimate kissing.

33 Reancourt was banished on pain of death should he return to Geneva while Beudant's banishment was on pain of flogging.

34 AEG, PC1: 971 (17–21 August 1561): Guillaume, son of Guillaume Branlard from Berry, aged thirty-three (a registered alien and carder) and Balthasard Ramel, from Provence, aged fifteen of sixteen.

35 Penetrative sex could not be proved though they had certainly fondled one another.

36 There is no surviving case but a Jean Fontanna (perhaps aged forty-four) had been previously prosecuted for sexual impropriety, perhaps sodomy, with François Puthod (aged eighteen to twenty). See AEG, PC1: 469 (18 April–28 May 1551). Fontanna was chained up for a year and Puthod was perpetually banished. The lawyers were convinced that anal penetration had taken place, though the defendants admitted only mutual masturbation. Fontanna, a citizen, was saved from death after a successful appeal to the city's larger council, Duex Cents. His heroic role in the Revolution against Savoy in the 1530s seems to have saved him this time (but, it appears, not in 1554–55) – assuming he is the same person, which is not certain.

37 AEG, PC1: 1078 (3–16 November 1562): Pierre, son of Jean Jobert from Auvergne, and Thibaud, son of Thibaud Lespingley from Tours. Both were lace-workers and registered aliens.

38 'Auroient use lung envers laultre de plus[ieu]rs villanes et infammes attochemens'.

39 A number of witnesses overheard this exchange: 'tu bougre' followed by 'cest moy'.

40 AEG, PC1: 1167 (29–31 December 1563): Hozias Lamotte, a student from Anduze.

41 The child (aged seven or eight) testified that after he was beaten on his bare bottom 'luy mist son quillet avec quoy il pisse dans son cul et sefforca dentrer en luy et luy fist mal'.

42 For more on Geneva's schools and, more generally, schools in France see W. G. Naphy, 'The Reformation and the Evolution of Geneva's Schools', in B. Kümin, ed., *Reformations Old and New: Essays on the Socio-economic Impact of Religious Change c. 1470–1630* (Aldershot: 1996), pp. 185–202. Cf. AEG, PC1: 1147 (16–19 August 1563) in which Claude Barbel, the teacher of year eight at Geneva's school, was sacked for beating three students in the mouth with a rod. Cf. L. Haas, *The Renaissance Man and His Children: Childbirth and Early Childhood in Florence 1300–1600* (Basingstoke: 1998) and B. A. Hanawalt, *Growing up in Medieval London: The Experience of Childhood in History* (Oxford: 1993).

43 AEG, PC1: 1168 (4–7 January 1564): Simon (aged nine, son of Michel Chastel, a registered alien); Pierre (aged eight, son of Pierre Roquet, a citizen and waggoner); Mathieu (aged seven, son of Jean Convenir, a registered alien).

44 AEG, PC1: 1359 (28 May–10 June 1566): Batholomy (aged fifteen or sixteen, son of Bastian Tecia, from Piedmont, a student and registered alien), Theodore (aged fifteen, son of Jean d'Aubigné, from Gascony), Emery (aged fifteen, son of Arnaud Garnier, from Gascony).

45 D'Aubigné (1552–1630) distinguished himself as a soldier in 1567 and later served as vice-admiral of Guyenne and Brittany under Henry IV. His most famous work is his *Histoire universelle* (1616–20). He was also known for his satirical wit, best seen in his *Aventures du baron de Foenesté* (1617) and his posthumously published *Confession catholique du Sieur de Saney* (1660).

46 They were not completely free of guilt since the court was concerned that they had not reported Tecia's advances immediately rather than discussing them amongst themselves.

47 AEG, PC1: 1818 (5–14 November 1600): Pierre (aged nineteen or twenty, son of François Dufour, a naturalised citizen) and Pierre (aged sixteen, son of Antoine Brilat, a shepherd).

48 AEG, PC1: 2350 (5–8 February 1617): Jean, son of Jacques de la Rue, aged eighty.

49 'Par plaisir e p[ar] le grnolte & p[ar] pauvrete confesse lavoir fair'.

50 'P[ar] plaisir avec toute ceux quil avec lesquelz il l'a commisery'.

51 All the trials took place in 1610. PC1: 2013 (12 January–2 February, Canal, executed); 2014 (20 January–13 March, Jean Maillet, *citoyen*, spying and murder); 2016 (31 January–24 February, Plongon, *citoyen*, fined 200 écus); 2017 (31 January–25 February, Bonoit; Felisat; Gaudy; sodomy, all executed); 2018 (31 January–3 March, Berjon, *citoyen*, banished); 2019 (31 January–3 March, Artaut; Bedeville; André; Destalle; sodomy); 2022 (1 February–17 April, Bodet, *bourgeois*, sodomy, fined 1,000 écus); 2031 (30 March–10 April, Buffet, fornication and sodomy, banished).

52 Marginalium: *C. de Adulter. L. cum vir autem ut non luxurientur contra naturam.*

53 Marginalium: *Ad leg. Conrel. De Sicar. L. infans ad s. sillania L. pro s. impubes c. si adver. Delict. L. pri.*

54 *C. de penis L. impunitas die L. tn. Xiv.*

7

Sexual identities:
a medieval perspective

SARAH SALIH

According to the *Golden Legend*, Jacobus de Voragine's popular preaching manual, the moment of Christ's birth was marked by miraculous occurrences all over the world. In Egypt idols shattered; in Rome a fountain of oil sprung up; throughout the Roman Empire, somewhat anticlimactically, Octavian built public roads.[1] The natural and the social worlds united to produce signs testifying to the inauguration of a new age. One conclusive miracle remained:

> And even the sodomites gave witness by being exterminated wherever they were in the world on that night, as Jerome says: 'A light rose over them so bright that all who practised this vice were wiped out; and Christ did this in order that no such uncleanness might be found in the nature he had assumed.' For, as Augustine says, God, seeing that a vice contrary to nature was rife in human nature, hesitated to become incarnate.[2]

The tale highlights a fundamental difficulty for anyone wishing to investigate conceptions of same-sex activities in medieval Christian Europe: such an investigation requires a search for a category of people who are, apparently, (1) monstrous and (2) non-existent. Jacobus's text establishes 'the sodomites' as a category at the very moment that all of the category's members are obliterated: it is produced only as an empty space. The process puts considerable strain on the conception of 'nature', always an ambiguous term in Christian sexual ethics, being able to denote either the bestial or the proper.[3] How, logically, can a vice contrary to nature also be rife in human nature? If the implication is that nature has become corrupted through the repeated practice of the vice, then nature's self-identical stability – its naturalness – is called into question. Miracles, by definition, are events which disrupt natural order: is the destruction of the sodomites, with the ensuing restoration of natural order, thus an anti-miracle? There is confusion also about agency: while the syntax of the opening sentence implies with grim irony that self-defining sodomites voluntarily offered themselves up for immolation, the comment attributed to Augustine sees them only as abject vessels of vice. It seems that the very invocation of the sodomite disrupts all the distinctions it is presumably intended to guarantee. Sodomy, famously labelled 'that utterly confused category' by Michel Foucault, also acts to confuse other categories, being at once unnatural and rife in nature, unspeakable and that which must be spoken.[4]

The destruction of the sodomites is equally problematic for the distinctions commonly used by histories of sexuality, the terms of which were set by Foucault's now-classic formulation:

> As defined by the ancient civil or canonical codes, sodomy was a category of forbidden acts; their perpetrator was nothing more than the juridical subject of them. The nineteenth-century homosexual became a personage, a past, a case history and a childhood, in addition to being a type of life, a life form, and a morphology, with an indiscreet anatomy and possibly a mysterious physiology.[5]

Thus, while premodern sexuality may be envisaged as consisting of a number of more or less transgressive acts, modern sexuality is claimed to be organised into identity categories which are saturated with meaning: whom a person desires can be assumed also to imply other details of their personalities and preferences.

Both theoretical and historical investigations suggest that this formulation is more useful as a schematic clarification of terms than as a statement about an historical process. As David M. Halperin argues, Foucault's claim was always genre-specific, and is 'a discursive analysis, not a social history'.[6] Halperin insists on a distinction between sexual identity and sexual orientation: however, his definition of orientation is so very rigorous as to leave room to search for less prescriptive forms of identity.[7] It is possible to use Foucault's conceptual distinctions without accepting his narrative statement. Meanwhile, queer theories which privilege incoherence are not necessarily committed to any such clear-cut narrative, and problematise the distinction by focusing on the insecurities and excesses of modern sexual identities. Eve Kokofsky Sedgwick argues that that modern understandings of sexual identity are less coherent than Foucault's account suggest, being complicated by the tension between minoritising and universalising, integrative and separatist views.[8] Judith Butler builds on Foucault's terms, arguing that the investigation of the excluded and the incoherent is imperative for modern studies of sexuality.[9]

The destruction of the sodomites only confirms the confusion: the passage clearly envisages a class of people called sodomites, whose transgressive pleasures are sufficient to define them, but in its stress on the prevalence of the vice it also offers some support to an acts-based theory of sexuality: perhaps some of those obliterated were just unlucky enough to be caught practising that particular vice on that particular night. After all, according to St Augustine, sexuality – in any form – is the marker of fallen, exiled and disunified humanity:

They experienced an unprecedented movement of their own disobedient flesh as punishment in kind, as it were, for their own disobedience. The soul, in fact, delighting now in its own freedom to do wickedness and scorning to serve God, was stripped of the former subjection of the body, and because it had wilfully deserted its own higher master, no longer kept its lower servant subject to its will.[10]

If the desires of the flesh mark the fallen state of medieval humanity, it is not unreasonable to suppose that the direction of those desires might be used to distinguish between categories of persons, but only within a framework in which the very existence of such desires testifies to the essential similarity between all imperfect humans. Those who eliminate desire by celibate practices and physical or mystical castrations thus mark themselves as saints, whose achievements are not available to the average Christian.[11]

Chronologies

Sedgwick's complication of the Foucauldian terms also challenges the narrative of the supersession of one form of sexual categorisation by another, pointing out that American law still enshrines an act-based understanding of sexuality, which thus cannot be discounted as 'an anachronistic vestige'.[12] The two ways of conceptualising sexuality may coexist and overlap. Her demonstration of the multiplicity of modern categories does not, however, engage with the premodern: might the earlier period be shown to be equally complicated? The status of the acts/identities narrative is contested for the early modern period, with, for example, Robert Shephard and Joseph Cady disagreeing within the space of a single volume as to the existence of 'homosexuality' in the seventeenth century.[13] Michael B. Young uses James I as a case study to discover the early modern existence of an identity based on sexual object choice, and approvingly cites James Saslow's argument that 'where homosexuality is concerned, "we should 'push back' the temporal frontier of an emerging modern consciousness, at least in embryonic form, well into the early modern period."'[14] Carolyn Dinshaw's conclusion that in some late medieval texts 'men who engaged in acts of male–male sex were thought to be visibly marked, known at least to others if not to themselves, grouped with others of the same kind, and defined by sexual desire' suggests firstly that such an emergence of modernity should be pushed back still further, into the late medieval, and secondly that the terms of the question may need further refinement.[15] If the emergence of the homosexual (rather like the rise of the bourgeoisie) can be discovered in any period a scholar chooses to examine, it may be that narrative is not the appropriate format for this discussion.

The question is of particular resonance for medievalists, owing to the peculiar status of the medieval in the grand narratives of Western historiography. As Sellar and Yeatman tell us, the Middle Ages are so called 'on account of their coming at the beginning', and the duality of the period, cited both as the origin of the modern and as its incomprehensible predecessor, is especially marked in the young sub-discipline of the history of sexuality.[16] While the post-modern may sometimes claim a special affinity with the premodern, the medieval is also simultaneously used to stand for the non-modern and the inno-cent.[17] The current form of the confusion can be traced to Foucault's remark-ably plural chronologies. In *History of Sexuality* a key moment of emergent modernity is, rather unexpectedly, 1215, when the Fourth Lateran Council ordered every Christian to undergo annual confession.[18] Foucault's medieval is both innocent and knowing, before subjectivity and its cradle.[19]

Jacqueline Murray deals with the problem by arguing that the traditional periodisation of medieval and early modern is inapplicable to questions of social history and choosing instead to stress continuity with the term 'pre-modern'.[20] Specialists of the early modern period do not always work with an assumption of such continuity. Alan Stewart, for example, highlights, whilst continuing to contribute to, the privileging of the early modern in sexual his-tory: 'Yet the reasons *why* homosexuality should be writ so large evidently require some thought. Why not medieval England, or the romantic period?'[21] Why, indeed, not medieval England? Stewart's arguments rest on an uneasy relationship with the medieval. As he admits, patronage, a key term in his analysis, was not an invention of the sixteenth century: yet his claim that 'the new utilitarian nature of the nobility's patronage of scholars' distinguishes the English Renaissance looks distinctly questionable in the light of, say, the claims made for the 'Lancastrian language policy'.[22] Meanwhile the medieval can also be silently appropriated, as when Stewart cites the specifically late-medieval architectural development of the closet as private space in aristocratic house-holds in order to inform analysis of the early modern.[23]

Medievalists, meanwhile, are by no means unanimous about the most effective way to conceptualise medieval sexual identities.[24] John Boswell's groundbreaking and controversial *Christianity, Sexual Tolerance and Homosexuality* is less essentialist than its reputation (and its own subtitle) suggest, devoting considerable space to the problem of terminology.[25] His definition of 'gay people' as 'persons who are conscious of erotic preference for their own gender' does not necessarily imply that such persons had any coherent theory of what that preference signified or whether and how they enacted it.[26] It is still too essentialist, however, for much recent scholarship. Allen J. Frantzen claims that 'The early Middle Ages (the later Middle Ages too, I would argue) lacked an identity that we might think of today as "the sexual subject" whose sexual practices inform, if they do not actually determine, both self-awareness and public identity'.[27] This does not mean that sexual preferences did not exist: 'we can speak of a sexual identity based on same-sex acts in the Anglo-Saxon period', but that these preferences are not equivalent to the modern sense of sexual orientation.[28] Karma Lochrie also affirms the narrative, arguing that 'The Middle Ages, after all, preceded the conception, invention, and normalisation of heterosexuality as we know it.'[29] That 'as we know it' indicates that Lochrie demands high standards of coherence and self-identity for such a heterosexuality. However, neither Frantzen nor Lochrie uncritically reproduces the Foucauldian narrative: apparent confirmation of the narrative's main features coexists with sharp critiques of the shortcomings of Foucault's medievalism.[30]

Other medievalists are willing to identify at least occasional sightings of sexual identities. Simon Gaunt's 'queer wishes' and Dinshaw's 'queer touches' are influential locutions which are cautious about locating essential sexual identities in other historical periods.[31] Dinshaw's discussion of the case of John/Eleanor Rykener makes the point that not only sexual identities but also sexual acts may be difficult to categorise: some of Rykener's male lovers apparently remained convinced that he was a woman.[32] However, both scholars also argue that in some circumstances relatively familiar sexual identities may be discerned in medieval texts. Dinshaw has been already cited: Gaunt concurs that the category of a man with a persistent inclination for sexual contact with men – not entirely identical with the modern homosexual – appears in certain contexts, and, crucially, also notes the genre-specific nature of sexual identities.[33] Mark D. Jordan finds that 'Peter Damian attributes to the Sodomite many of the kinds of features that Foucault finds only in the nineteenth-century definition'.[34]

On closer examination the apparent polarity looks more like a continuum. Caution is justified by the demonstration that medieval terms do not match modern ones: that there is no medieval category which corresponds to the modern 'sexuality'; that medieval terms such as 'sodomy' fluctuate and may include any non-reproductive sexual act, as well as sins which are not sexual at all.[35] Nobody claims that medieval sexual identities were identical in all respects to the modern versions. The disagreement is about what precisely constitutes a sexual identity category: how stable, how permanent, how recognisable it should be: whether it is recognised by medical, legal, religious discourses. Frantzen distinguishes the Anglo-Saxon sodomite from the modern homosexual on the grounds that 'the kind of identity created by the term "sodomite" was not exclusive to sexual behaviour in the Middle Ages': but then nor do modern identity categories refer exclusively to sexual behaviour: this is what makes them identity categories rather than neutral descriptions of individual tastes.[36] Rather than spend any more time worrying about which conceptualisations of identity are to be permitted to count, I intend to consider some of the variables of how they come into visibility. Dinshaw's latest formulation calls for a radical openness which refuses to choose between the alterity and the familiarity of the medieval: she argues that queer history must always be contingent.[37] I would agree that, though conceptions of sexual identity appear in some places in late medieval culture, they do not neatly correspond to modern formulations and may not be engaged in the same cultural work. The male sodomite is to be privileged as an initial test case: as Jordan argues, to name sodomy 'was to isolate the erotic in its pure state' and thus to produce a repository for all erotic anxieties.[38] The question of whether the premodern was able to conceptualise sexual identities has been answered: in some instances it demonstrably could. Once we have acknowledged that, further questions arise: what kinds of identities could it produce; why does this con-ceptualisation remain marginal; when does it appear, in which genres, which circumstances, implicated in which networks of relations; interacting in what ways with other categories of gender, age, social status, religious profession? It is impossible to do a full survey here, so I intend to concentrate on the effects of genre to enquire further what the discursive circumstances are in which a conceptualisation of sexual identity is both possible and desirable, narrowing the question to investigate some of the range of relations between acts and identities according to genre.

Genres

As we have seen, it is possible to claim that sexual identities became thinkable in Western culture as a by-product of the practice of confession: thus this way of conceptualising the self should be more commonplace following the Fourth Lateran Council of 1215. Unfortunately, the evidence complicates any such narrative, as the history of the tale of Lanval will show. In its earliest extant ver-sion, the lay of Lanval, written in Anglo-Norman in the mid twelfth century by a woman known for convenience as Marie de France, the eponymous hero is propositioned by King Arthur's nameless wife. He rejects her for two reasons, the unspoken one being that he already has a fairy mistress whose existence he is sworn to conceal. The reason he proclaims, emphatically, to the queen is the bond of homosocial loyalty between lord and vassal: 'I have long served the king and do not want to betray my faith. Neither you nor your love will ever lead me to wrong my lord!' It is the queen's response to this rebuff which is of interest here. She answers, 'unwisely':

> I well believe that you do not like this kind of pleasure. I have been told often enough that you have no desire for women. You have well-trained young men

and enjoy yourself with them. Base coward, wicked recreant, my lord is unfortunate to have suffered you near him. I think he may have lost his salvation because of it!

The queen identifies Lanval as an outsider to her courtly world of compulsory heterosexuality, in which she takes her damsels to meet knights who 'took the girls by the hand, and the conversation was not uncourtly'.[39] She has no term for what she means, and can only describe the acts involved, but she clearly conceives of the existence of a kind of man who takes his pleasure with other men, and who thus refuses the love of women: she believes sexual object choice to be exclusive. Borrowing Foucault's terms, she imagines Lanval as a personage, a past, and a case history. In the specification of young men as Lanval's lovers, she may imply the existence of a pederastic model of male–male sexuality. She also believes such behaviour to be threatening to homosociality: Lanval is a spiritual danger to those men with whom he has such bonds. Gender and status identities are at stake, for the accusation of recreance claims that Lanval has failed to perform the aristocratic and military masculinity of the knight. Lanval himself evidently accepts the same assumptions, for, equally unwisely, he is driven to defend his heterosexual potency by revealing the existence of his supremely lovely fairy mistress, who promptly abandons him. Author and characters share a conception of sexual identity different in detail from the modern 'homosexual', but nevertheless firmly based on same-sex object choice.

We can trace some of the variations in medieval conceptions of sexuality by following the career of this text in its later English version. The omissions and additions in Thomas Chestre's late-fourteenth-century version, *Sir Launfal*, register unease about the hero's gender performance.[40] Chestre makes explicit the anxiety of masculinity present in the tale, introducing battles and tournaments to give Launfal the chance to show off his heroic prowess and successfully defend challenges to 'hys manhod'.[41] The confrontation with the queen has quite lost the clarity of Marie's version: Launfal rejects her with the words: 'I nell be traytour' without specifying whether to the king or to his mistress. The queen's accusation has also lost force and specificity: 'Thou lovyst no woman, ne no woman the.'[42] However, chivalric romance is always shadowed by queerness: as Kathleen Coyne Kelly puts it, 'it does not take much effort to recover those moments when spears and swords substitute for, and perhaps extend, phallus and penis' – and what is excluded returns in another form.[43] Chestre's version actually gives Launfal a couple of loyally devoted younger knights, who share his 'chamber by my orchard-syde' as if in an attempt to translate the scandalous accusation of Marie's original into properly secured homosocial structures.[44] Far more attention is given to Launfal's relationships with his peers, especially his 'lefly frende' Gawain.[45] Same-sex activity has become both unspeakable and potentially everywhere.

The difference between the two versions is the opposite of that implied by the Foucauldian chronology: it is the pre-1215 text which has a conception of sexual identity and the post-1215 text which wishes to obscure it. These differences do not comprise a straightforward narrative. Gaunt's analysis of the comparable accusation scene in the twelfth-century *Roman d'Enéas* revives the much-debated claim that in the twelfth century 'courtly romance simultaneously "discovers" the individual, woman and love' to argue that 'it is striking that in the *Enéas* that the heterosexual is produced in opposition to the homosexual. Homosexuality is within culture as well as excluded from it, because it is a crucial element in the definition of the dominant model of sexuality.'[46] This makes logical and theoretical sense: just as the modern term 'heterosexual' is a back-formation from 'homosexual' therefore, if the twelfth-century romance invented heterosexuality, it should also have invented homosexuality simultaneously.[47] The interpretation is strengthened by the fact that this accusation is apparently only permitted to appear in circumstances which identify it as being untrue: that is, in between heterosexual acts, as if it were a default condition to which any man might revert if he were to neglect continual performance of heterosexual desire. Perhaps Jacobus was right: the category of sodomites exists, but there is no one in it.

However, it is less clear why, having invented two sexualities simultaneously, the genre should then, apparently, only remember one: why, in the later versions of the Lanval story, does courtly heterosexuality no longer need its homosexual other? The queen's belief in the exclusivity of sexual object choice does not disappear from medieval culture altogether – it recurs in the thirteenth-century Parisian prostitutes who shouted 'sodomite' at those clerics who refused their offers – but has vanished from chivalric romance.[48] It is possible to speculate: perhaps the process of naturalising heterosexuality was so successful that it no longer needed its other. Perhaps, also, there was a different other which the generally secular bias of modern criticism has neglected. The form of heterosexuality constructed by twelfth-century romance, unsatisfactorily but generally known as 'courtly love', is widely acknowledged to have been influenced by erotic mysticism, a genre to which queer moments are endemic owing to the disruption caused by the direction of desires to the divine.[49] Thus it may be the generic difference between secular and mystical eroticism which is at stake in the queen's accusation and Lanval's denial, but not, primarily, sexuality in the modern sense. The process is of organising erotic impulses into genre-specific categories at the moment of the formation of a new genre of erotic literature.

The theory and practice of confession have a foundational, but problematic, place in histories of sexuality. Foucault's account privileges confession as a locus of self-production: 'Everyone in Christianity has the duty to explore who he is, what is happening within himself, the fault he may have committed, the temptations to which he is exposed. Moreover, everyone is obliged to tell these things to other people and, hence, to bear witness against himself.'[50] Individuals are thus asked to construct themselves by reporting on their acts. That confession may make possibe self-production is clear enough for compulsive penitents such as Margery Kempe, who 'schewyd ... al hyr maner of levyng fro hyr chyldhod' to every cleric she met: she used the space of the confessional to tell and refine the story of her whole life.[51] Jerry Root summarises the consensual position: 'Confessional practice makes available to both simple and learned a technique of self-production ... this institutional practice became powerful and attractive enough [to change] the way people were able to talk about themselves', and goes on to trace this new sense of self in the literature of late medieval England.[52]

However, confessional discourse also features prominently in those works which reject the notion of medieval sexual identities: Frantzen relies in part on a detailed study of penitential evidence, as does Lochrie. A brief examination of the handful of relevant passages in one text offering basic instruction in confessional practice, The Book of Vices and Virtues, will help to test whether the sodomite can be found lurking in the confessional. The initial brief discussions of the commandments informs us that 'in this comaundement is forbode al synne agens kynde, in what manere that it be do, or in his owne persone or in otheres': thus the category of sins against nature includes autoerotic activities as well as those performed with a partner.[53] Confessions are to be organised in terms of the seven deadly sins, which themselves come with sub-divisions into different branches and degrees of sin.[54] The relevant deadly sin here is lechery, which may be subdivided in various ways: there are five stages – looks, words, touches, kisses, 'the dede' – there is lechery of the heart, which has four degrees, and lechery of the body, which the text neglects to sub-divide.[55] Then come the fourteen branches of lechery: between unbound persons; men with prostitutes; men with bound women; men with virgins; men with married women; acts 'agens kynde and agens the ordre of wedloke' within marriage; three kinds of incest; women with clerics; lay people with religious; monks with nuns; prelates with anyone: so far the list seems to deal only with other-sex acts, although there is some room for ambiguity in the descriptions of the eleventh and thirteenth branches.[56] Branch fourteen is the one that we are interested in:

> The last is so foule and so hidous that it scholde not be nempned, that is synne agens kynde, that the devel techeth to a man or to a womman in many wises that mowe not be spoken, for the matere is so foul that it is abhomynacioun to speke it; but natheles be it man or womman that be gilty ther-of he mote telle it openly

in his schrifte to the prest as it was y-don. ... This synne is so myslykyng to God,
that he made reyne fier and stynkynge brymston upon the citees of Sodom and
Gomorre, and sunke in-to helle fyve citees.[57]

The account has all the elements commentators usually find: horror, demonic
involvement, unspeakability combined with an imperative to speak; invocation
of Sodom, and a remarkable vagueness as to what acts might be included in the
category. Thus the vast majority of imaginable sexual acts are proscribed: sins
against nature are not exclusive to same-sex contexts, but may also occur in
marriage or indeed alone. There are many circumstances which affect the
degree of sin. Object choice matters – nuns and prostitutes are inappropriate
sexual objects – and the gender of the object choice matters, but not only is
there is no concept of sexual identity in any of this, there is no conception
either of same-sex acts as a discrete category. A later reference under the first
state of chastity suggests that 'lechery that is agens kynde' is a bad habit which
young people may be taught, or fall into, but with no suggestion that such sins
might be especially difficult to unlearn, and with the clear implication that
there is no class of persons with an innate propensity to them.[58] The emphasis
on the unspeakability of acts 'agens kynde' amounts to a constructionist position: people will only be able to commit such acts if they have first learnt to
articulate them.

This is, of course, only one example of the genre. Another, *Handlyng
Synne*, discerns seven types of lechery, all other-sex acts, and devotes its entire
446-line commentary on the sixth commandment to the regulation of marriage.[59] Its definition of sexual sin, in fact, is synonymous with heterosexuality:
its standard paraphrases for sexual activity are variations on 'doing things with
women' – 'with wymmen to rage', 'with womman to do flesshely dedes'.[60]
Kissing between men and women is 'grete peryl', but a kiss of forgiveness
between two knights is narrated with approval, and rewarded with a further,
more detailed embrace from Christ:

> wyth the tokene he gan hym blesse,
> And kneled down, the cros to kesse.
> The crucyfyx, that there was leyd,
> Hys armes fro the cros upbreyd,
> And clepd the chylde hym betwyx,
> And aftyrward kyst hym, that crucyfyx.[61]

Handlyng Synne either takes literally the ban on mentioning same-sex acts, or is
utterly unaware of any possibility of such acts. It is as if Jacobus were right, and
the sodomites and all their works have been eliminated from Western Chris-
tendom. No one attempting to use this text as the basis for constructing a personal identity would be able to centre this identity on the direction of their

desires: indeed, its silences might seem tacitly to permit such desires, whilst admitting them to language only in disguise. This analysis, brief as it is, confirms that confessional literature does not produce sexual subjects, and that its categories of the erotic are, to modern habits of thought, utterly incoherent.

Perhaps we have been misunderstanding the genre. Lochrie offers a valuable corrective to the overemphasis on sex in the Foucauldian model, pointing out that 'sexuality itself was only one aspect of a system devoted to the surveillance of the individual, and it was not always the most verbose'.[62] If confession constructs a subject, there is no reason to privilege sexuality as the grounds of this construction: to judge from confessional literature, it would be just as likely that a subject centred on its tendency to wrath or gluttony might emerge. Confessional discourse constructs a composite sinner, one who might be guilty of anything from incest to coining to inattention in church: it is not the place to look for delineations of particular kinds of sinners. Other details of confessional practice suggest that perhaps the confessional is less useful for the production of identities than is sometimes supposed. Penitential literature does not provide access to confession itself, but to a textualised prescription of it. No parish priest could possibly, practically, interrogate all his parishioners about the full range of sins specified in the vast *summae*: the Easter confessions would take him all year. And what are the parishioners supposed to be doing in the interval between their annual confessions: do they revert to pre-1215 modes of self-perception? The fear that the ordinary laity can hardly be expected to remember a full year's sins is addressed in the proviso that forgotten and unspoken sins may be included in absolution.[63] If confession is so bound up with identity, are we to suppose, for example, that medieval Christians had identities and their Jewish neighbours did not?

Circumstances thus suggest that confession could only have functioned as the theatre of self-production for the confessional elite, professed religious and lay enthusiasts such as Kempe, who made a point of crafting and retelling their confessions. Even for regular penitents, the self thus produced is not necessarily a stable identity. The process of confession is not conducive to coherent self-formation, because the penitent must renounce at the same time as they acknowledge. Admitting that they have committed certain acts, in that admission they refuse to be defined by those acts and promise to stop doing them. Confession is a repeated interruption of an individual's history: after confession, penance and restitution may remind the individual of their previous sins, but also of their intention never again to be that sinner. Sexuality appears to be act-specific when viewed through the lens of penitential discourse, because confession is act-specific. How often a sin has been committed is one factor which may affect the severity of the penance, but one amongst many – with whom, when, for what motive, where, to whose knowledge – and with no suggestion that it has a significance of a different order. The whole process is designed to ensure that sins, even repeated sins, do not solidify into identities: *Handlyng Synne* tells an exemplum of the devil's inability to recognise a former sinner who had made his confession.[64]

Visitations

Penitential and visitation evidence have significant generic similarities. They are based on the same set of clerical moral values and use similar formats. In both, individuals must bear witness to their actions in response to a pre-scripted, but almost infinitely flexible, set of questions. Thus differences between the two, even if only in nuance, are worth noting. When Bishop Alnwick of Lincoln visited New College, Leicester, in 1440, he was informed that 'master John Dey, canon of the place, is defamed of the vice of sodomy'.[65] The charge was upheld after an investigation, and Dey deprived of his place. The punishment is far more serious than that allotted to other transgressors, such as Ralph Welles, who was 'defamed with Alice Norys ... of whom he has begotten offspring, and with Joan the wife of William Heuse of Leicester, and with Alice Spensere, of whom he has begotten offspring', but who was allowed to deny the charges and promise not to do it again.[66] The bishop's sentence of Dey makes much rhetorical play with the unspeakability of sodomy: 'you, master John Dey ... were revealed and accused to us ... of that damnable and hateful vice of sodomy, by the name whereof alone the air is defiled, committed in damnable wise by you, as it was said, with divers persons', but apparently nevertheless does not mind polluting the air by mentioning the name of the vice, in a paradox noticed by Dinshaw in her identification of the concept of 'the *aforementioned* unmentionable vice' in the interrogation of John/Eleanor Rykener.[67] In fact the early-twentieth-century editor is far more circumspect than the fifteenth-century bishop: Thompson not only omits the crucial testimony of Dey's partners but also notes the omission itself only in Latin, leaving a tantalising glimpse of what William Bentley saw through the 'snekhole'.[68] Bishop Alnwick wants to make sodomy public, Thompson to conceal it again, even in defiance of the old-fashioned scholarly convention that those who can read Latin are not susceptible to corruption.

Stewart argues that the sixteenth-century commissioners seeking hopefully for monastic sodomy use a distinction between same-sex and other-sex acts which is essentially spatial:

> Incontinence [heterosexual] is a literal *transgression* of those walls, a going beyond the bounds of the monastic institution. Sodomy, in sharp contrast, is

literally *embedded* within the institution, dependent on the organisational requirements whereby men share sleeping quarters and are forced into intimate situations with boys.[69]

The situation at New College is comparable: Alnwick cannot, structurally, deal with Dey within the institution. His general injunction ordered, amongst other things, that women should be prevented from entering the college: their exclusion reconstitutes that college as an institution of masculine purity.[70] Dey's punishment is parallel: presumably recognised as at the least a centre of sodomitical activity in the college, he is metaphorically feminised by exclusion from the masculine community. The punishment confirms Lochrie's identification of sodomy as a 'female perversion' that threatens men with feminisation.[71] Alnwick is working with a sense of sexual identity, though one which is in no way explicit: Dey has done this before, is likely to do it again, is incurable, and must be removed for the good of the community: no lesser discipline is likely to change his behaviour. The general injunction does not mention him: he has come, briefly and pragmatically, into visibility and can now disappear again: he is no longer the community's problem. Other moments in the visitation records – such as the complaint that at Markby Priory 'brother John Alforde is wont to have youths lying with him of a night in his bed in the dorter' – suggest the possibility of sexual acts between males, but, as long as no one says the word 'sodomy', there is no particular fuss.[72] Once it has been said, however, its subject, the sodomite, may be identified, and excluded from the company of chaste men. Dinshaw's account of John/Eleanor Rykener suggests that his interrogators had difficulty classifying his crime: prostitution was a female crime and sodomy not in their jurisdiction.[73] They appear to have been mystified by this man who had sex with women as a man, with men as a woman, and it is unclear whether he was ever actually charged with anything. Perhaps the difference is spatial as well as generic: a Rykener can be lost in London's streets more easily than a Dey in Leicester College.

The different ways in which visitation and confessional discourses conceptualise sexual identities can be connected to their different purposes. Handbooks of sins need to be all-encompassing enough to anticipate whichever sins penitents may offer. They belong to a disciplinary discourse which needs to be universally applicable, and can only weaken its usefulness by describing types of sinners as well as types of sin. Visitations, belonging to a largely similar disciplinary discourse, differ in that they are dealing with a named and circumscribed group of individuals, and, in some instances, sorting these individuals into types of sinners is exactly what is necessary to discipline them successfully. Whether a sexual identity comes into visibility is thus dependent on the particular needs of the genre: whether acts constitute identities depends on whether you need them to. Pope Leo IX, writing in a disciplinary context in which the question of incorrigibility did matter, made a further distinction: acts of masturbation, mutual masturbation and interfemoral intercourse were forgivable if occasional acts, but not if habitual practice had allowed them to become an identity. Anal intercourse, however, was so significant that even a single such act would constitute an identity.[74]

The example of medical texts confirms the importance of genre. Joan Cadden argues that 'evidence might indicate that a construct suggesting some dimensions of our notion of "homosexual" was operating in medicine, but not in law or literature. Thus any historical finding, whether of silence or positive evidence, must be evaluated … in the context of the particular cultural site in which it was generated.'[75] There is some evidence that medical texts are best equipped to conceptualise a particular kind of body which desires particular kinds of pleasures. Cadden goes on to discuss a medical text which naturalises some men's capacity for anal pleasure as a physical irregularity which maybe either innate or acquired.[76] Jordan, examining similar material, concludes: 'There is no need to wait for the nineteenth century "homosexual" in order to have same-sex behaviour reduced to a medical identity.'[77] Hildegard of Bingen's account of humoral physical types includes sexual desires and behaviours among the defining features of each type: phlegmatic men are soft-fleshed and effeminate, and 'can be loved in sexual embrace because they like to cohabit with men and with women'.[78] Hildegard's account refuses the heterosexualising grid so often found in such rationalisations, and offers instead a naturalisation of desire for the same: 'in their natural weakness, they love women because women too are weak, and because in her weakness woman is like a boy'. So phlegmatic men, themselves womanlike, desire what is womanlike, which may be women or each other. The neutrality of tone in this example is particularly interesting, coming as it does from an author who in her theological works vehemently denounced all sins of unchastity, and found in same-sex acts an offensive confusion of categories: 'A man who sins with another man as if with a woman sins bitterly against God and against the union with which God united male and female. Hence both in God's sight are polluted, black and wanton, horrible and harmful to God and humanity, and guilty of death.'[79] The contrast between the two indicates that genre may be more significant than authorship: Hildegard does not have a single view of same-sex eroticism, but conforms to generic standards. While theology conceptualises sexual matters under the heading of reproduction, medical discourses also delineate individual bodies' needs for balance.[80]

Conclusion

None of the above examples has found a sexual identity category which consists of a '*conjunction* of sexual morphology and sexual subjectivity', although medieval texts clearly can, when they need to, conceptualise the existence of men who desire other men.[81] The implications of the category are variable: it may imply effeminacy and gender confusion; it may include distinctive personal habits of dress and demeanour; it may be considered innate, habitual or situational; it may imply a particular physicality; it may or may not imply age-differentiated relationships. These characteristics do not necessarily solidify across genres to form a coherent figure of The Medieval Sodomite. Medieval texts find it possible to conceptualise a sexual identity based on object choice, but this is not their primary principle of categorisation.

A brief comparison of some female sexual identities may help to elucidate some of the other main points of medieval sexual identity categorisation. Women's sexual identity categories are far more visible and definable than men's, because they are about women as property. I have argued previously that the holy virgin – she whose desire for God is legible in her public demeanour – constitutes a sexual identity category: she is a coherent figure, with a partic-ular personal history and a particular kind of body.[82] Her opposite, the whore, is equally coherent: she is legally disadvantaged, available to all, and great efforts are made in sumptuary legislation and residency regulations to ensure that 'whore' functioned as a fully saturated category, that every detail of such a woman's persona spoke of her sexual behaviour.[83] Conduct books attempt to do the same for wives and marriageable girls, offering sets of regulations designed to ensure that every detail of their dress and demeanour testifies to the proper regulation of their sexuality.[84] A woman's public appearance has to make it clear to whom she belongs: the virgin to God; the secular woman to husband and father; the prostitute to everyone, so that the precise terms of her availability are immediately legible.

For men, as sexual subjects rather than sexual objects, categorisation by sexuality is less pressing. It is well known that genres such as estates literature typically characterise women by sexual, men by occupational status.[85] Men were identified as virgins only in exceptional cases. For other men certain forms of sexual behaviour may have been considered more appropriate than others are, but they are not the basis of definitions. Male sexual desire might be considered as a temporary or age-specific phase, as it is in the play 'Mundus et Infans', in which the protagonist is named 'Love-Lust-Liking' for the period of adolescence, apparently to abandon sexual desire when he achieves manhood.[86] In this instance sexuality defines his identity, but that identity is not lifelong. For the sodomite, hovering between monstrosity and non-existence, the extent to which he came into visibility may also be the measure of his distance from masculinity. Medieval productions of sexual subjects are not benign: most typically, they call such subjects into being in order to control, expel or obliterate them. If modern histories of sexuality are to evade complicity in such obliterations, they must disavow the innocence of the Middle Ages.

NOTES

I am grateful to Tom Betteridge and Robert Mills for their comments on drafts of this article, and to Catherine Lyon and John McCullough for general encouragement.

1 Jacobus de Voragine, *The Golden Legend: Readings on the Saints*, trans. William Granger Ryan (Princeton: 1993), I, pp. 40–1. See Sherry L. Reames, *The Legenda Aurea: A Re-examination of its Paradoxical History* (Madison, Wisconsin and London: 1985) for further information about this text's history.

2 *Golden Legend*, I, p. 41. Megan McLaughlin's e-mail 'Non-festive Holiday Query' to med-gay list, 19 December 2000, led me to this passage.

3 For just a few of the works dealing with the problems of the medieval category of nature, see James A. Brundage, 'Let Me Count the Ways: Canonists and Theologians Contemplate Coital Positions', *Journal of Medieval History* 10 (1984), p. 88; John Boswell, *Christianity, Social Tolerance, and Homosexuality: Gay People in Western Europe from the Beginning of the Christian Era to the Fourteenth Century* (Chicago: 1980), pp. 11–15; Mark D. Jordan, *The Invention of Sodomy in Christian Theology* (Chicago: 1997), p. 80; Karma Lochrie, *Covert Operations: The Medieval Uses of Secrecy* (Philadelphia: 1999), pp. 207–20.

4 Michel Foucault, *The History of Sexuality: An Introduction*, trans. Robert Hurley (Harmondsworth: 1978), p. 101.

5 *Ibid.*, p. 43.

6 David M. Halperin, 'Forgetting Foucault: Acts, Identities, and the Histories of Sexuality', *Representations* 63 (1998), pp. 93–120, 97, 99.

7 *Ibid.*, p. 109.

8 Eve Kokofsky Sedgwick, *Epistemology of the Closet* (London: 1994), pp. 85–90.

9 Judith Butler, *Bodies that Matter: On the Discursive Limits of 'Sex'* (New York: 1993), p. 22.

10 Augustine of Hippo, *The City of God Against the Pagans*, 7 vols, trans. George E. McCracken, Philip Levine, William M. Green, Loeb Classical Library (London: 1966), Book 13, ch. 13.

11 Jacqueline Murray, 'Mystical Castration: Some Reflections on Peter Abelard, Hugh of Lincoln and Sexual Control', in Murray, ed., *Conflicted Identities and Multiple Masculinities: Men in the Medieval West* (New York: 1999), pp. 73–91.

12 Sedgwick, 1994, p. 47. See also Karma Lochrie, 'Don't Ask, Don't Tell: Murderous Plots and Medieval Secrets', in Louise Fradenburg and Carla Freccero, eds, *Premodern Sexualities* (New York: 1996), pp. 137–52.

13 Robert Shephard, 'Sexual Rumours in English Politics: The Cases of Elizabeth I and James I', in Jacqueline Murray and Konrad Eisenbichler, eds, *Desire and Discipline: Sex and Sexuality in the Premodern West* (Toronto: 1996), pp. 101–22; Joseph Cady, 'The "Masculine Love" of the "Princes of Sodom" "Practising the Art of Ganymede" at Henry III's Court: The Homosexuality of Henry III and his *Mignons* in Pierre de L'Estoile's *Mémoires-Journaux*' in the same, pp. 123–54.

14 Michael B. Young, *King James and the History of Homosexuality* (New York: 1999), p. 4.

15 Carolyn Dinshaw, *Getting Medieval: Sexualities and Communities, Pre- and Postmodern* (Durham, North Carolina: 1999), p. 195.

16 W. C. Sellar and R. J. Yeatman, *1066 and All That* (London: 1930), p. 30; Paul Freedman and Gabrielle M. Spiegel, 'Medievalisms Old and New: The Rediscovery of Alterity in North American Medieval Studies', *American Historical Review* 103 (1998), pp. 677–704.

17 See, amongst others, David Aers, 'A Whisper in the Ear of Early Modernists: or, Reflections on Literary Critics Writing "the History of the Subject"', in Aers, ed., *Culture and History*

1350–1600: Essays on English Communities, Identities and Writing (Brighton: 1992), pp. 177–
202; Nancy F. Partner, 'Did Mystics Have Sex?', in Murray and Eisenbichler, 1996,
pp. 296–311; Lee Patterson, 'On the Margin: Postmodernism, Ironic History and Medieval
Studies', *Speculum* 65 (1990), pp. 87–108.

18 Foucault, 1978, p. 58.

19 See Ross Balzaretti, 'Michael Foucault, Homosexuality and the Middle Ages', *Renaissance and
Modern Studies* 37 (1994), pp. 1–12; Carolyn Dinshaw, 'Getting Medieval: *Pulp Fiction,
Gawain, and Foucault*', in Dolores Warwick Frese and Katherine O'Brien O'Keefe, eds, *The
Book and the Body* (Notre Dame: 1997), pp. 116–63, 136–49; Karma Lochrie, 'Desiring Fou-
cault', *Journal of Medieval and Early Modern Studies* 27 (1997), pp. 3–16, for discussions of the
ambiguities of Foucault's medievalisms.

20 Jacqueline Murray, 'Introduction', in Murray and Eisenbichler, eds, 1996, pp. ix–xxviii,
xii–xiii.

21 Alan Stewart, *Close Readers: Humanism and Sodomy in Early Modern England* (Princeton: 1997),
p. xxii.

22 Stewart, 1997, p. xxvi; John H. Fisher, 'A Language Policy for Lancastrian England', in
Daniel J. Pinti, ed., *Writing After Chaucer: Essential Readings in Chaucer and the Fifteenth Century*
(New York: 1998), pp. 81–99. I am not arguing with Stewart's analysis as such, only with
its chronological specificity.

23 Stewart, 1997, p. 167.

24 The literature on medieval sexual identities, especially transgressive ones, is large and
expanding at a considerable rate: to review it in detail is impossible here. Vern L. Bullough
and James A. Brundage, eds, *Handbook of Medieval Sexuality* (New York: 1996), reviews the
field at the time of writing: however, it is developing rapidly. As well as those cited, the history of recent criticism on Chaucer's Pardoner can be read as a distillation of medievalists
doing sexuality.

25 Boswell, 1980, pp. 41–3; see also Boswell, 'Categories, Experience and Sexuality', in
Edward Stein, ed., *Forms of Desire: Sexual Orientation and the Social Constructionist Controversy*
(New York: 1990), pp. 133–73.

26 Boswell, 1980, p. 43.

27 Allen J. Frantzen, *Before the Closet: Same-sex Love from* Beowulf *to* Angels in America (Chicago:
1998), p. 4.

28 Frantzen, 1998, p. 179.

29 Lochrie, 1999, p. 201.

30 Lochrie, 1999, pp. 15–24, criticises Foucault for nostalgia and reductionism; Frantzen,
1998, pp. 7–13 discusses his historical shortcomings.

31 Simon Gaunt, 'Straight Minds/"Queer" Wishes in Old French Hagiography: *La vie de Sainte
Euphrosine*', *GLQ: A Journal of Lesbian and Gay Studies* 1 (1995), pp. 439–57, 441; Carolyn Dinshaw, 'Chaucer's Queer Touches/a Queer Touches Chaucer', *Exemplaria* 7 (1995), pp. 76–92.

32 Dinshaw, 1999, pp. 109–10; for more on this recently discovered text see David Lorenzo
Boyd and Ruth M. Karras, 'The Interrogation of a Male Transvestite Prostitute in Fourteenth
Century London', *GLQ: A Journal of Lesbian and Gay Studies* 1 (1995), pp. 459–65; Boyd and
Karras, '"Ut cum muliere": A Male Transvestite Prostitute in Fourteenth Century London',
in Fradenburg and Freccero, eds, 1996, pp. 99–116.

33 Simon Gaunt, *Genre and Gender in Medieval French Literature* (Cambridge: 1995), pp. 80–3.

34 Jordan, 1997, p. 163.

35 Jordan, 1997, p. 156; Lochrie, 1999, pp. 179–92; Frantzen, 1998, p. 214.

36 Frantzen, 1998, p. 174.

37 Dinshaw, 1999, pp. 38–9.

38 Jordan, 1997, p. 176.

39 *The Lais of Marie de France*, trans. Glyn S. Burgess and Keith Busby (London: 1986), p. 76.

40 See A. C. Spearing, *The Medieval Poet as Voyeur: Looking and Listening in Medieval Love
Narratives* (Cambridge: 1993), pp. 106–14, for a discussion of this poem as masculine fantasy.

41 A. J. Bliss, ed., *Sir Launfal* (London and Edinburgh: 1960), p. 67.

42 *Ibid.*, p. 72. Middle English characters have been modernised in this and other Middle English quotations.

43 Kathleen Coyne Kelly, 'Malory's Body Chivalric', *Arthuriana* 6 (1996), p. 62.

44 Bliss, 1960, p. 56.

45 *Ibid.*, p. 77.

46 Gaunt, 1995, pp. 71, 85.

47 *OED*.

48 James A. Brundage, 'Prostitution in the Medieval Canon Law', in Judith M. Bennett *et al.*, eds, *Sisters and Workers in the Middle Ages* (Chicago: 1989), pp. 79–99, 95.

49 For queer readings of mystical texts see: Karma Lochrie, 'Mystical Acts, Queer Tendencies', in Lochrie, Peggy McCracken and James A. Schultz, eds, *Constructing Medieval Sxuality* (Minneapolis: 1997), pp. 180–200; Susannah Mary Chewning, 'The Paradox of Virginity within the Anchoritic Tradition: The Masculine Gaze and the Feminine Body in the *Wohunge* Group', in Cindy L. Carlson and Angela Jane Weisl, eds, *Constructions of Widowhood and Virginity in the Middle Ages* (New York: 1999), pp. 113–34; Sarah Salih, 'Queering *Sponsalia Christi*: Virginity, Gender and Desire in the Early Middle English Anchoritic Texts', *New Medieval Literatures* 5 (forthcoming); Robert Mills, 'Ecce Homo', in Samantha J. E. Riches and Sarah Salih, eds, *Gender and Holiness: Men, Women and Saints in Late Medieval Europe* (London: 2002), pp. 152–73.

50 Michel Foucault and Richard Sennett, 'Sexuality and Solitude', *Humanities Review* 1 (1982), pp. 10–11.

51 Sanford Brown Meech and Hope Emily Allen, eds, *The Book of Margery Kempe*, EETS o.s. 212 (Oxford: 1940), p. 38.

52 Jerry Root, *'Space to Speke': The Confessional Subject in Medieval Literature* (New York: 1997), p. 3.

53 W. Nelson Francis, ed., *The Book of Vices and Virtues*, EETS o.s. 217 (London: 1942), p. 4.

54 *Ibid.*, p. 177.

55 *Ibid.*, pp. 43–4.

56 *Ibid.*, pp. 44–6.

57 *Ibid.*, p. 46.

58 *Ibid.*, p. 244.

59 Frederick J. Furnivall, ed., *Robert of Brunne's 'Handlyng Synne'*, EETS o.s. 119 (London: 1901), pp. 58–73, 234–8.

60 *Ibid.*, p. 281.

61 *Ibid.*, pp. 131, 132, 257

62 Lochrie, 1999, p. 41.

63 Lesley Smith, 'William of Auvergne and Confession', in Peter Biller and A. J. Minnis, eds, *Handling Sin: Confession in the Middle Ages* (Woodbridge: 1998), pp. 95–107, 104.

64 Furnivall, 1901, p. 381.

65 A. Hamilton Thompson, ed., *Visitations of Religious Houses in the Diocese of Lincoln Vol. II: Records of Visitations held by William Alnwick, Bishop of Lincoln 1436–1449 Part 1* (London: 1919), p. 188.

66 *Ibid.*, pp. 188–9.

67 *Ibid.*, p. 197; Dinshaw, 1999, p. 105.

68 Thompson, 1919, p. 197.

69 Stewart, 1997, p. 51.

70 Thompson, 1919, p. 201.

71 Lochrie, 1999, p. 185.

72 A. Hamilton Thompson, ed., *Visitations of Religious Houses in the Diocese of Lincoln Vol. III: Records of Visitations held by William Alnwick, Bishop of Lincoln 1436–1449 Part 2* (Oxford: 1927), p. 222.

73 Dinshaw, 1999, pp. 103–4.

74 Peter Damian, *Book of Gomorrah: An Eleventh-century Treatise Against Clerical Homosexual Prac-tices*, trans. Pierre J. Payer (Waterloo, Ontario: 1982), p. 96.

75 Joan Cadden, 'Sciences/Silences: The Natures and Languages of "Sodomy" in Peter of Abano's *Problemata* Commentary', in Lochrie, McCracken and Schultz, eds, 1997, pp. 40–57, 41–2.

76 *Ibid.*, p. 46.

77 Jordan, 1997, p. 123.

78 Hildegard of Bingen, *On Natural Philosophy and Medicine: Selections from Cause et cure*, trans. Margret Berger (Cambridge: 1999), p. 61.

79 Hildegard of Bingen, *Scivias*, trans. Columba Hart and Jane Bishop (New York: 1990), Book 2, Vision 6, Part 78.

80 Cadden, 1997, pp. 44–5.

81 Halperin, 1998, p.108. Emphasis in original.

82 Sarah Salih, *Versions of Virginity in Late Medieval England* (Cambridge: 2001).

83 Ruth Mazo Karras, *Common Women: Prostitution and Sexuality in Medieval England* (Oxford: 1996), pp. 14–24.

84 On conduct books see Felicity Riddy, 'Mother Knows Best: Reading Social Change in a Courtesy Text', *Speculum* 71 (1996), pp. 66–86; Claire Sponsler, *Drama and Resistance: Bodies, Goods and Theatricality in Late Medieval England* (Minneapolis: 1997), pp. 50–74; Bar-bara A. Hanawalt, 'At the Margins of Women's Space in Medieval Europe', in Hanawalt, *'Of Good and Ill Repute': Gender and Social Control in Medieval England* (Oxford: 1998), pp. 70–87; Kim M. Phillips, 'Bodily Walls, Windows and Doors: The Politics of Gesture in Late Fif-teenth-century English Books for Women', in Jocelyn Wogan-Browne *et al.*, eds, *Medieval Women: Texts and Contexts in Late Medieval Britain: Essays for Felicity Riddy* (Turnhout: 2000), pp. 185–98.

85 Jill Mann, *Chaucer and Medieval Estates Satire: The Literature of Social Classes and the General Prologue to the Canterbury Tales* (Cambridge: 1973), p. 121.

86 G. A. Lester, ed., *Three Late Medieval Morality Plays* (London: 1981), p. 117.

8

Boys' buttocks revisited: James VI and the myth of the sovereign schoolmaster

ALAN STEWART[1]

Among prominent early modern men James VI of Scotland is perhaps most readily claimed today as homoerotically invested. His series of intimate relationships with male favourites, passionately attested to in private letters and physically expressed in public, has left recent scholars certain that King James is that rare breed, the Renaissance homosexual: James 'did have sex with his male favourites, and it is nonsense to deny it', as one critic recently insisted.[2] Such assertions are of course unverifiable, but this chapter will interrogate James's recorded responses to a site of great sodomitical anxiety – the early modern schoolroom. By examining James's educational experience, I explore how James reacted against that experience to forge a new way of considering his relationship to his country, his counsellors and his son.

Sodomitical anxiety in the early modern schoolroom

In 1669 a *Children's Petition* was published, a 'Modest Remonstrance' opposing 'that intolerable grievance our Youth lie under, in the accustomed severities of the school discipline of this Nation'.[3] According to a later source, the papers for this book were brought to the publisher Roger LeStrange 'by a Knight of his Acquaintance, and the Book was Presented by a Lively Boy (with a Servant of that Knight attending him) to the Speaker, and to several Members of the House, as a Petitition in behalf of the Children of this Nation'.[4] The 'Children' allege that 'our sufferings are of that nature as makes our Schools to be not meerly houses of Correction, but of Prostitution, in this vile way of castigation in use, wherein our secret parts, which are by nature shameful, and not to be uncovered, must be the Anvil exposed to the immodest eyes, and filthy blows of the smiter';[5] the passage ends with Greek words relating to pederasty and a Latin citation of the scriptural episode where the men of Sodom call on Lot's guests to come outside so that they may know them. The 'Children' call on the gentlemen in Parliament, some of whom 'are not so old as to forget what was unhandsome',[6] to put an end to this abuse. The petition failed to reach Parliament, but a 1698 pamphlet entitled *Lex Forcia* (an allusion to the punitive Roman Forcian law) attempted to revive the debate thirty years later, this time by stressing the vulnerability of the flogger to dangerous accusations: 'those that keep Boys and Girls to Attend them, or be Taught by them, [are warned] to forbear this Punishment after they come to their Teens, seeing Casuists who occasionally touch on such things, must and cannot but Brand it for a Spice, or Degree, of this Enormity, which is therefore to be Abandoned by Modest Persons.' The pamphlet signs off resignedly, saying 'If the Nation will not take the Warning, but will be Wicked, and a Sodom, let it be Wicked still.'[7]

With their allusions to prostitution, 'secret parts' and the shame provoked by their exposure, these late-seventeenth-century texts are quite explicit about the sexual nature of beating – indeed the author of *Lex Forcia* links the beating of schoolboys to what he claims is a recent vogue for flagellation in adult sexual relations.[8] In the use of the term 'Enormity' and the repeated references to Sodom, they also reveal the sodomitical nature of beating. Anxiety about the beating schoolmaster is a trope of educational literature from at least Quintilian onwards, and was a particular concern for sixteenth-century humanist writers. But whereas the seventeenth-century texts are quite blatant in stressing sodomitical anxiety, provoked perhaps by the need to articulate strongly the cause for the proposed political reforms, earlier texts are at once less explicit and more complex. In this chapter I aim to explore more closely these earlier texts, and to demonstrate that sodomitical anxiety is not merely a literal fear of sexual assault on the schoolboy by the schoolmaster but a much more nuanced understanding of the place of the pedagogue – and of humanist pedagogy in general – in a rapidly changing society.

Several critics have turned over the past few years to the physical conditions of early modern education for boys.[9] Among other issues they have focused on the place of beating in the educational curriculum, embedded to the extent that the initiation ceremonies for the Master of Grammar at both Cambridge and Oxford required the graduand to prove his grammatical worth by giving a display of his beating hand.[10] There are innumerable accounts of vicious corporal punishment in early modern humanist tracts: Desiderius Erasmus of Rotterdam, in his *De pueris instituendis* (1512), for example, paints a picture of a four-year-old child confronted by 'an unknowen scholemaster, rude of manners, not verye sober, and sometyme not well in hys wytte, often lunatike, or havynge the fallyng sycknes, or frenche pockes'. The schoolhouse is 'a tormentyngge place: nothynge is hearde there beside the slappynge upon the hande, beside yorkynge of roddes, besyde howlynge and sobbinge and cruell threatnynges'. He recalls how he witnessed a boy beaten by a monitor on the command of his master until he was 'almost in a sounde': the master justifies it on the ground that the boy 'must be made lowe' ('humiliandus'). On another occasion a boy is forced to swallow excrement stuffed into his mouth, and is then hanged up naked and beaten. A third episode concerns a young gentleman who arrives at university to learn the liberal sciences: he is daubed with and forced to swallow urine, vinegar and salt; finally he is hoisted up and his back smashed into a wall. Erasmus inscribes himself in this abuse of pedagogical power: he claims to have been beaten quite arbitrarily by a master at the age of fourteen.[11]

Such images of violent pedagogy have naturally appealed to Renaissance scholars influenced by Michel Foucault's analysis of techniques of discipline. Richard Halpern, for example, argues that 'the ideological function of Tudor schooling must ... be understood to include not only the transmission of doctrine or governing representations, but also the imposition of certain productive or disciplinary practices. The schools hammered in ideological content and also laid down economics of recreation and labor, punishment and reward. They thus participated in the disciplinary "accumulation of men" which, according to Foucault, complemented, and reinforced the accumulation of capital.' This 'hammering in' of ideological content took place literally on schoolboys' bodies.[12]

In Halpern's analysis 'the Tudor pedagogue often exercised a sovereign, sometimes unpredictable form of violence'. These tortures, he argues, 'clearly worked as a political ritual, in which the pedagogue both assumed and reinforced the sovereign authority of the monarch or magistrate'.[13] He quotes the educationalist Richard Mulcaster, headmaster of both Merchant Taylors' and St Paul's Schools (1561–86 and 1596–1608, respectively): 'the *rod* may no more be spared in schooles, then the *sworde* may in the *Princes* hand. By the *rod* I mean *correction* and *awe*'.[14] Mulcaster, as Halpern shows, saw beating as 'a means of testing the social and political dispositions of students'.[15] To his own question 'what wit is fittest for learning in a monarchie', Mulcaster answers: 'That child ... is like to prove in further yeares, the fittest subiect for learning in a *monarchie*, which in his tender age sheweth himselfe obedient to scholeorders, and eitheir will not lightly offend, or if he do, will take his punishment gently: without either much repyning, or great stomacking.'[16]

To take Mulcaster's verdict as typical would be misleading: he was, as Halpern readily admits, 'bucking the general trend'.[17] While Mulcaster was known to be (in Thomas Fuller's words) '*Plagosus Orbilius*',[18] 'somewhat too severe, and given to insult too much over children that he taught'[19] (a charge also levelled at Eton's Nicholas Udall and Westminster's Dr Richard Busby),[20] many sixteenth-century educational writers wrote passionately against the corporal punishment of boys. Halpern concedes, then, that the situation is more complex than it at first appears: 'the sixteenth century simultaneously witnessed both an intensification of physical punishment in schools *and* the humanist alternative of persuasion'.[21] Recent work by Rebecca Bushnell and Mary Thomas Crane has attempted to explain this *aporia*.[22] Bushnell argues that 'the real life of the early modern classroom complicated' the scenario as described by Mulcaster and Halpern: 'Although the master might have imagined himself as a monarch, it was unlikely that his students, their parents, or the larger community recognized his absolute rule ... Teachers' complaints offer ample evidence of their low social status, misrule was common in the classroom, and masters were still mocked in poems and plays.'[23] Crane, less accepting of the humanists' version of events, proposes that humanist educators mediated between old and new cultural codes by replacing an aristocratic martial training with a non-violent humanist curriculum and then by including in that curriculum 'the actual violence of corporal punishment and the metaphoric violence of a coercive cultural code as substitutes for the old displays of violence as power ... an internalization of symbolic violence designed to replace the openly violent codes of feudalism' so that the humanist programme will appear equivalent to the aristocratic codes it seeks to replace.[24] While providing nuanced readings of beating as a politicised practice, none of these commentators explores its sexual or sodomitical coding. In what follows I shall suggest that the contradictions laid bare in these analyses have their roots not merely in the relationship between state and subject, nor in the claimed humanist persuasive alternative to its predecessor in the education market, but in an unresolved contradiction between education and family, and specifically in the uneasy transaction between father and schoolmaster.

In his *The Scholemaster* (published in 1570) Roger Ascham quotes Sir Richard Sackvile as revealing that he was subjected to 'a fond Scholemaster' who 'before I was fullie fourtene yeare olde, drave me so, with feare of beating, from all love of learninge, as nowe, when I know, what difference it is, to have learninge, and to have litle, or none at all, I feele it my greatest greife, and finde it my greatest hurte, that ever came to me, that it was my so ill chance, to light upon so lewde a Scholemaster'.[25] A century later, Marchamont Nedham claimed that 'the great indiscretion and intemperance of Masters in that [beating], hath brought a very great contempt and hatred upon the Profession it self; and not to speak of the ill use some have made of it to lewdness (of which Instances are not wanting, but that they are odious) it being a kinde of uncovering of nakedness'.[26] As Jeffrey Masten has astutely pointed out, 'lewd' here is a keyword, which 'recurs with striking (as it were) frequency' in humanist discussions of beating. Whereas Nedham's 'lewdness' is helpfully self-glossed as simply an 'odious' 'uncovering of nakedness', Ascham's is less straightforward. 'Which of the following concurrently available meanings', Masten asks, 'apply to Ascham's "lewde" beating schoolmaster: lay (not clerical); common, vulgar, base; unlearned; wicked; lascivious?' The answer, of course, is that Ascham's 'lewde' schoolmaster might be simultaneously lay, common, vulgar, base, unlearned, wicked, *and* lascivious: that his lasciviousness is part of a nexus of qualities associated with the demonised schoolmaster. But since, 'as the *OED* points out, "lascivious" is the only meaning that eventually survives',[27] Nedham, a century later, points to a more narrowly sexual lewdness. How might this apparent shift help us to understand the sodomitical component of the sixteenth-century beating schoolmaster?

George Buchanan, royal tutor and beater

To investigate this I turn to another beating schoolmaster: the famed humanist scholar George Buchanan, who spent his final years as tutor to the young king of Scots, James VI. James VI's education has recently been analysed by Rebecca Bushnell in her study of humanist pedagogy, *A Culture of Teaching*. Buchanan's schoolroom, she notes, was 'a place for oppositional thinking and politics at the same time that it was meant to fashion a king': Buchanan blithely alternated his duties as tutor with prolific writing that sought to demonise James's mother, Mary Queen of Scots, and to provide a history of Scotland that gave great agency to the aristocracy at the expense of the royal family. Beyond the obvious interpersonal implications of this scenario for Buchanan and James, its contradictions and tensions, Bushnell argues, 'bring into relief the paradoxes underpinning the image of the humanist teacher as it developed in England in the sixteenth century', the teacher supposedly the sovereign of the schoolroom, but in reality socially undervalued and underpaid. As a result, 'the master was the prince if his authority was accepted as socially legitimate. If not accepted he became the tyrant. In that case the violence of corporal punishment, rather than reinforcing absolutism, disabled its premise by rendering it illegitimate.'[28]

James's tutors, Buchanan and Peter Young, 'his pedagogues for his instruction in literature and religion',[29] were appointed perhaps in 1569, and certainly by 1570, when James was three or four years old;[30] the king shared his schoolroom with at least three other boys, the young earl of Mar (son of his guardian), his cousin Sir William Murray, Lord Invertyle, and Walter Stewart, Lord Blantyre. We know a good deal about James's education, thanks to a manuscript in the British Library (Additional Ms. 34, 275) that, in its account of the staggered acquisition of books, details James's curriculum, at heart a basic (if somewhat outdated) classical humanist education, but heavier than most in Greek, history and politics.[31] In the margins of the manuscript are recorded the young James's witticisms – many of them turning on multilingual wordplay or punning – dotingly transcribed by Peter Young, who also left a short account of James's daily regime.[32]

The young king's education also gave rise to a significant number of heavily loaded anecdotes, several of which found their way into George Mackenzie's 1722 life of Buchanan, passed on, he claimed, from the Earl of Cromarty, who heard them from his grandfather, Lord Invertyle, one of James's fellow scholars.[33] These stories have not helped Buchanan's reputation: they usually involve his pupil getting hurt, and he has come down to posterity as an irritable, irascible and potentially violent schoolmaster. Even at the time, Sir James Melville commented that, in his teaching methods, 'Mester George was a stoik philosopher, and loked not far before the hand';[34] James himself is said to have referred to the 'violence of his humour and heat of his spirit',[35] and Francis Osborn famously records another verdict: 'King *James* used to say of a Person in high place about him, that *he ever trembled at his approach, it minded him so of his Pedagogue.*'[36] Other sovereigns had their 'whipping boy' – the supposed surrogate for the kingly buttocks who absorbed the wrath of their master.[37] While Peter Young ('gentiller and laith till offend the kyng at ony tyme', according to Melville) allegedly allowed James a whipping boy, the anecdotes concerning Buchanan and James emphatically dismiss such a possibility.[38] One story tells of how his fellow pupil, the Master of Erskine, 'having a tame Sparrow, the King would needs have the Sparrow from him, and he refusing to give it, they fell a struggling about it, and in the Scuffle the Sparrow was killed, upon which the Master of *Erskine* fell a crying, *Buchanan* being informed of the Matter, gave the King a Box on the Ear, and told him, *That what he had done, was like a true Bird of the bloody Nest of which he was come.*'[39] On one level, a typical boys' scuffle, brought to a halt by the the schoolmaster's intervention. But what does it mean that Buchanan can give the king a box on the ear, and refer to his family – the royal family – as 'the bloody nest'?

To pursue this we need to consider the transactions that bring about the boy's education. The notion of education as a contractual arrangement between father and schoolmaster is commonplace in humanist writings: in Juan Luis Vives's *Linguae latinae excitatio* (1539) a father hands his son over to the schoolmaster Philoponus, saying 'I bring you this boy of mine to make of him a man from the beast.' Philoponus replies, 'This shall be my earnest endeavour. He shall become a man from a beast, a fruitful and good creature out of a useless one.' A social contract is struck, as the father witnesses: 'We share the responsibility then; you to instruct zealously, I to recompense your labour richly.'[40] But corporal punishment by the schoolmaster – or in other words, power over the body of another man's son – was an ill-defined grey area, as even Richard Mulcaster realised. Mulcaster's comments, quoted above, working the analogy between schoolmaster and sovereign, rod and sword, in fact come in the midst of a discussion of a remedy 'to helpe schoole *inconveniences*': namely, 'to set downe the schoole *ordinaunces* betwene the maister, and his scholers in a publicke place, where they may easily be seene & red'. The intended audience of these ordinances is the parent; the display is intended

> to leave as litle uncertaine or untoucht, which the parent ought to know, and whereupon misliking may arise, as is possible. For if at the first entry the parent condiscend, to those orders, which he seeth, so that he cannot afterward plead either ignorance, or disallowing, he is not to take offence, if his childe be forced unto them, when he will not follow, according to that fourme, which he himselfe did confirme by his owne consent.[41]

These ordinances should cover such matters as 'the *maner* of teaching, the ascent in fourmes, the *times* of admission, the *prevention* to have formes equall, the *bookes* for learning' and so on; 'But', Mulcaster insists, 'he must cheifly touch what *punishment* he will use, and how much, for every kinde of fault, that shall seeme punishable by the *rod*'.[42]

In his insistence on a pre-agreed contract between schoolmaster and parent about beating, Mulcaster acknowledges the growing power of parents in the question of the physical disciplining of students. As Halpern argues, 'Whereas medieval schoolteachers were generally clerics supported by the church, their Renaissance succesors were frequently dependent on tuition and fees paid by parents and gifts given by them, and thus schoolmasters were accountable to them.'[43] The question of social rank and wealth is important here: Halpern opposes Lawrence Stone's contention that corporal punishment in schools was 'a standard practice applied to rich and poor, young and old, regardless of rank', arguing that 'though true', this line 'obscures probable differences in the severity and frequency of such punishment',[44] citing John Brinsley who in 1612 mentions 'that extreame sharpnes used ordinarily in schools amongst the poore children'. This would seem to suggest, as Halpern deduces, that 'wealthier children enjoyed the benefits of at least relative leniency'.[45] But if 'the pedagogue both assumed and reinforced the sovereign authority of the monarch or magistrate', as Halpern puts it, what happens when the student supposedly *under* that pedagogue actually is a monarch with sovereign authority?

In his discussion of Buchanan's vexed relations with James, Mackenzie's longest anecdote is perhaps the most revealing:

> The King one Day having got prescribed him for his Theme, the History of the Conspiracy at *Lauder* Bridge in King *James* the III. Time, where *Archibald* Earl of *Angus* obtain'd the Name of *Bell the Cat*, from his telling them the Fable of some Rats that had combin'd against a Cat, whom they resolved to seize, and to tye a Bell about his Neck, to warn them for the future, by the ringing of that Bell of their Danger, but as they were going to put their Project in Execution, one of the old Rats asked which of which of them would be the first that would seize upon the Cat? This Question put them all in a profound Silence, as it did likewise the

Conspirators, which the Earl perceiving, told them that he would *Bell the Cat*. The King having I say got this for his theme, as he was diverting himself after Dinner with the Master of *Erskine*, the Earl of *Mar*'s eldest Son, *Buchanan* desired the King to hold his Peace, for he disturbed him in his Reading, the King taking no notice of this, he reprov'd him for a second Time, and told, *That if he did not hold his Peace, he would whip his Breech*, the King answered, *That he would gladly see who would Bell the Cat*. Upon this, in a Passion *Buchanan* throws the Book from him, and whips the King severely, the old Countess of *Mar* who had her Apartment near them, hearing the King cry, run to him, and taking him up in her Arms, asked what the Matter was? The King told her, that the Master (for so *Buchanan* was called) had whipt him, *She asked how he durst put his Hand on the Lord's Anointed?* To which he made this unmannerly Reply, *Madam, I have whipt his Ar —, you may kiss it if you please*.[46]

Mackenzie's story, like so many anecdotes, takes some further unpacking (I am assuming for my present purposes that, even if this tale is not 'genuine', it can speak to us about perceived pedagogical relations).[47] The much-used fable – older than its application here – is of the mice or rats who decide to receive advance warning of the approach of their arch-enemy, the cat, by placing a bell around the cat's neck.[48] The point of this fable is: it's a great idea, but what rat would be brave or foolhardy enough to 'bell the cat'? So when Buchanan says he will whip the king's breech, James retorts by daring him to do it – it's a great plan to whip the king's breech, but is Buchanan brave enough to bell the cat? Sadly for James he is. As Bushnell notes, the anecdote plays out the battle between Buchanan and James 'explicitly in terms of the language of sovereignty, tyranny and rebellion'. The fable has been set for James at a precise historical moment: the 'Lauder crisis' of 1482, when the nobles were conferring secretly in Lauder Kirk about how to remove the royal favourites from around James III. Archibald Earl of Angus allegedly leapt up and said, 'I sal bell the cat', gaining himself a long-standing nickname. The story reveals how a sovereign's supposedly absolute rule – and the sway of his unsuitable favourites, an obsession of Buchanan's – can be successfully challenged. For Buchanan, as Jenny Wormald has observed, 'The rebellion of 1488 could be transformed into a great constitutional act. Even more important, so could the events of 1567 [the forced abdication of Mary Queen of Scots, which resulted in James's accession].'[49] But if Buchanan's aim was to force an identification between James VI and his ancestor James III (one of Buchanan's most despised kings of Scots), he failed: 'Perversely, the child James reversed the equation so that the schoolmaster became the tyrant and the child-king the rebel.' This reversal, however, failed to turn the tables completely, as Bushnell notes: 'James, in identifying himself with the conspirator Archibald, at once undermined his own authority while challenging his tutor's. Buchanan was quick to reestablish his mastery, but through exactly the kind of eruption of violence which he would condemn in a king.'[50]

Over Bushnell's analysis I would lay another reading. In the 'belling the cat' anecdote, the struggle for James's authority – is he God's anointed, is he subject to the schoolmaster? – is physically played out on his buttocks: you may kiss his arse, I shall whip it. Simultaneously and importantly, it is played out between the schoolmaster and Annabella Erskine, the old Countess of Mar, wife of James's guardian. The Countess here is clearly a surrogate mother: she comes running when she hears 'her' child cry, and 'tak[es] him up in her Arms', physically comforting him and challenging the authority of the schoolmaster. In making this challenge, I shall argue, the Countess fulfils the function of the mother in a familiar triangulation of father–mother–schoolmaster competing for the schoolboy.

James VI's rites of passage

Implicit in the father–schoolmaster transaction is an assumed link between education and the 'manning' of the boy: education starts (usually around the age of seven) when the boy is taken away from women and placed in male company. Beating is an integral part of this education, as Walter Ong discusses in his influential 1959 essay 'Latin Language Study as a Renaissance Puberty Rite'. Ong argues that 'the Renaissance teaching of Latin involved a survival, or an echo, devious and vague but unmistakably real, of what anthropologists, treating of more primitive peoples, call puberty rites'. Borrowing Arnold van Gennep's notion of *rites de passage*, Ong outlines the process whereby the male child learns Latin, removed from his family and placed in an all-male didactic environment (what van Gennep calls a 'marginal' environment). Through Latin study the boy inculcates 'corage', but flogging is an integral part of this process: 'the boy must acknowledge the equation of learning and flogging, and thereby face courageously into learning as into an initiation, something of itself taxing and fearsome'.[51]

This rites of passage is clearly staged by and for men. As Pierre Bourdieu observes in his critique of *Rites de passage*, van Gennep's theory conceals one of the rites' essential effects, 'namely that of separating those who have undergone it, not from those who have not yet undergone it, but from those who will not undergo it in any sense, and thereby instituting a lasting difference between those to whom the rite pertains and those to whom it does not pertain'.[52] 'Those who will not undergo it in any sense' are women, and a result of this is the assumed opposition, not of schoolmaster to parent but of schoolmaster to *mother*, which becomes a constant trope in early modern writings. One early

Tudor schoolbook admonishes a 'wanton boy': 'Thoughte *thu* haue ben brought vp here afore *with* thi mother wantonly, yet y co*n*sell the to put owt of thi mynd *tha*t wantones here, for and if *thu* do not *thu* shall sa here-after *that thu* hast a grett caus to co*m*playn.' The mother disrupts the boy's attendance at school, as he reveals: 'I wakydd a grett part of *thi*s nyght *and* abowte day I begane to fall fast *and* heuy a-slepe, *and* so thawghe the owre *that* was a-powntyd me to to go to scole in was cum*m*e, yet my mother co*m*mandyd *that* ther shuld no noyse be mayd *and* wold not let me be callyd vp. Therfor my mother is the cause of my late co*m*yng.'[53] A manuscript written by a master of grammar at Magdalen School in the last years of the fifteenth century, develops this opposition at length. One section elaborates on how 'All the richest menys Children everywher be loste [corrupted] nowaadais in ther youghe at home'. It particularly deplores the mother, portraying her as mollycoddling: 'The mother must have them [children] to play withall stede of puppetes [dolls], as children were borne to japes and tryfullys. thei bolde them both in worde and dede to do what thei liste, and with wantonnes and sufferance shamfully they renne on the hede [headlong].' In particular, the manuscript reveals how the beating of the boy was differently received by the boy's father and mother:

> I wyll make youe an example by a cosyn of myne that [was sent] to his absey [ABC, primary school] hereby at the next dore, and if he come wepynge after his maister hath charede away the flees from his skynne, anone his mother loketh onn his buttockys yf the stryppys be a-sen. And the stryppys appere, she wepyth and waileth and fareth as she were made. then she complayneth of the cruelte of techers, saynge she hade lever [rather] se hire childe were fair buriede than so to be intretide. These wordes thei spake and suche other infinite, and other while for the childrenys sake ther begynneth afray betwixte the goode mann and his wyffe, for what he commaundeth, she forbyddeth. And thus in processe of tyme, when thei cum to age, thei waxe bolde to do all myschevousness, settynge litell to do the greatest shame that can be.[54]

Read through this model, the experience undergone by James is notably uneasy. In James's case there is no decisive rites of passage into an Ongian marginal male world of Latin and beating. James's education starts too early, at the age of four, when he is still, muddlingly, in the care of women; it may well be that the Countess presides over his general well-being long after his seventh birthday (and hence her conflict with Buchanan). Later, in his *Basilikon Doron*, James exhorts his eldest son Henry to 'honoure ... thame that are in loco parentum unto you, sicc as youre gouernouris & upbringaires & youre præceptouris', placing the maternal surrogates ('upbringaires') alongside the male pedagogues ('præceptoris').[55] Whereas, as Vives and Erasmus writes, the boy's education is usually transacted between father and schoolmaster, James's father is murdered when the prince is eight months old: his surrogate father, the Earl of Mar, died in 1572 when James was just five. James, as he himself writes, was 'alone, without father or mother, brother or sister, king of this realm and heir apparent of England' – a state he describes, tellingly, as 'my nakedness', echoing the language of the de-breeched, beaten boys of *The Children's Petition*.[56] This strengthens the struggle between schoolmaster and (surrogate) mother: Sir James Melville records that 'my Lady Mar was wyse and schairp, and held the King in great aw [i.e. the king was in awe of her]; and sa did Mester George Buchwhennen'.[57] Even in Melville's prose James is held taut between the mother and the master.

Buchanan plays on the struggle by deriding and demonising the motherly role. In official accounts of the Countess of Mar's job, she is twice described as 'gouuernant of his hienes persone and mowth in his infancy'[58] – the king's mouth being technically the term for 'the provision and serving of his food and drink',[59] but also irresistibly suggesting an early stage of nursing (although in reality James's wet-nurse was another woman, Helen Little).[60] Indeed, throughout his writings, Buchanan (like many classical and humanist authors) opposes his male, man-building pedagogy to female, childish wet-nursing, developing the metaphor in his political writings of the 1570s and 1580s, all of them dedicated to his royal pupil. Their message is consistent: James should avoid flatterers. In his dedicatory epistle to *De iure regni apud Scotos* (1579) Buchanan pays lip service to the notion that the king's natural qualities will protect him, but immediately contradicts that confidence by pointing to the seductive threats surrounding the king – all figured in the trope of nursing:

> I know … that your nature ever impels you to avoid that wet-nurse [nutricula] of tyrants and disease of legitimate governments, flattery; and that you dislike the absurdities and artificial customs of courts no less than you do those persons who appear to despise everything which is in good taste, and who love and practice such absurdities and customs: who season their speech with such terms as Your Majesty, My Lord, Your Excellency, and other expressions even more disgusting. Although your natural goodness and the correctness of your principles protect you for the present from these ills, I am, none the less, apprehensive lest that suave wet-nurse [altrix] of vice, bad company, turns your tender mind in a worse direction; and I am especially so, because I am not unaware of the ease which our senses present us with temptations. I, therefore, present this book to you not merely as a guide [monitorem], but also as an importunate critic [flagitatiorem] – one even lacking, at times, in respect – which, in the age while your disposition is plastic, may go with you through the dangers of flattery, not only to show you the way, but also, once you have entered upon it, to keep you in it – to check you and draw you back if you would stray.[61]

In the 'belling the cat' anecdote Buchanan further reduces this nurturing role: he claims the right to whip the boy's arse, while allowing the Countess to kiss it, obscenely inverting the oral nursing metaphor that usually sustains James's relations with women into a figure of anilingus.

Buchanan fashions a male pedagogy that neurotically insists on its distance from the evil wet-nurse, and which asserts its right to teach in physically aggressive terms (the acoustic closeness of 'flagitatiorem' to 'flagellum', although they are not etymologically linked, raises the spectre of beating). Put more strongly, Buchanan insists on a model of education that erases the parent in favour of the tutor. But by his own standards, Buchanan's education of James must be said to have failed. James not only wilfully misreads Buchanan's political lessons but, as soon as he could, worked to suppress his old tutor's writings. Even fifteen years after Buchanan's death, he advises his son Henry to avoid 'sicc infamouse inuectiues as buchananis or knokisis croniclis' and to 'use the lau upon' any who possessed copies.[62]

More importantly, I would argue that, as a direct result to his experience, James proposes a different *model* of education to his son in *Basilikon Doron*, one that seeks to evade what he perceived as the evils of the father–master transaction, figured as beating. In his dedicatory epistle he stresses his position not only as king (as the title suggests) but as father. Whom could he dedicate the book to, he asks Henry, 'quhomto I saye can it sa iustlie appartaine as unto you my dearest sonne, since I the authoure thairof as youre naturall father man [must] be cairfull for youre godlie & uertuouse education as my eldest sonne and the first fruictis of goddis blessing touardis mee in my posteritie, and as a king man tymouslie [timely, in good time] prouyde for youre training up in all the pointis of a kings office'.[63] At the most fundamental level, then, *Basilikon Doron*, is the timely advice not only of a king to a young prince who will be king but of a father to a son. This paternal advice is something James himself – fatherless at the age of eight months – signally lacked, but which he feels compelled to provide – and the reason why is clarified in a figure he employs: 'ressaue & uellcome this booke then as a faithfull præceptoure & counsailloure unto you, quhilke because my affaires uill not permitte me euer to be present uith you I ordaine to be a resident faithfull admonisher of you.'[64] James cannot be with his son, a situation not in itself peculiar: Henry, like James before him, was placed shortly after his birth in the charge of the Earl and Countess of Mar, and despite his mother's protests (Queen Anna wanted him with her at Holyrood) he remained there until 1603.[65] But the book suggests a new educational possibility. *Basilikon Doron* becomes a textual 'præceptoure & counsailloure'[66], a 'resident faithfull admonisher', explicitly replacing the flesh-and-blood Buchanan of James's childhood. Unlike a counsellor, *Basilikon Doron* lacks human failings: 'ye uill find it a iuste & impartiall counsailloure nather flattering you in any uyce nor importuning you unseasonablie at unmeit times, it uill not cum uncalld nor speake unspearid [unquestioned] at'.[67] James casts *Basilikon Doron* as a respectful, silent tutor or counsellor, available when needed.

This is a direct strike at his old master's model for royal counsellor. Buchanan, as we have seen, designs his *De iure regni apud Scotos* to be a 'flagita-tiorem', an importunate critic, 'one even lacking in respect'. James insists that *Basilikon Doron* will not be guilty of 'importuning you unseasonablie at unmeit times, it uill not cum uncalld nor speake unspearid at'. Underlying these two texts are radically different notions of the role of counsel and of education. James attempts to erase the importunate counsellor in favour of a 'resident faithfull admonisher', a 'faithfull præceptoure & counsailloure', that repetition (in a single sentence) of 'faithfull' underscoring that the pedagogical pro-gramme is to be subjugated to *a priori* loyalty.

In opposing Buchanan's pedagogy, however, James does not simply subvert his tutor's rhetoric, and replace the schoolmaster with the wet-nurse. Instead, I would argue, he attempts to dispense with the master – and thus with the dangerous father–master contract – altogether. In one striking passage, explain-ing a king's fatherly duty to the kirk, James rejects schoolmasterly figures: 'to ende my aduyce anent the kirke estait cherishe na man maire then a goode pastoure, hate na man maire then a proude puritane, thinking in ane of youre fairest styles to be be calld a louing noorishe father to the kirke.'[68] The figure did not go unnoticed: in 1619 Sir James Sempill dedicated a book 'To the Most Noble and truly sacred Prince; Defender of Christ's Faith, and Nourish-father of his Church James'.[69] While the *OED* glosses 'nourish-father' as 'a foster-father',[70] James's consistent opposition to the tropes of Buchanan's prose demands that we understand 'noorishe father' as simultaneously father and wet-nurse.

Conclusion

But ultimately James cannot repress the schoolmaster. In one telling sentence he charges Henry, 'by the fatherlie authoritie I haue ouer you that ye keepe it [*Basilikon Doron*] euer uith you als cairfullie as alexander did the iliades of homer'.[71] Alexander was of course the son of a great ruler, Philip of Macedon – but, by referring Henry to Alexander's reading, James cannot help but invoke a missing character: Alexander's tutor, the most famous of tutors, Aristotle. Indeed, when an English ambassador set out to praise Buchanan, he could find no better way than to invoke Alexander: 'I thought the Kinge your Maister more happie that had *Buchanan* to his Maister, then *Alexander* the *Great*, that had *Aristotell* his instructor.'[72] Even as he articulates a model of education that con-flates father and wet-nurse, and suppresses the beating schoolmaster, James cannot but invoke the master. The humanist model of education is too far entrenched in the mind of the humanist pupil-king: now, whether the grown pupil-father like it or no, the schoolmaster will 'cum uncalld'.

NOTES
1 Some of the materials for this chapter were first presented at the University of Maryland at College Park: I am grateful to Donna Hamilton for her generous invitation to speak there.
2 Michael B. Young, *King James and the History of Homosexuality* (New York: 1999), p. 135. See also David Bergeron, *King James and Letters of Homoerotic Desire* (Iowa City: 1999).
3 *The Children's Petition* (London: 1669), title page.
4 *Lex Forcia: Being A Sensible Address to the Parliament, for an Act to remedy the Foul Abuse of Children at Schools* (London: 1698), B2r.
5 *Children's Petition*, A5r.
6 *Ibid.*, A12r.
7 *Lex Forcia*, C4r, Ev.
8 *Ibid.*, B3v–B4r.
9 See Richard Halpern, *The Poetics of Primitive Accumulation: English Renaissance Culture and the Genealogy of Capital* (Ithaca: 1991); Rebecca W. Bushnell, *A Culture of Teaching: Early Modern Humanism in Theory and Practice* (Ithaca: 1996); Alan Stewart, *Close Readers: Humanism and Sodomy in Early Modern England* (Princeton: 1997).
10 Stewart, 1997, p. 93.
11 Translated by Richard Sherry in *A Treatise of Schemes & Tropes* (London: 1550), Lviiv, Mijv, Mvr–v, Mvii v–Mviiir.
12 Halpern, 1991, pp. 21–45 at 26–8.
13 *Ibid.*, p. 26.
14 Richard Mulcaster, *Positions Wherein those Primitive Circumstances be Examined, which are Necessarie for the Training up of Children* (London: 1581), Mmiijr, cit. Halpern, 1991, pp. 26–7.
15 Halpern, 1991, p. 27.
16 Mulcaster, 1581, Tiijv, cit. Halpern, 1991, p. 27.
17 Halpern, 1991, p. 36.
18 Thomas Fuller, *The History of the Worthies of England* ed. J. F. Fuller, 4 pts London: 1662), s.v. Westermerland, 3rd sequence of pages, 149–50. The commonplace reference is to Horace's schoolmaster: see Stanley F. Bonner, *Education in Ancient Rome: From the Elder Cato to the Younger Pliny* (Berkeley: 1977), pp. 143–5.
19 This passage derives from a comic anecdote (source uncertain) about Mulcaster beating a schoolboy, quoted by William Barker, 'Introduction' to his edn, Mulcaster, *Positions Concerning the Training Up of Children* (Toronto: 1994), pp. xi–lxxxvi at lxv.
20 On later criticism's pathologisation of Udall as *the* beating schoolmaster see Elizabeth Pittenger, '"To Serve the Queere": Nicholas Udall, Master of Rebels', in Jonathan Goldberg, ed., *Queering the Renaissance* (Durham, North Carolina: 1994), pp. 162–89; Stewart, 1997, pp. 116–21. The author of *Lex Forcia* (1698) dubs Busby 'that transcending Rabbi … famous for this Geare [beating]' (8).
21 Halpern, 1991, p. 35.
22 Mary Thomas Crane, *Framing Authority: Sayings, Self, and Society in Sixteenth-century England* (Princeton: 1993); Bushnell, 1996.
23 Bushnell, 1996, p. 25.
24 Crane, 1993, pp. 55–6.
25 Roger Ascham, *The Scholemaster* (London: 1570), Bijv.
26 M[archamont] N[edham], *A Discourse Concerning Schools And School-Masters, Offered to publick Consideration* (London: 1663), B4v.
27 Jeffrey Masten, review of Stewart, *Close Readers*, in *Shakespeare Studies* 28 (2000), pp. 361–5 at 364–5. His glossing of 'lewde' is here based on the *Oxford English Dictionary* entry, s.v. 'lewd'.
28 Bushnell, 1996, p. 71.
29 In the Act of Caution, 1572. Historical Manuscripts Commission, *Report on the Manuscripts of the Earl of Mar and Kellie Preserved at Alloa House, N.B.* [hereafter *HMC Mar*] (London: 1904), p. 30.

30 Certainly by 30 July 1570 Buchanan was in place: the Regent (Lennox) signed a precept to allow 'Mr George Munro, servant to Mr George Buchanan, into the King's household, and to give him his daily allowance'. Lennox to Master and Steward of the King's House-hold, 30 July 1570, Stirling. *HMC Mar*, 22. On Buchanan see I. D. McFarlane, *Buchanan* (London: 1981).

31 BL Additional Ms. 34, 275, discussed in George F. Warner, ed., 'The Library of James VI: 1573–1583 From a Manuscript in the Hand of Peter Young, His Tutor', *Miscellany of the Scottish History Society* (Edinburgh: 1893), pp. ix–lxxv.

32 Thomas Smith, *Vitæ quorundam eruditissimorum et illustrium virorum* (London: 1707), Fff2*v*, in his life of Petrus Junius [Peter Young]. T. W. Baldwin has reconstructed James's changing curriculum on the basis of this evidence in 'The Textbooks of King James of Scotland' in *William Shakspere's Small Latine & Lesse Greeke*, 2 vols (Urbana: 1944), 1: 532–56 (ch. 14).

33 George Mackenzie, 'The Life of Mr. George Buchanan', *The Lives and Characters of the most Eminent Writers of the Scots Nation*, vol. 3 (of 3) (Edinburgh: 1722), pp. 156–83.

34 Sir James Melville of Halhill, *Memoirs of His Own Life*, ed. T. Thomson (Edinburgh: 1827), p. 262.

35 Cited in D. Harris Willson, *King James VI and I* (Oxford: 1956), p. 21.

36 Francis Osborn, *Advice to a Son: Or Directions For your better Conduct*, 6th edn. (Oxford: 1656), B7*r*.

37 For Edward VI's whipping boy see Bushnell, 1996, pp. 53–62.

38 Melville of Halhill, 1827, p. 262; for the whipping boy see Robert S. Rait and Annie I. Cameron, *King James's Secret: Negotiations Between Elizabeth and James VI Relating to the Execu-tion of Mary Queen of Scots, From the Warrender Papers* (London: 1927), p. 3.

39 Mackenzie, 1722, p. 180.

40 Juan Luis Vives, *Linguae latinae exercitatio* (Basel: 1541), a6*r*; trans. Foster Watson as *Tudor School-boy Life* (London: 1908), p. 10. 'Pa[ter]. Hunc filiolum meum ad te adduco, ut ex belua hominem facias. Phil[oponus ludimagister]. Dabo in eam rem operam sedulam. fiet: reuertetur ex pecude homo, ex nequam frugi & bonus ... Pa. Partiamur inter nos igitur hanc curam: tu ut sedulò institutas, ego ut benigne compensem tuam operam.'

41 Mulcaster, 1994, Mmijv.

42 *Ibid.*, Mmijv–Mmiijr.

43 Halpern, 1991, pp. 35–6.

44 Lawrence Stone, *The Family, Sex, and Marriage in England, 1500–1800* (London: 1977), p. 163, quoted and discussed in Halpern, *Poetics*, p. 279, n. 67.

45 John Brinsley, *Ludus literarius: Or, The Grammar Schoole* (London: 1612), ¶3*r–v*, quoted in Halpern, 1991, p. 279, n. 67. Despite the attractiveness of Halpern's reading to this argu-ment, it is by no means clear from the context (a dedicatory epistle to Prince Henry) that Brinsley is using 'poore' here to denote the students' poverty.

46 Mackenzie, 1722, pp. 179–80.

47 Norman McDougall argues that because Buchanan does not tell this story in his *Historia* – and the 'bell the cat' story is first related to Angus in print only in David Hume of Godscroft, *The History of the Houses of Douglas ad Angus* (Edinburgh: 1644), p. 226 – it must be of seven-teenth-century, rather than sixteenth-century, origin. See MacDougall, *James III: A Political Study* (Edinburgh: 1982), p. 297, n. 65. The *Dictionary of the Scottish Tongue* notes that 'The attribution of the phrase to Archibald, Earl of Angus, in 1482, does not appear in early sources' (1, p. 227 s.v. Bell v.1) and cites David Fergusson, *Fergusson's Scottish Proverbs; from the Original Print of 1641*, ed. Erskine Beveridge (Edinburgh: 1924), p. 64: 'It is weill said, but wha will bell the cat.' This predates Hume of Godscroft's use; but the phrase appears not to be present in the c. 1598 manuscript version.

48 This fable appears in the Latin collection of the Englishman Odo de Cheriton in the early thirteenth century, in the tales of French Franciscan Nicol Bozon (c. 1320) and in William Langland's *Piers Plowman*. See MacDougall, 1982, p. 297, n. 74.

49 Jenny Wormald, *Court, Kirk and Community: Scotland, 1470–1625* (London: 1981), p. 147. See also Maurice Lee, Jnr, *Great Britain's Solomon: James VI and I in His Three Kingdoms* (Chicago: 1990), pp. 34–5.

50 Bushnell, 1996, pp. 66–7.

51 Walter J. Ong, 'Latin Language Study as a Renaissance Puberty Rite' (1959) rpt in *Rhetoric, Romance and Technology: Studies in the Interaction of Expression and Culture* (Ithaca: 1971), pp. 113–41 at 115; for a recent elaboration see Bruce R. Smith, *Homosexual Desire in Shakespeare's England: A Cultural Poetics* (Chicago: 1991), pp. 83–4. For the classic 'rites of passage' formulation see Arnold van Gennep, *Les Rites de passage: étude systématique des rites* (Paris: 1909), trans. Monika B. Vizedom and Gabrielle L. Caffee as *The Rites of Passage* (London: 1960).

52 Pierre Bourdieu, *Ce que parler veut dire: l'économie des échanges linguistiques* (Paris: Arthème Fayard, 1982), trans. Gino Raymond and Matthew Adamson, ed. John B. Thompson, as *Language and Symbolic Power* (Cambridge: 1991), p. 117.

53 BL Royal Ms. 12.B.XX, fols 35–49, quoted in Nicholas Orme, *Education and Society in Medieval and Renaissance England* (London: 1989), pp. 145, 139.

54 William Nelson, ed., *A Fifteenth-century School Book from a Manuscript in the British Museum (MS. Arundel 249)* (Oxford, 1956), pp. 13–14. 'Ditissimi cuiusque filii passim in euo puerili corrumpuntur hiis diebus, idque domi apud parentes, quod plane miserandum est … Matris oportet apud se retinere qui cum pro puppis nugentur perinde quasi ad iocum et nugas nascerentur liberi. Eos animant et verbis et rebus quo licenter omnia factitent. ita lasciuiis et licentia effeminati fede precipites eunt … faciam vobis exemplar de quodam propinquo meo qui hic in vicino apud domum propriam primis incumbit elimentis. is ut domum redit plorans (postquam a cute pulices preceptor abegerit) actutum mater nates spectat visura plage si appareant. Ast si viderit extare vibices in fletum et luctum tota soluitur ut que foret mente capta. tum seueritatem magistrorum queritur malle se ingemens sepultum videre quam eo more tractari filium. hec et ad hunc modum infinita verba faciunt. interdum quoque prolis causa turba oritur inter maritum suam et coniugem, quin que ille mandat hecque inhibet. ita procedente tempore quium ad etatem maturem peruenerint euadunt ad omnia scelera perpetranda paruifacientes flagitium committere fedissimum' (pp. 102–3).

55 James VI, *The Basilicon Doron of King James VI*, ed. James Craigie, 2 vols (Edinburgh: 1944), 1, p. 155 (I quote throughout from James's holograph version of 1598, BL Royal Ms. 18. B. xv).

56 James VI, 'Letter to the People of Scotland', 22? October 1589, in G. P. V. Akrigg, ed., *Letters of King James VI & I* (Berkeley: 1984), p. 98.

57 Melville, 1827, p. 262.

58 *Acts of the Parliaments of Scotland*, 12 vols (n.p., n.pub., 1814–75), 3: 149/2. See also *Register of the Privy Council of Scotland* (Edinburgh: 1877 and continuing), 2 689: 'the cair of the attendance upoun his hienes mowth and dyet continewing as afoir in the charge of the Lady Countesse of Mar' (1578).

59 *A Dictionary of the Older Scottish Tongue* ed. William A. Craigie (Chicago: 1931 and continuing), 4, pp. 389–90 s.v. 'mouth', 2.

60 'Royal establishment for attendance of James VI', 10 March 1567/8, Stirling. *HMC Mar*, pp. 18–20 at 18.

61 'Video … te naturæ quodam instinctu ab adulatione, quæ & tyrannidis est nutricula, & legitimi regni grauissima pestis, adeo abhorrere, vt solœcismos & barbarismos aulicos, non minus oderis, quam qui sibi omnis elegantiæ censores videntur, eos ament, & affectent, & velut sermonis condimenta passim Maiestates, Dominationes, illustritates, & si qua alia magis sunt putida aspergant. ab hoc te errore quanquam & naturæ bonitas, & institutio rectorum in præsentia vendicent, tamen non nihil subueriri cogor, ne blanda vitiorum altrix, praua consuetudo animum adhuc tenellum in peiorem partem detorqueat: præsertim cùm non ignotem quàm reliqui nostri sensus facile sese præbeant seducendos. Hunc igitur ad te non modo monitorem sed etiam flagitatiorem importunum, ac interim impudentem misi. qui in hoc flexu ætatis trans adulationis scopulos te comitetur: nec moneat modo, sed in via semel inita

continèat, & si quid deflexeris, reprehendat, & retrahat.' George Buchanan, *De ivre regni apvd Scotos, dialogvs* (Edinburgh: apud Iohannem Rosseum, pro Henrico Charteris, 1579), A2v; trans. Charles Flinn Arrowood as *The Powers of the Crown in Scotland* (Austin: 1949), pp. 37–8.

62 James VI, 1944, 1, p. 149.

63 *Ibid.*, 1, p. 6–7.

64 *Ibid.*, 1, p. 9. The odd term 'admonisher' interestingly echoes Thomas Wilson, in a dedicatory epistle to Sir William Cecil, praising Sir John Cheke: 'the sayd Sir Iohn Cheeke … was your brother in lawe, your deare friende, your good admonisher, and teacher in your yonger yeares'. *The Three Orations of Demosthenes Chiefe Orator among the Grecians, in favour of the Olynthians*, trans. Thomas Wilson (London: 1570), *ijr.

65 Willson, 1956, p. 117; Roy Strong, *Henry, Prince of Wales and England's Lost Renaissance* (London: 1986), p. 9.

66 'Præceptor' is a standard term for 'an instructor, a teacher' in Scots; t does not seem to have the negative connotations that Ascham gives to the teaching by precepts.

67 James VI, 1944, 1, p.10.

68 *Ibid.*, 1, pp. 80–1.

69 Sir James Sempill, *Sacrilege Sacredly Handled, that is, According to Scripture Onely* (London: 1619).

70 *OED* s.v. 'nourish-father', 10: 561.

71 James VI, 1944, 1, pp. 9–10.

72 Cited in Baldwin, 1944, 1, p. 537.

9

'Kiss me with the kisses of his mouth': gender inversion and Canticles in godly spirituality[1]

TOM WEBSTER

In a work of practical divinity notable only for its typicality, the godly minister Thomas Brooks pressed his congregation to practise self-examination. Only by 'a serious examination of a man's own estate, he may know whether he be Christ's spouse or the devil's strumpet, whether there be a work of grace upon his heart or not'.[2] It is the former, positive, analogy that will be the centre of attention here rather than the latter, for nuptial imagery applied to and accepted by godly men proves to be quite common once one keeps an eye open for it. In addition, it should be stressed, this is not a matter of ministers spraying mixed congregations with a variety of analogies in the hope that different ones would strike true with different sections of their flock. In a sermon delivered to MPs during a fast held by the House of Commons, plainly an exclusively male congregation, Stephen Marshall pleaded with them to maintain orthodoxy: 'As a man who finds his wife faithful in the marriage bed, judgeth that she loves him, and that her heart is one with his ... [thus with you], they that are are interpreted to keep all his commandments.'[3] This was a plea following a more positive image delivered by Marshall's friend Cornelius Burges, in a sermon to the same people on the same day. For Burges the covenant between God and the magistrate was that '*this joyning of ourselves to the Lord*, is such, as is usually made by *marriage*; ... and admits us to the participation of all the most intimate, neerest and choysest expressions of the deerest love of God, which can be found between the husband and the wife'.[4] A recurring appetite for the imagery of Canticles in particular can be explored as a source for the negotiation of godly masculinity in public and private, a route to a greater appreciation of the multi-faceted, and usefully unstable, nature of masculine Puritan identity. This examination will accommodate a brief case study of examples in seventeenth-century England and one of the allies from Scotland. Ambitions are small in that they are limited to the particular discourse of godly ministers (as Puritan clergy called themselves).

Representing masculinity and femininity in clerical discourse

The initial assumption regarding the *self*-application of the nuptial imagery of Canticles for godly ministers is that it was fraught with anxiety and can be co-opted for the 'crisis of masculinity' thesis. That the findings of this study do not support this line is not, however, to suggest that it holds good generally or even that godly masculinity was a stable construct, free of fears. One of the many criticisms of theatre by the Puritans related to the matter of men taking on women's roles, for the practice of transvestism entailed the risk of 'degeneration' of masculinity, a 'risk' exacerbated by the inherently friable nature of the godly self.[5] William Prynne was clear in his condemnation, worrying that a male actor would 'degenerate into a woman with his veiled face'.[6] This instance can be taken as evidence of a more general disquiet about gender relations in this period. Susan Amussen has argued that this is a transitional age for masculinity, particularly fraught with tension as gender boundaries were seen to be dangerously fluid, partly owing to the dominance of the idea of the 'one-sex' body.[7] In terms of the clergy, to adopt gender reversal might be seen as particularly dangerous, for to lose 'proper' masculinity would be, of course, to remove the possibility of fulfilling their vocation.

The issues take on different levels, then, when we examine the experience and identity of the clergyman once we focus on the fact that he was exactly that: a clergy*man*. Ministerial identity has to be understood as drawing upon and relating to conceptions of masculinity and femininity.[8] Even a superficial discussion reveals ambivalences in clerical discourse that have profound consequences for identity, piety and experience. The Reformation had, of course, considerable effects on these gender implications, to which we will return. Despite the loss of the status of the priest standing in for God made male flesh, the advent of clerical marriage reduced the sexual ambivalence of their forebears and placed them in a site less easily contained as a 'third sex'.[9] In this situation it is possible to see the minister as a type of masculinity writ large, a kind of superman. He draws fully upon the power of patriarchy supported by a patriarchal reading of Scripture. This received the full support of the epithets supplied by clerics for clerics. There is a rich variety of masculine callings and attributes attached to the ministerial image.[10]

However, there is also a strong element in clerical discourse that works against the minister's place in contemporary masculinities. The idea of 'ministry' placed clergymen in a number of roles that were antithetical to early modern masculinity. 'Ministry' has connotations of service, of nurturing and caring; the sacraments, despite Reformation changes, still located the clergy as providers of food and sustenance; spiritual comfort, a central pastoral duty, and the whole rhetoric of ministry modified clerical masculinities. A related reading of Canticles, as an allegory for Christ as the husband of the Church, offered clergymen a range of positions. It should be noted that the boundary between Church and the individual believer was very permeable, further complicating the matter. Richard Sibbes made it clear that 'Every Christian soul is the spouse of Christ as the whole church is'.[11] In his treatment he slipped easily between the Christ and Church relationship to the Christ and Christian relationship, occasionally having the Church as the means by which Christ could kiss the individual believer.

> They love his appearance, but because this shall not be yet, though the church be still in expectation of it, therefore she desireth to hear his words, and to have him kiss her with his mouth in his word. But this is not all; but let me find his Spirit now walking with me here and further, 'kiss me with his mouth' [Canticles 1.2], by increasing his graces in me, manifesting his love unto me more and more. This is the desire of the church, and of every Christian soul, that Christ would thus kiss her; that he would reveal himself every day more and more unto her, in his word, in his sacraments, by his Spirit, by his graces, by increasing of them. This is the desire of the church and of every Christian soul, that Christ would thus 'kiss her with the kisses of his mouth.'[12]

In this system the clergy were part of the feminine Church both institutionally and individually but could also take on the part of the masculinised Church to the individual Christian when the Church was Christ's representative. Thus the ministry could be the best man. As John Cotton had it, 'The Church as it is the House of God; so it is also the spouse of Christ; Ministers are the friends of the Bridegroom, and of the Bride. The ministers have done their work in preparing the Bride for the Bridegroom; as also in ministering to her when she is married'.[13] Sibbes had the minister as a panderer: 'Christ give his spouse a taste of his love in his word, by sending his ambassadors, his ministers with his love-letters, the gospel of peace, giving therein a taste of his love, as also by his Spirit, by his sacrament, by his graces.'[14] Elsewhere he took multiple inflections further.

> Those that bring together these two different parties, are the friends of the bride; that is, the ministers, as it is, John iii. 23. They are the *paranymphi*, the friends of the bride, that learn of Christ what to report to his spouse, and so they woo for Christ, and open the riches, beauty, honour, and all that is lovely in him, which is indeed the especial duty of ministers.[15]

Paranymphi were either the best man or the bridesmaid but more often the latter. Others took this opportunity with relish; ministers could be breast-feeding mothers. The minister is 'a Father to beget us with the immortal seed of the word, a Mother to nourish us up in the same'.[16] For John Collinges ministers

> are Fathers and Mothers too, Gal. 4. 19. *My little Children* (saith Paul) *with whom I travel in birth, till Christ be formed in you* [Gal. 4.29]. They are nursing Fathers,

and nursing Mothers. The word is the Saint's milk. As new born Babes desire the sincere milk of the word, that you may grow thereby [I Pet. 2.2]. If the word be milk, the Minister's mouth is the breast, through which this milk runs into the bowels of the people.[17]

The richness of clerical self-promotional imagery is intended to do more than remind us of the richness of Scriptural language. The main point is to make it clear that clerical masculinity was, both by context and by choice, ambivalent. A space was opened up where ministers could see themselves in female roles and accordingly, in certain circumstances, appropriate 'women's symbols'.[18] Indeed, as will emerge, it may not be excessive to argue that Puritan clerical piety drew upon, was perhaps even structured through, a series of male/female oppositions which the clergy were able to negotiate through the ambivalence of their gender identity. In addition it becomes clear that this was a positive and productive dimension to their spirituality, a source of reassurance and empowerment more than of anxiety and insecurity.

If we turn from the public sphere of the sermon and the treatise to the relative privacy of the spiritual journal, the sense of 'self' in self-application becomes more internal, less of a public-relations exercise than the material we have surveyed so far. Gender inversion, related strategies and a particular delight in Canticles runs through the diary of Samuel Rogers, a young minister in the 1630s. The breast-feeding analogy is taken on board; when he complains of 'heartlesse preaching, litle life in it', he prays, 'for my heart is ready to decay; thou canst help meanes; oh some milke to nourish my pore soule'.[19] He was more likely to turn straight to the Lord, to cut out the middleman, as it were. '[T]he Lord strengthens mee to hange at the breasts of a promise and to sucke for milke; and though but litle comes, yet I am still strengthened to sucke; oh I will wait upon the Lord, it is good dying while I lye at gods feete, looking up though troubled.'[20] He adapts Canticles 2.5 in requests for succour: 'For myne owne part, the Lord inlarges my heart, and gives matter, Lord also cleare up the coast, and refresh me with thy flagons of love',[21] almost turning the Christ-figure maternal. Elsewhere, the figure becomes ambiguous, when he asks for 'more of this love, ever ravish my love with thy flagon of love' or 'more of thy selfe and thy loves, ravish mee with thy flagons'.[22]

The most frequent appearances of Canticles are in pleas to lessen the distance between Rogers and Christ: 'wilt thou give mee thy Christ, and wilt not thou make me tast of his sweetnes, oh some of his sweetnes; and thy countenance thorough him, that may ravish my soule, as with love'; 'Oh that my husband would kisse me, with the kisses of his mouth and refresh my pore decayed soule and raise it up somewhat'.[23] The as-yet-undelivered promise of the betrothed comes through in one such plea: 'oh more Lord, more, more of thy selfe whose love I have tasted; but oh the vaile the vaile to be removed'.[24] The sense of distance makes the embraces and kisses a clearly intense attraction. '[O]h when will I see him, when shall I lye in the embraces of Jesus Christ; when will he kisse mee with the kisses of his mouth, amongst those that excell in virtue'; 'why standest thou afar of[f], oh my deare god, why hidest thou thy selfe from mee; my heart is yet fixed, grieves for my loosenes, folly; I will come unto thee, oh my first husband, oh hugge me in thyne armes, and I shall be safe'.[25] Such moments of a sense of neglect and the related sense of inadequacy are when Rogers makes explicit his 'wifely' status to Christ as husband: 'oh pore wretch that I am, that the Lord should looke upon me; be my husband; I a wife, that walke not as I should'.[26]

   At the same time, the embraces of Christ appear in Rogers's best days. He wrote his diary shortly before he retired each day and the best days had a recurring theme, a confidence that 'I will sleep between the breasts of my beloved'.[27] 'The Lord is now sweetly neere to my soule, ... I will now throw myselfe upon thy allsufficiencye oh Lord; and rest in thy bosome this night expecting thy holy saboath.'[28] 'I will lye downe in faith, and peace; the Lord hath drawne neere my soule, and I will praise him; and lye downe in the armes of my first husband.'[29] The passivity won from human physical limitations is rewarded: 'oh good the L[or]d is, and therefore I come unto him; yea in his armes lye downe; weake, and tyred in bodye; but with my spirit up; I will sleep in Christes armes'.[30] One of his best days ended with Rogers at his most passive: 'A litle recovered; the bridegrome hath taken me into his chamber, and comforted mee with his loves, and some calmnes, and serenitye hath come into my troubled spirit.'[31] Finally, lest the impression be given that Rogers had only one image of Christ, a good day produced the following (though it is noteworthy that only one figure is repeated). 'I have discussed, this night, about the blessed union with Christ, and my heart rejoices in Christ, my head, vine, spouse, foundation, teacher, my King; I do not have that in which the world glories, but I have Christ, my husband, in whose arms this night I shall safely be sheltered.'[32]

Samuel Rutherford and the joys of dependency

It might be complained that the treatment of the nuptial imagery so far has been a little too focused, almost monomaniacal, hardly representing a full exploration of the possibilities offered by Canticles. To broaden the analysis, it proves useful to trace the theme in the epistles of Samuel Rutherford, the primary theologian, political theorist and minister of mid-seventeenth-century Scotland. Canticles and the sensuous imagery offered therein was such a prominent element in his spirituality, both internal and pastoral, that, according to an

eighteenth-century source, his published letters were employed as a porno-
graphic reading source (although whether this is a recognition of potential
eroticism or a judgement on the limitations of the press is open to debate).[33]

In his pastoral work Rutherford turned to the attractions of the Bride of
Christ on many occasions. Much of the advice is for patience, a matter of being
betrothed rather than being married, the consummation to come on Judgement Day. Marion McNaught was encouraged to 'wait upon the times of the
blowing of the sweet south and north wind of His gracious Spirit, that may
make you cast a sweet smell in your Beloved's nostrils; and bid your Beloved
come down to His garden, and eat of his pleasant fruits' [Canticles 4.16].[34] For
Viscountess Kenmure it is noteworthy that Christ was characterised by a principal part of masculinity, an unmistakable voice:

> For this is the house of wine, where ye meet with your Well-Beloved. Here it is
> where He kisseth you with the kisses of His mouth, and where ye feel the smell of
> His garments; and they have indeed a most fragrant and glorious smell. Ye must,
> I say, wait upon Him, and be often communing with Him, whose lips are as lilies,
> dropping sweet-smelling myrrh, and by the moving thereof He will assuage your
> grief; for the Christ that saveth you is a speaking Christ; the Church knoweth Him
> by His voice [Canticles 2.8], and can discern His tongue amongst a thousand.[35]

There is still a sense of anticipation, but one which mixes with what verges on
an implied sexual relationship in slightly later advice to Kenmure: 'When your
Head shall appear, your Bridegroom and Lord, your day shall then dawn, and
it shall never have an afternoon, nor an evening shadow. Let your child be
Christ's; let him stay beside you as thy Lord's pledge, that you shall willingly
render again, if God will.'[36] This was taken to its furthest when the Viscountess became a widow, with his comfort almost tending to be celebratory:

> I trust your Lord shall remember that, and give you comfort now at such a time
> as this, wherein your dearest Lord hath made you a widow, that ye shall be a free
> woman for Christ, who is now suiting for marriage-love of you. And therefore,
> since you lie alone in your bed, let Christ be as a bundle of myrrh, to sleep and
> lie all the night betwixt your breasts [Canticles 1.13], and then your bed is
> better filled than before.[37]

On occasion, however, the vision was gender-free, although it might be noted
that the following instances were both in letters to women. To Lady Culross:
'O that all the virgins had part of the Bridegroom's love whereupon He maketh
me to feed!'[38] In a particularly visionary missive to Lady Kilconquhair, his
counsel was as follows.

> But let us come near, and fill ourselves with Christ, and let His friends drink,
> and be drunken, and satisfy our hollow and deep desires with Jesus. Oh, come

all and drink at this living well; come, drink, and live for evermore; come, drink and welcome! 'Welcome,' saith our fairest Bridegroom.[39]

Part of the attraction of this imagery is that it provided a vivid collection of ways of differentiating between intellectual and 'real' experiences of Christ, the latter clearly being preferable. For Rutherford, those with notional conversion 'talk of Christ by the book and the tongue, and no more; but to come nigh Christ, and hause [close with, clasp round the neck] Him, and embrace Him, is another thing'.[40] This search for experiential veracity makes the sensual nature of many of his comforts more comprehensible. It could be by scent; it could be tactile or visual.[41] At its best, closeness to Christ stimulated many of the senses. 'I would seek no more happiness than a sight of Him so near-hand, as to see, hear, smell, and touch, and embrace Him.'[42]

Rutherford tested his capacity for hyperbole to communicate the sensuous joy of union with Christ:

> And oh, what a fair One, what an only One, what an excellent, lovely, ravishing One, is Jesus! Put the beauty of ten thousand worlds of paradises, like the garden of Eden in one; put all trees, all flowers, all smells, all colours, all tastes, all joys, all sweetness, all loveliness, in one: oh, what a fair and excellent thing would that be! And yet it would be less to that fair and dearest Well-beloved, Christ, than one drop of rain to the whole seas, rivers, lakes, and fountains of ten thousand earths. Oh, but Christ is heaven's wonder, and earth's wonder! What marvel that His bride saith, 'He is altogether lovely!' [Canticles 5.16].[43]

That this linguistic challenge could never be met took him into the depths of sensuality and to a heightened sense of his own lack and desert.

> What heaven can be there liker to hell, than to lust, and green [desire], and dwine [pine], and fall a swoon for Christ's love, and to want it? Is not this hell and heaven woven through-other? Is not this pain and joy, sweetness and sadness, to be in one web, the one the weft, the other the warp? Therefore, I would that Christ would let us meet and join together, the soul and Christ in each other's arms. Oh what meeting is like this, to see blackness and beauty, contemptibleness and glory, highness and baseness, even a soul and Christ, kiss each other! Nay, but when all is done, I may be wearied in speaking and writing, but, oh, how far am I from the right expression of Christ of His love? I can neither speak nor write feeling, nor tasting, nor smelling: come feel, and smell, and taste Christ and His love, and ye shall call it more than can be spoken. To write how sweet the honeycomb is, is not so lovely as to eat and suck the honeycomb [Canticles 5.1]. One night's rest in a bed of love with Christ will say more than the heart can think, or tongue can utter.[44]

The sense of failure and an unearned love very clearly links us back to the sense of humility sought after by the godly. The disciplines of self-denial and self-examination are designed to turn the necessary condition of selfishness to the creation of a self-abnegating selfhood. For Rutherford Canticles provided what almost amounts to an escape clause, as a route to, and recognition of, dependency and passivity normally unavailable to early modern masculinity.

It comes as no surprise then to find sickness play a part in this search. Rutherford's illness, however, is largely metaphorical. At one point, while he was celebrating Christ's presence, his desire seems almost beyond satiety: 'I have for the present a sick dwining life, with much pain, and much love-sickness for Christ.'[45] First in his list of things that moved him 'since it hath pleased my Lord to turn my moon-light into day-light' was the following:

> He hath yoked me to work, to wrestle with Christ's love; of longing wherewith I am sick, pained, fainting, and like to die because I cannot get Himself; which I think a strange sort of desertion. For I have not Himself, whom if I had, my love-sickness would cool, and my fever go away; at least, I should know the heat of the fire of complacency, which would cool the scorching heat of the fire of desire. (And yet I have no penury of His love!) And so I dwine, I die, and He seemeth not to rue [take pity] on me.[46]

The opening masculinist image of wrestling might be noted but there is also a note of unsatisfied desire, an ever-heightened demand, almost a whinge, with an implicit recognition of the desirability of delay. At a later point the latter is given the emphasis and made more explicit: 'I have a dwining, sickly, and pained life, for a real possession of Him; and am troubled with love-brashes [fits] and love-fevers; but it is a sweet pain.'[47] There was an intense desire for the communion to be without end, almost an impatience that it was not yet so.

> Oh, but it is long to that day when I shall have a free world of Christ's love! Oh, what a sight to be up in heaven, in that fair orchard of the new paradise; and to see, and smell, and touch, and kiss, that fair Field-flower, that evergreen Tree of Life! ... Christ, Christ, Christ, nothing but Christ, can cool our love's burning langour. O thirsty love! wilt thou set Christ, the well of life, to thy head, and drink thy fill? Drink, and spare not; drink love, and be drunken with Christ! Nay, alas! the distance betwixt us and Christ is a death. Oh if we were clasped in [each] other's arms! We should never twin [separate] again, except heaven twinned and sundered us; and that cannot be.[48]

Rutherford proved to be more successful in experiencing the joys of dependency and passivity when he had a certain dependency imposed upon him when he was sent into internal exile in Aberdeen: 'It pleaseth my Well-beloved to dine with a poor prisoner.'[49] His spiritual discomfort was eased even with the prospect of this exile. Shortly before his departure he assured Marion McNaught that 'I am well and my soul prospereth. I find Christ with me. I burden no man; I want nothing; no face looketh on me but it laugheth on me. Sweet, sweet is the

Lord's cross. I overcome my heaviness. My Bridegroom's love-blinks fatten my weary soul.'[50] A positive role of satisfaction in adversity was beginning to emerge. Impotence and (forced) passivity improved his capacity to employ his spiritual impotence and passivity.

> If I had a lease of Christ of my own dating (for whoever cometh nigh-hand, and taketh a hearty look at Christ's inner side, shall never wring nor wrestle themselves out of his love-grips again), I would rest contentedly in my prison, yea, in my prison without light of sun or candle, providing Christ and I had a love-bed, not of mine, but of Christ's own making, that we might lie together among the lilies, till the day break and the shadows flee away [Canticles 2.17].[51]

He is taken to such spiritual heights that he almost pities those in the kingdom who are free: 'Oh, if all the kingdom were as I am, except my bonds! They know not the love-kisses that my only Lord Jesus wasteth on a dawted [fondled] prisoner.'[52] He is happy to relinquish central parts of his masculinity; first, his physique (and his active role as a wooer): 'It was not my flattering of Christ that drew a kiss from his mouth ... If He bear me on His back, or carry me in his arms over this water, I hope for grace to set down my feet on dry ground, when the way is better.'[53] Finally, he finds comfort in the loss of the central element of clerical masculinity, speaking, that is, preaching the Word of God: 'My dumb Sabbaths broke my heart, and I would not be comforted. But now He whom my soul loveth is come again, and it pleaseth Him to feast me with the kisses of His love.'[54] In his sufferings from political vagaries he finds an almost unprecedented pleasure.

> I cannot but write to my friends, that Christ hath trysted [met] me in Aberdeen; and my adversaries have sent me here to be feasted with love banquets with my royal, high, high, and princely King Jesus. Madam, why should I smother Christ's honesty? ... I shall not again quarrel Christ for a gloom [frown], now He hath taken the mask off His face, and saith 'Kiss thy fill;' and what can I have more when I get great heaven in *my little arms*? Oh how sweet are the sufferings of Christ for Christ![55]

Once we recognise that Rutherford's imposed worldly passivity was necessary to take him beyond any remnant of reluctance to embrace spiritual passivity fully, it proves fruitful to read these moments with a sensitivity to the depth of his activity. In the last instant, for instance, he is at his most passive, but it is noteworthy that he is still *invited* to 'Kiss thy fill', that is, he is not simply a recipient. In the following passage, there is a certain diffidence in his passivity when he stresses that, if he had the choice, he would not exchange Christ's love for the best of worldly goods. The very last sentence virtually empowers Rutherford through a mutual love, a reciprocity that almost makes Christ and Rutherford's soul equals. Having almost accused him of a spiritual audacity, of having 'got above himself,' he is licensed, or licenses himself, by directly quoting Scripture, rather than simply alluding to it.

> I would not want the visitations of love, and the very breathings of Christ's mouth when He kisseth, and my Lord's delightsome smiles and love-embracements under my sufferings for Him, for a mountain of gold, or for all the honours, court, and grandeur of velvet kirkmen. Christ hath the yolk and heart of my love. 'I am my Beloved's, and my Well-Beloved is mine.' [Canticles 6.3][56]

Scripture also gave Rutherford wine, or drink generally, as a route to passivity and joy, implicitly or explicitly, and in different ways. It was implicit in advice to his female pastoral charges, as in advice to Lady Kenmure, directing her to the 'house of wine, where ye meet with your Well-Beloved'.[57] It could be a matter of contrast, when he enthused about 'my Bridegroom's kindness, whose love is better than wine' (Canticles 1.2).[58] At its most positive, he is invited to go to Christ, the well of life, and drink his fill: 'Drink, and spare not; drink love, and be drunken with Christ!'[59]

A more common image is sharing a bed and/or sleeping with Christ. It should be noted, however that this is not necessarily sexual, for early modern sources also saw male 'bedfellows' as confidantes, as friends with no sexual undertones.[60] This much granted, the visions are open to different readings. 'I sleep in His arms all the night, and my head betwixt His breasts. My Well-Beloved is altogether lovely'[61] is an image suffused with passivity and security. 'One night's rest in a bed of love with Christ will say more than heart can think, or tongue can utter.'[62] Similarly, there is rest here but, when this is read as a conclusion to the section quoted above, it is the climax to a mixture of pleasure and human inadequacy.[63] The same applies to the following: 'Oh, what would I give to have a bed made to my wearied soul in His bosom!'[64] A particularly appropriate request is contained in the next vision. Rutherford will be content in prison, 'providing Christ and I had a love-bed, not of mine, but of Christ's own making, that we might lie together among the lilies, till the day break and the shadows flee away'.[65] Obviously the bed being made by Christ is a matter of self-abnegation but it seems reasonable to expect that a theologian was unlikely to make as good a bed as a man whose stepfather was a carpenter.

Conclusion

I would like to address a couple of important issues which open a route to explanation. The main issue that needs addressing is the matter of the gendered soul. In an otherwise stimulating essay Richard Godbeer assuages the fears of later male members of the godly by pointing out that Christ was to marry the *souls* of men and women rather than men and women *per se*. Because souls were seen either as sexually indeterminate or female, adopting nuptial imagery should not be seen as a threat to masculinity.[66] The first problem is that this ignores the fluidity and instability of the 'one-sex' outlook touched upon earlier. The second is that it seems to assume an assumed community of Cartesians *avant la lettre*. There was a more strongly established school that ranked souls by gender and maintained a sense of corporeality for the sake of individuality.[67] In any case this is a matter that is rarely stressed in the exegeses of Canticles with which I am familiar. John Preston, for instance, writes quite explicitly that '*Christ* comes and tels a man, I will have thee … and saith to him; I am willing to marry thee'.[68] Moreover, and perhaps crucially, we are addressing experience, and religious history is the richer for the fact that the relationship between theology and experience is dialogic; rhetorics, discourses and outlooks that are related but separate cross over, interact, and blur boundaries. The details are to be explored rather than reassuringly 'clarified'.

The same plea can be repeated, in a less defensive tone, regarding the second issue. The early modern period has been particularly shy about exploring masculinities. The medieval and modern periods have, for some reason, proved to be more inclined to address these issues.[69] In particular Connell explores the relationship between hegemonic masculinity and subordinate and especially marginal masculinities, with the later being defined (by the hegemonic masculinity) as inadequate or beyond the category of 'properly masculine', the most obvious modern example being homosexuality, defined as the 'other', in this case effeminate. At the same time, of course, the group declared marginal can work through, and transform, this projection to its own advantage.[70] Surely, once we have moved beyond the definition of 'man' as the 'norm', this is a model worth exploring in history?

To return to the particular focus of this chapter, it would be inaccurate to describe the clergy as wholly subordinate; perhaps marginal in a sense, but clearly a particularly positioned form of masculinity. R. N. Swanson has splendidly explored this issue for medieval clergy, their (sort of) counterparts. He took Herdt's study to the earlier period and, observing that the period's definition of masculinity rested on three activities, from each of which the clergy were excluded, revealed the inadequacy of sexual dimorphism here. Religious men 'became extraneous to contemporary gender constructions'. Accordingly, he studied 'the constructed "third gender" of the clergy which, for want of a better term, is here called "emasculinity"'.[71] While I find his account of the medieval clergy persuasive, I am not happy with his conclusion regarding the Reformation, characterised by 'the affirmation of a masculine priesthood, made evident in marriage'; 'they were, unmistakably, men'.[72] My objection would be the traditional 'well, it's a bit more complicated than that'. The Reformation brought a different gender identity for clergy, it is true, but one characterised by new problems, new opportunities, new social and spiritual issues.

The under-addressed issue in this conclusion is why Canticles exercised such an attraction over the godly clergy examined here. The broad context helps to explain to availability of the option of nuptial imagery. That this was a period of transition for masculinities in general can be accepted as a given and that was sharpened, as has been seen, for clergy. However, this does not, in itself, provide a causal scheme; it merely opens the option, makes the adoption a possibility. On one level the attraction is clear within the accepted *mentalité* of godly ministry. Subordination and humility were seen as spiritually valuable and, in these eyes, they were assets more readily available to women, properly trained, than men. 'Men's spirits are hardier, doe not so easily feare Majesty, tremble at judgements, beleeve promises, shun sinne, love God, as women: so that when they are in the way, none are better.'[73] Thus the weaknesses and dangers of femininity could be turned to sources of valuable obedience and a useful sense of inadequacy. At its worst, this led to gender reversal in times of a sense of distance, as we have seen.

However, we can find a path to a more deeply rooted need satiated by this spiritual style if we read these experiences against the early modern 'mystic speech' identified by Michel de Certeau. This may seem surprising, as de Certeau works through the language, primarily, of St Teresa of Avila, St John of the Cross and Angelus Silesius.[74] There are, of course, differences. He looks at the creation of a space from which to speak, a locus and authority denied on several grounds, partly through social destabilisation, questioned tradition and institutional inadequacies but also through a broader deprivation of locus, a loss. The differences help to explain the different solutions but it is worthwhile pointing out the similarities too. When he writes of a 'divided Christianity', the 'community of saints', of how his subjects 'were obliged to distinguish themselves in order to mark the place of a new beginning' and the two obsessive topoi of 'the mythic image of paradise lost, and the eschatological or apocalyptic image of the new Jerusalem', the similarities are striking.[75] The issues of perceived marginalisation and unjust disempowerment fit Rogers and Rutherford very nicely, and it is no stretch to accommodate the other figures noted above. As a source of reassurance for Rogers we need only read his private searches against Sibbes's identification of a *'wondrous comfort'*: 'God will not suffer his own to want ... . When we are once of Christ's family, and not only of his family, but of his body, his spouse, can we think he will suffer us to want that which is needful?'[76] Furthermore, when de Certeau treats the creation of a voice of authority through the creation of an 'I' in a position of indubitable validity, Rutherford, in a Protestant form, fits well. He found his own linguistic efforts inherently failing to capture the full communion with Christ;

these efforts all finished with the adoption of the voice of Scripture, the ultimate written authority and source of stability.

   This may take us closer, but the specificity of Canticles still needs tightening. According to Paul Ricoeur, part of the impact of the Reformation was
to diminish the 'pure' allegorical reading of the monastic paradigm and to make
available an erotic reading of Canticles. Such a reading was delayed by a different understanding of sexuality and left Canticles in a transitional phase, oscil-
lating between the personal and the institutional.[77] This resembles the shifts
identified in Richard Sibbes's treatment above. In particular, the profitable tension of this reading allows a space for the negotiation of the huge vertical space
between human and divine. As Ricoeur sees it,

> love introduces an element of reciprocity that can imply crossing the threshold
> between the ethical and the mystical. Where ethics maintains the vertical dimen-
> sion, mysticism attempts to introduce reciprocity; the lover and the loved occupy
> equal reciprocal roles. Reciprocity is introduced into verticality by means of the
> language of love and thanks to the metaphorical resources of the erotic.[78]

This spatial combination of the vertical and the horizontal runs through
Sibbes. At one point Christ 'hath my soul, my affections, my body, and all. He
hath a propriety in me, and a peculiarity in me. He hath my affection and love
to the uttermost, as I have his, for there is an intercourse in these words.'[79] At
another point he surveys different sorts of kiss, concluding that 'here is the
kiss of a superior to an inferior, "Let him kiss me with the kisses of his mouth,"
that is, let him shew me further testimony of his love by his presence; let me
enjoy further communion with him still'.[80] Canticles allows the godly divine
to have his cake and eat it, as it were. That is, the gender reversal creates a
space for humility and for an intimate and anticipatory, even demanding, relationship with Christ without lessening the proper distance between divine
and human.

NOTES
1 The Old Testament book of Canticles is also known as the Song of Songs or the Song of
   Solomon. In its various guises this has been given as a paper to the inter disciplinary seminar
   at the University of Edinburgh, an opportunity I owe to Roisín Higgins, and at a web-semi-
   nar in Toronto, which I owe to Frank Bremer. I benefited from both discussions and owe a
   great deal to Diane Willen in particular, whose thoughts took me in a very different direction. I am also grateful to John Morrill, who read and criticised an early version, and to
   Claire Higgins, who took time to read a late version, and to Ann Milović for patience, toleration and ideas. Any faults which remain are, of course, my own.
2 Thomas Brooks, Heaven on Earth: A Treatise on Christian Assurance (Edinburgh: 1982, first published 1654) p. 26.
3 Stephen Marshall, A Sermon Preached before the House of Commons (1641), p. 41.
4 Cornelius Burges, The First Sermon Preached to the House of Commons (1641), p. 25. I am grateful to Mike O'Brien for drawing the last two quotations to my attention
5 Laura Levine, 'Men in Women's Clothing: Anti-theatricality and Feminization from 1579 to

1642', *Criticism* 28 (1986), pp. 12–43; Katherine Eisaman Maus, 'Playhouse Flesh and Blood: Sexual Ideology and the Restoration Actress', *English Literary History* 46 (1979), pp. 604–17.

6 William Prynne, *Histrio-Mastix: The Player's Scourge or Actor's Tragedy* (1633), p. 197.

7 Susan Dwyer Amussen, '"The Part of a Christian Man": The Cultural Politics of Manhood in Early Modern England', in *eadem* and Mark A. Kishlansky, ed., *Political Culture and Cultural Politics in Early Modern England* (Manchester: 1995), pp. 213–33, with some space devoted to the clergy, pp. 222–4; Thomas Lacquer, *Making Sex: Body and Gender from the Greeks to Freud* (Cambridge, Massachusetts: 1990) pp. 134–42; David Underdown, 'The Taming of the Scold: The Enforcement of Patriarchal Authority in Early Modern England', in Anthony Fletcher and John Stevenson, eds, *Order and Disorder in Early Modern England* (Cambridge: 1985), pp. 116–36.

8 It is plain that what follows in the rest of this section draws open earlier work in my *Godly Clergy in Early Stuart England: The Caroline Puritan Movement, c. 1620–1643* (Cambridge: 1997), pp. 72–3, 101–5, 126–8. However, I would be the first to point out that my conclusions have been substantially modified by subsequent reading and discussion.

9 See Gilbert Herdt, ed., *Third Sex, Third Gender: Beyond Sexual Dimorphism in Culture and History* (New York: 1994).

10 Instances are given in my *Godly Clergy*, pp. 101–5. The earlier work also provides a broadening of this analysis into the secular sphere.

11 Richard Sibbes, *The Spouse, Her Earnest Desire after Christ* (first published 1638), in A. B. Grosart, ed., *The Complete Works of Richard Sibbes*, vol. II (Edinburgh: 1862), p. 202.

12 *Ibid.*, p. 203.

13 John Cotton, *The Way of Congregational Churches Cleared* (1648), pt II, p. 27.

14 Sibbes, 1862, p. 204

15 Sibbes, *Bowels Opened; or, Expository Sermons on Canticles* (first published 1639), in *Works*, vol. II, p. 24.

16 *A Parte of a Register* (1593), p. 203. This may be linked to the gender flexibility of God; God was portrayed as a breast-feeding maternal figure: Elaine Hobby, *Virtue of Necessity: English Women's Writing 1649–1688* (London: 1988), p. 42; Diane Purkiss, 'Producing the Word, Consuming the Body: Women Prophets of the Seventeenth Century,' in Isobel Grundy and Susan Wiseman, eds, *Women, Writing, History, 1640–1740* (London: 1992), pp. 152–3

17 John Collinges, *Elisha's Lamentation for Elijah* (1657), p. 8.

18 Caroline Walker Bynum, 'Women's Stories, Women's Symbols: A Critique of Victor Turner's Theory of Liminality', in *Fragmentation and Redemption: Essays on Gender and the Human Body in Medieval Religion* (New York: 1991), pp. 27–51.

19 Q[ueen's] U[niversity] B[elfast] Percy Ms. 7, fol. 71.

20 QUB Percy Ms. 7, fol. 180. For (slight) biographical details of Rogers see Webster, 1997, pp. 136–8 and *passim*.

21 QUB Percy Ms. 7, fol. 117. The source for 'cleare up the coast', a fairly frequent phrase, is probably I Chron. 4.10, a plea for protection.

22 QUB Percy Ms. 7, fol. 138, 146.

23 QUB Percy Ms. 7, fol. 154, 61.

24 QUB Percy Ms. 7, fol. 152.

25 QUB Percy Ms. 7, fols 218, 222. The 'first husband', a recurring phrase, is from Hosea 2.7 and answers the question as this is an account of an adulterous woman.

26 QUB Percy Ms. 7, fol. 274. On other occasions he uses the motifs of 'black' or 'uncomely' from Cant. 1.5.

27 QUB Percy Ms. 7, fol. 236.

28 QUB Percy Ms. 7, fol. 116.

29 QUB Percy Ms. 7, fol. 181.

30 QUB Percy Ms. 7, fol. 229.

31 QUB Percy Ms. 7, fol. 235.

32 QUB Percy Ms. 7, fol. 373. 'Disserui hac nocte de beata unione cum Christo; et exultat cor meum cum Christo, capite meo, vite, coniuge, fundamento, magistro, Rege meo; non habeo id quo gloriatur mundus, sed habeo Christum maritum meum, in cuius ulnis hac nocte tutus latebo' (my translation).

33 John Coffey, *Politics, Religion and the British Revolutions: The Mind of Samuel Rutherford* (Cambridge, 1997), p. 104; cf. pp. 85–6, 88–9, 93–4, 104–9 for examinations of the place of the Canticles in Rutherford's preaching as well as his correspondence. I am grateful to John for discussing Rutherford's spirituality with me.

34 Andrew A. Bonar, ed., *Letters of Samuel Rutherford* (Edinburgh: 1863), vol. I, p. 93.

35 *Ibid.*, I, p. 52.

36 *Ibid.*, I, p. 179.

37 *Ibid.*, I, pp. 117–18. It may come as little surprise that this advice has caused certain critics more than a little discomfort, as Coffey notes: Coffey, 1997, p. 105n. Cf. Samuel Clarke, *A Collection of the Lives of Ten Eminent Divines* (1662), pp. 322–3, where Robert Harris writes to his wife about the time after his death when he wants to 'thank you for your faithfulness, and resign you to the Husband of Husbands, the Lord Jesus'.

38 Bonar, 1863, I, p. 190.

39 *Ibid.*, II, p. 98.

40 *Ibid.*, I, p. 179.

41 *Ibid.*, I, pp. 181, 52, 93 (scent, using Canticles 1.2.); I, p. 423 (touch); I, p. 200, II, p. 188 (sight).

42 *Ibid.*, II, p. 57.

43 *Ibid.*, II, p. 97.

44 *Ibid.*, II, p. 99.

45 *Ibid.*, I, p. 432; cf. QUB Percy Ms. 7, fols 310; Webster, 1997, p. 127.

46 Bonar, 1863, I, p. 285.

47 *Ibid.*, I, p. 456.

48 *Ibid.*, I, p. 209.

49 *Ibid.*, I, p. 181.

50 *Ibid.*, I, p. 155.

51 *Ibid.*, I, p. 446.

52 *Ibid.*, I, p. 248.

53 *Ibid.*, I, p. 295.

54 *Ibid.*, I, p. 388.

55 *Ibid.*, I, p. 178. My emphasis.

56 *Ibid.*, II, p. 93. The 'velvet kirkmen' are the High-Church clergy who accepted, and promoted, the shifts to Anglican practices which caused Rutherford's opposition and exile.

57 *Ibid.*, I, p. 52.

58 *Ibid.*, I, p. 188.

59 *Ibid.*, I, p. 209.

60 Alan Bray, 'Homosexuality and the Signs of Male Friendship in Elizabethan England', *History Workshop Journal* 29 (1990), pp. 3–8; and Michael Rey, 'The Body of the Friend: Continuity and Change in Masculine Friendship in the Seventeenth Century', in Tim Hitchcock and Michèle Cohen, eds, *English Masculinities 1660–1800* (London: 1999).

61 Bonar, 1863, II, p. 188.

62 *Ibid.*, II, p. 99.

63 See above, pp. 151–2.

64 Bonar, 1863, I, p. 432.

65 *Ibid.*, I, p. 446.

66 Richard Godbeer, '"Love Raptures": Marital, Romantic and Erotic Images of Jesus Christ in Puritan New England', in Laura McCall and Donald Yacovone, eds, *A Shared Experience: Men, Women, and the History of Gender* (New York: 1998), p. 67.

67 C. W. Bynum, *The Resurrection of the Body in Western Christianity* (New York: 1995), pp. 8–11. See also Hilary Hind, *God's Englishwomen: Seventeenth-century Radical Sectarian Writing and Feminist Criticism* (Manchester: 1996), p. 44 and Purkiss, 1992.

68 John Preston, *The Breast-plate of Faith and Love* (5th ed. 1634), 1st pag., pp. 197–8.

69 For instance, R. W. Connell, *Masculinities* (Cambridge: 1995); D. M. Hadley, ed., *Masculinity in Medieval Europe* (London: 1999); C. Lees, ed., *Medieval Masculinities: Regarding Men in the Middle Ages* (Minneapolis: 1994); D. D. Gilmore, *Manhood in the Making: Cultural Concepts of Masculinity* (London: 1990); M. Roper and J. Tosh, eds, *Manful Assertions: Masculinities in Britain since 1800* (London: 1991).

70 Connell, 1995, pp. 76–81.

71 R. N. Swanson, 'Angels Incarnate: Clergy and Masculinity from Gregorian Reform to the Reformation', in Hadley, 1999, pp. 160–77, quoted pp. 167, 160.

72 *Ibid.*, p. 176.

73 Daniel Rogers, *Matrimoniall Honour* (1640), p. 309. More generally, see the examples in Amanda Porterfield, *Female Piety in Puritan New: The Emergence of Religious Humanism* (Oxford: 1992), pp. 40–79.

74 Michel de Certeau, *Heterologies: Discourse on the Other*, trans. Brian Massumi (Minneapolis: 1986), pp. 80–100.

75 *Ibid.*, p. 87. This is taken further, of course, in de Certeau's *The Mystic Fable: Volume One: The Sixteenth and Seventeenth Centuries*, trans. Michael B. Smith (Chicago: 1995), see esp. pp. 137–42; cf. Louis Bouyer, *Orthodox Spirituality and Protestant and Anglican Spirituality* (London: 1969), pp. 134–8, 140–2, although I do not share his dismissal of Rutherford; Gordon Rupp, 'A Devotion of Rapture in English Puritanism', in R. B. Knox, ed., *Reformation, Conformity and Dissent: Essays in Honour of Geoffrey Nuttall* (London: 1977), esp. pp. 125–6. Canticles was commonly used in an apocalyptic context: Bryan W. Ball, *A Great Expectation: Eschatological Thought in English Protestantism to 1660* (Leiden: 1975), pp. 239–42.

76 Sibbes, *Bowels Opened*, p. 179.

77 Paul Ricoeur, 'The nuptial metaphor,' in *idem* and André LaCocque, *Thinking Biblically: Exegeticaland Hermeneutical Studies*, trans. David Pellauer (Chicago: 1998), pp. 293–4; E. A. Matter, *The Voice of My Beloved: The Song of Songs in Western Medieval Christianity* (Philadelphia: 1990).

78 Ricoeur, *Critique and Conviction*, trans. Kathleen Blamey (Cambridge: 1998), p. 185.

79 Sibbes, *Bowels Opened*, p. 175.

80 Sibbes, *The Spouse*, p. 202.

Epilogue

ALAN BRAY

Readers beginning here are making a mistake, although an understandable one. Twenty years ago my *Homosexuality in Renaissance England* was one of the first attempts to map out the study of the history of homosexuality, in those early pioneering days. Twenty years on, this epilogue is a reflection on how I think that map might now be redrawn.[1]

Let me introduce this, at first obliquely, by recalling a controversy in which my book figured. This is not because the terms of that debate have an enduring significance. Quite the reverse: they would quickly come up against their inherent limits. What I want to do here is rather to draw out of that controversy a point that was not grasped at the time: a wider point and one that suggests that the controversy in one important respect was not what it seemed.

My argument in *Homosexuality in Renaissance England* – that the modern homosexual identity was a product of history, not immutable and above historical change – figured in the debates that followed between an 'essentialist' and a 'constructionist' view of the history of homosexuality, albeit that these were terms coined in polemical debate rather than by their supposed proponents. These two parties, if such they were, were defined in terms less of the conclusions they came to than of the questions they asked: the first in those contemporary terms where the politics of the 'homosexual' identity were foremost, the latter by contrast in historic terms. It was argued that without the second the answers given would not be true, but without the other – it was also argued – they would not be of use.

What was not grasped in this debate was that my *Homosexuality in Renaissance England* was in these terms an 'essentialist' rather than a 'constructionist' work. Let me illustrate this. Take this claim: 'In such circumstances historians should be watchful for signs, however difficult to detect, that for someone involved in a homosexual relationship the nature of that relationship might not have been as obvious to him *as it is to them*.' I have added the emphasis here. The first part of this formulation attracted a sometimes scandalised attention that

set the homosexual identity at issue; but some twelve years later a bright graduate student at The Johns Hopkins University was to point out that the homosexual identity lay implicit in its terms: as much as the Empire State Building
once lay in the Indiana quarry from which it was hewn, in prehistoric majesty
– as in that great *Fortune* caption.[2]

The origin of my book was the extent to which, as it seemed to me, the
exotic language of 'sodomy' could be held suspended from the physical intimacy
that pervaded sixteenth- and seventeenth-century culture. This was evidently
the detective story where the clue was that the dog did *not* bark. The title of my
'Homosexuality in Renaissance England' was an oxymoron. This would be the
enduring part of the book rather than the narrative it went on to recount of how
that exotic language of 'sodomy' acquired an identity and a referent on which it
could seize – and with bloody results – as English society emerged into the eighteenth century. Twenty years later, that disjunction does not appear as sharp as
it did then. Ubiquity on the one hand and identity on the other are two poles
between which sexuality can be set; and not only over time: they can coexist
within the same culture, even within the mind of the one individual. This is not
to say that they do not have a history, although the analogy of an archaeology
might be more apt; and the coming of civil society in late-seventeenth-century
England was I think a moment in that history: but the faultline one sees opening
up there did not pass away with the apparent triumph of civil society.

Important though that point is, there is also – alongside this – a second
reflection on my book which I have primarily in mind in this epilogue. Let me take
a step back. I have suggested a definition of the – admittedly pejorative – term
'essentialism' as an approach shaped by contemporary *political* questions. In this
sense my work was then 'essentialist', taken up with the modern homosexual
identity if not in historical then in political terms. Later I (and my book) would
acquire a place in academia – I will always owe a debt to Nuffield College in
Oxford and to Birkbeck College in London – but in 1982 the context for my book
lay elsewhere. It was written not in a university but mostly late at night after a
day's work as a British career civil servant. Its material context was rather in the
homosexual subcultures of Britain, elsewhere in Europe and in North America
that in the early 1970s were becoming increasingly articulate and questioning. My
book was an attempt to find an answer to that question 'What then are we?' – a
project that led me directly to the politics of identity. Twenty years on, these politics do not now signify as they did then, and it is that fact that sets the context for
this piece. The question I want to ask here is whether we are on the edge of a trap
that is most apparent to an authoritarian political right that has grasped the faultline in the politics of homosexuality more perceptively than its proponents.

The changes of course have been immense: within only a single generation
from illegality to the possibility of same-sex marriage; but the dilemma that has

opened up has lain perhaps in not grasping fully that with that transition the significance of the politics of identity has changed. William Cornwallis – in seventeenth-century England – warned that two men might become sworn brothers simply because both were rich, and it is not difficult to see the fears he was manipulating: the fear of an ethic without altruism, of friendship as mutual self-advancement.[3] Has an authoritarian right grasped that the fautline in that fear can be displaced to other ends?

Some years after completing my book I made a visit to Cambridge to give a lecture, a visit that was for me to be a catalyst. While finishing breakfast in college the following morning, I was joined by my host, Jonathan Walters, then a graduate student in the university. Our walk that morning was to the chapel of Christ's College to see the monument to Sir John Finch and Sir Thomas Baines by the communion table there, near where they were buried together in the same tomb in 1682. 'What', I was asked, 'do you make of this?' The two sides of the monument, each surmounted by a portrait of one of the two men, were linked within the design by a knotted cloth that appeared to symbolise the love knot or the marriage knot. Later I would read the Latin manuscript in the British Library in which Sir John Finch had indeed described his friendship with Sir Thomas Baines in terms of a marriage (as a 'Connubium'); but what equally, if not more, drew the eye of the viewer was the design of the woodwork set above the communion table nearby, where the same imagery of the monument's inscription – of a single heart and the mingling of their bodies in death – reappeared: but there made universal. I had written a book that had turned on how the friendship of that world I had described had *not* been understood. What if I were to write a book that turned on how it was understood? Was this what I was seeing – and would it address those concerns that I had brought with me on that visit to Cambridge? Whatever the ethic that had left its trace in this monument, it pointed in the most emphatic terms beyond the good of these two friends who lay there together in death.

The difficulty I had in answering the question put to me that day was in grasping that I was standing with this monument near the far shore of a continent that already by then stretched back for more than half a thousand years. When, at the suggestion of the Oxford historian Diarmaid MacCulloch, I saw the great memorial brass to John Bloxham and John Whytton in the chapel of Merton College, Oxford, standing together side by side beneath their canopies, I knew that I had found the perspective that I was looking for: that and the scale of the task that now faced me. The result was the silence of the years that followed and my later book. Its title *The Friend* was a gesture to Marcel Mauss's great work of structural anthropology. The subtitle I gave it was *How Friendship, the Family and Religion Fell in Love.*[4]

The ethic that first became apparent to me in the tomb monument of Sir John Finch and Sir Thomas Baines did not prove to justify in any simple sense the juxtaposed bodies that the language of 'sodomy' had condemned. The two were not symmetrical. It was rather something more important and more fundamental. The effect of that ethic was rather to draw back into friendship and its ethical uncertainties a judgement of those very diverse acts, motives and circumstances that the abstraction of 'sodomy' has set aside. Later when Jacques Derrida's *Politics of Friendship* appeared I recognised the same project.[5] Jacques Derrida's book addressed the dilemma foreseen by Michel Foucault – the dilemma of resistance caught up in the very process that produced it – and is likely in the next generation of writings to play the same role that Michel Foucault's *History of Sexuality* played in the last.[6] Derrida's book is a book about the political problem of friendship but one where the history of friendship plays a defining role. It does this, first, because Derrida draws on premodern articulations of friendship – Montaigne as a paradigm – to convey a fracture in the problematic politics of friendship. On the one side of this fracture is an aspiration to universality: on the other is the pull of proximity, the friend as someone who is near to you in a friendship that grows with presence in the same place. The first, as he puts it, tends directly to a politist concord and one based on reciprocity – the point being that reciprocity is something that can in principle be replaced. The second, by contrast, is irreplaceable. It belongs to the experience of mourning and the moment of loss. Its rhetoric is one that both confides and at the same time at the last refuses to commit the death of the friend – unique and irreplaceable – to a universalisable discourse. It is I think this rhetoric that I saw in the tomb of Sir John Finch and Sir Thomas Baines and its setting. Yet Derrida insists that he is not here speaking of a simple fracture, between a Judaeo-Christian model on the one hand and a Kantian (and classical) model on the other. That would be to misunderstand the book. Nor does this fracture in his view depoliticise the Greek model or shift the nature of the political. This is despite the fact that he comes very close to saying all three. Crucially he draws back from characterising these as two different, antagonistic or incompatible models. While the one has the draw of narcissism, the other has the power for him within its own terms to become the other and thus, by a supplementary ruse, to address that very narcissism. Indeed much of the book is taken up with deconstructive readings designed to tease out how each of these two apparently incompatible models implies the other by such a supplementary ruse. The question the book asks is rather this: Is there today another way of apprehending the universality of the singular that would still justify the old name of democracy?

That word 'still' is a clue here, for in asking this question Derrida is responding to a precise historical change, which he characterises in the final pages of the book as the collapse of an Enlightenment confidence in the possibility of universality in friendship: the abyss, as he puts it, that is opening up beneath it today. It is not difficult at the turn of the twentieth century to recognise this abyss. Its voice is that of a persuasive exemplarist logic – 'exemplarist' in the claim that the instance of a universal can stand for that universal – that friendship's universality can be displaced to a commitment to nationalism, patriotism, ethnocentrism: to country, nation, state, even land and blood and to their economic and androcentric equivalents: to what Derrida's book calls 'the raging quest for identity'. These are the terms that Derrida uses, and he does not include sexual identity in that list. Yet has it acquired a place there? With the same exemplarist logic, has *sexual* identity become part of that displacement?

Although at times one can glimpse in Derrida's book the political programme he has in mind, he is resistant to articulating an alternative programme: fearful of the degree to which the ground can give way beneath it, in a similar exemplarist transformation. This is rather Derrida as a philosopher of language, analysing – and implicitly urging us to analyse – the dominant and hegemonic usages of language that make possible this exemplarist logic. What he urges in this book is for us to grasp the rhetorical effects that, in a word, are also *political* strategies 'through symptoms and disavowals whose rhetoric we must learn to decipher and whose strategy to outwit'. Could the recovery of the past play a part in this? There is of course no return to the forms of friendship of the past, but the recovery of their ethics might play a part in imagining a cultural space for change today. Where, then, would this change the map that we laid out twenty years ago? Would it not lie in a cultural space opened up in the transformation of sexuality into ethics, of identity into the politics of friendship?

NOTES
1 Alan Bray, *Homosexuality in Renissance England* (London: 1982).
2 Elizabeth Pittenger in *Queering the Renaissance*, ed. Jonathan Goldberg (Durham, North Carolina: 1994), p. 167 – the quotation from my book is taken from p. 68 of the 1995 edition.
3 William Cornwallis, *Essayes* (London: 1600) fol. D8v.
4 Alan Bray, *The Friend: How Friendship, the Family and Religion Fell In Love* (Chicago: 2002).
5 Jacques Derrida, *Politiques de l'amitié suivi de L'oreille de Heidegger* (Paris: 1994), trans. George Collins as *Politics of Friendship* (London: 1997). The direct quotations below are from pp. 106 and 237 of the 1997 translation.
6 Michel Foucault, *La Volonté de savoir* (Paris: 1976), trans. Robert Hurley as *The History of Sexuality: An Introduction* (Harmondsworth: 1984).

Index

Bkfst
Gym
Write Paper
Tutor
Write Paper
Hand in Paper

need 2 retar
stuff

- Study 4 MIS Test
- Poly Sci 911 Paper
  email 4 Proj.
- Do Artist td
  email girl 4
  project ideas.
- Do abstract &
  hand in @ office hours.

- Read Cod
  Print all this
  weeks documents.

- Figure out topic
        c/ Research
  paper.